easy Computer Basics

Michael Miller

Part 1
Understanding How Your Computer Works .... Pg. 2

Part 2
Setting Up Your Computer .... Pg. 14

Part 3
Using Microsoft Windows XP .... Pg. 28

Part 4
Working with Files and Folders .... Pg. 58

Part 5
Using Microsoft Works .... Pg. 74

Part 6
Using Microsoft Word .... Pg. 80

Part 7
Connecting to the Internet .... Pg. 94

Part 8
Playing Music and Movies .... Pg. 132

Part 9
Working with Pictures .... Pg. 152

Part 10
Adding New Devices to Your System .... Pg. 180

Part 11
Setting Up a Wireless Home Network .... Pg. 196

Part 12
Protecting Your Computer .... Pg. 212

Part 13
Taking Care of Your Computer .... Pg. 222

W9-BKA-116

Contents

1 Understanding How Your Computer Works 2

Getting to Know Your System Unit 4

Inside the Case 6

Hard Disk Drives: Long-term Storage 7

CD and DVD Drives 8

Keyboard 9

Mouse 10

Sound Cards and Speakers 11

Video Cards and Monitors 12

Printers 13

2 Setting Up Your Computer .14

Connecting the Mouse and Keyboard .16

Connecting the Monitor 17

Connecting the Audio System 18

Connecting a Parallel Printer 20

Connecting a USB Printer 21

Connecting the Modem 22

Connecting the System Power Cable 23

Powering On 24

Logging On to Windows XP 26

Shutting Down 27

13.59

3 Using Microsoft Windows XP **28**

Pointing and Clicking 30

Double-clicking 31

Right-clicking 32

Dragging and Dropping 33

Hovering 34

Moving a Window 35

Scrolling a Window 36

Resizing a Window 37

Maximizing, Minimizing, and Closing a Window 38

Using the Windows Start Menu 39

Opening a Program 40

Creating a New Shortcut on the Desktop 41

Switching Between Programs 42

Using Menus 43

Using Toolbars 44

Managing PC Resources with My Computer 45

Managing Windows with the Control Panel 46

Changing the Size of Your Desktop 48

Selecting a New Desktop Theme 49

Personalizing the Desktop Background .50

Changing the Color Scheme 51

Setting Up Additional Users 52

Using a Screensaver 54

Getting Help in Windows 56

4 Working with Files and Folders 58

Changing the Way Files Are Displayed 60

Sorting Files and Folders 61

Navigating Folders 62

Navigating with the Folders Pane 63

Creating a New Folder 64

Renaming a File or Folder 65

Copying a File or Folder 66

Moving a File or Folder 67

Deleting a File or Folder 68

Restoring Deleted Files 69

Emptying the Recycle Bin 70

Compressing a File 71

Extracting Files from a Compressed Folder 72

5 Using Microsoft Works **74**

Launching a Program 76

Starting a New Task 77

Opening an Existing Document 78

Managing a Big Project 79

6 Using Microsoft Word **80**

Creating a New Document 82

Saving a Document 84

Opening an Existing Document 85

Entering Text 86

Editing Text 87

Formatting Text 88

Formatting Paragraphs 90

Applying Styles 91

Checking Your Spelling 92

Printing a Document 93

7 Connecting to the Internet **94**

Setting Up a New Internet Connection 96

Surfing the Web with Internet Explorer 102

Saving Your Favorite Pages 106

Returning to a Favorite Page 107

Revisiting History 108

Searching the Web with Google 109

Finding News and Other Information Online 110

Shopping for Bargains at Shopping.com 114

Bidding for Items on eBay 116

Setting Up an Email Account 120

Reading an Email Message 124

Replying to an Email Message 125

Composing a New Email Message .126

Sending a File via Email 127

Adding Contacts in Windows Messenger 128

Instant Messaging with Windows Messenger 130

8 Playing Music and Movies **132**

Playing a CD 134

Ripping a CD to Your Hard Disk 136

Creating a Playlist 138

Playing a Playlist 140

Burning a Music CD 141

Connecting an iPod to Your PC 144

Transferring Songs to Your iPod via iTunes 146

Creating Smart Playlists for Your iPod 147

Connecting Other Portable Music Players 148

Playing a DVD 150

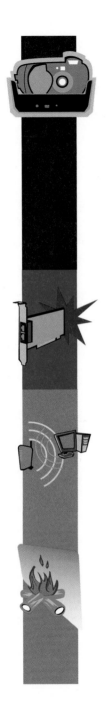

9 Working with Pictures **152**

Transferring Pictures from a Digital Camera 154

Transferring Pictures from a Memory Card 160

Scanning a Picture 164

Printing a Photo 168

Ordering Prints Online 170

Quick Fixing a Photo with Adobe Photoshop Elements 172

Removing Red-Eye 176

Cropping Your Photo 178

10 Adding New Devices to Your System **180**

Adding a Device via USB or FireWire 182

Adding New Internal Hardware 184

Using the Add Hardware Wizard 190

11 Setting Up a Wireless Home Network **196**

Setting Up Your Network's Main PC 198

Connecting Additional PCs to Your Wireless Network 208

Sharing Files and Folders Across Your Network 210

12 Protecting Your Computer **212**

Defending Against Computer Attacks with a Firewall 214

Protecting Against Computer Viruses 216

Fighting Email Spam 218

Cleaning Spyware from Your System 220

Blocking Pop-up Ads 221

13 Taking Care of Your Computer **222**

Deleting Unnecessary Files 224

Defragmenting Your Hard Disk 226

Checking Your Hard Disk for Errors 228

Restoring Your Computer After a Crash 230

Glossary **232**

Index **238**

EASY COMPUTER BASICS

International Standard Book Number: 0-7897-3420-6

First Printing: July 2005

09   08   07   06   4   3

Library of Congress Catalog Card Number: 2005924990

Printed in the United States of America

U. K. International Standard Book Number: 0-7897-3510-5

First Printing: July 2005

09   08   07   06   4   3   2   1

TRADEMARKS

WARNING AND DISCLAIMER

Associate Publisher
Greg Wiegand

Managing Editor
Charlotte Clapp

Acquisitions Editor
Michelle Newcomb

Development Editor
Todd Brakke

Project Editor
Seth Kerney

Production Editor
Megan Wade

Indexer
Erika Millen

Team Coordinator
Sharry Lee Gregory

Technical Editor
Mark Hall

Designer
Anne Jones

ABOUT THE AUTHOR

Michael Miller is a successful and prolific author with a reputation for practical advice, technical accuracy, and an unerring empathy for the needs of his readers.

Mr. Miller has written more than 60 best-selling books in the past 15 years. His books for Que include *Absolute Beginner's Guide to Computer Basics, Absolute Beginner's Guide to eBay, Tricks of the eBay Masters,* and *Bad Pics Fixed Quick.* He is known for his casual, easy-to-read writing style and his practical, real-world advice—as well as his ability to explain a wide variety of complex topics to an everyday audience.

You can email Mr. Miller directly at easycomputer@molehillgroup.com. His website is located at www.molehillgroup.com.

DEDICATION

To Mark and Stephanie—always glad to visit.

ACKNOWLEDGMENTS

Thanks to the usual suspects at Que, including but not limited to Greg Wiegand, Michelle Newcomb, Sharry Gregory, Todd Brakke, Seth Kerney, Mark Hall, and Megan Wade.

TELL US WHAT YOU THINK!

As the reader of this book, *you* are our most important critic and commentator. We value your opinion and want to know what we're doing right, what we could do better, what areas you'd like to see us publish in, and any other words of wisdom you're willing to pass our way.

As an associate publisher for Que, I welcome your comments. You can email or write me directly to let me know what you did or didn't like about this book—as well as what we can do to make our books stronger.

Please note that I cannot help you with technical problems related to the topic of this book, and that due to the high volume of mail I receive, I might not be able to reply to every message.

When you write, please be sure to include this book's title and author as well as your name and phone or fax number. I will carefully review your comments and share them with the author and editors who worked on the book.

Email: feedback@quepublishing.com

Mail: Greg Wiegand
         Que Publishing
         800 East 96th Street
         Indianapolis, IN 46240 USA

For more information about this book or others from Que Publishing, visit our website at www.quepublishing.com. Type the ISBN of the book (excluding hyphens) or the title of the book you're looking for in the Search box.

IT'S AS EASY AS 1-2-3

Each part of this book is made up of a series of short, instructional lessons, designed to help you understand basic information.

1 Each step is fully illustrated to show you how it looks onscreen.

2 Each task includes a series of quick, easy steps designed to guide you through the procedure.

3 Items that you select or click in menus, dialog boxes, tabs, and windows are shown in **bold**.

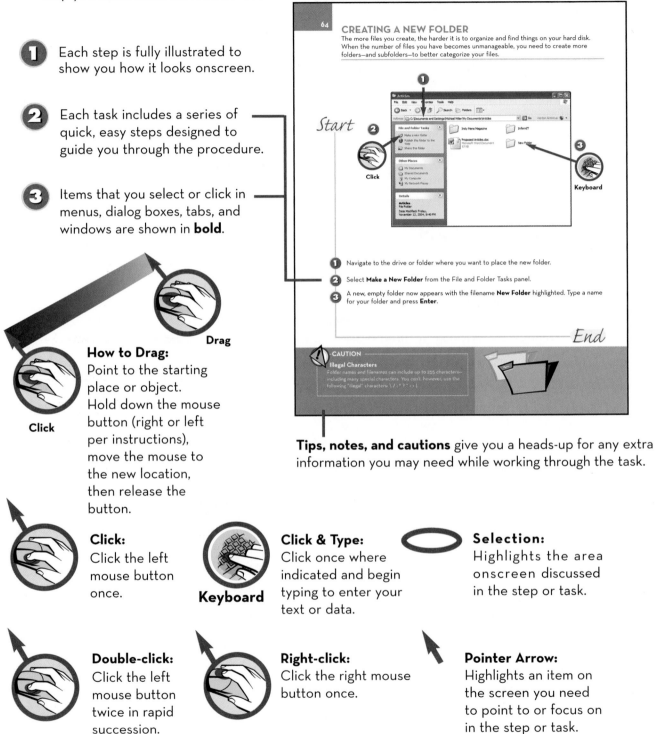

64 **CREATING A NEW FOLDER**
The more files you create, the harder it is to organize and find things on your hard disk. When the number of files you have becomes unmanageable, you need to create more folders—and subfolders—to better categorize your files.

Start

Click

Keyboard

1 Navigate to the drive or folder where you want to place the new folder.

2 Select **Make a New Folder** from the File and Folder Tasks panel.

3 A new, empty folder now appears with the filename **New Folder** highlighted. Type a name for your folder and press **Enter**.

End

CAUTION
Illegal Characters
Folder names and filenames can include up to 255 characters—including many special characters. You can't, however, use the following "illegal" characters \ / : * ? " < > |

Tips, notes, and cautions give you a heads-up for any extra information you may need while working through the task.

Drag

How to Drag:
Point to the starting place or object. Hold down the mouse button (right or left per instructions), move the mouse to the new location, then release the button.

Click

Click:
Click the left mouse button once.

Double-click:
Click the left mouse button twice in rapid succession.

Keyboard

Click & Type:
Click once where indicated and begin typing to enter your text or data.

Right-click:
Click the right mouse button once.

Selection:
Highlights the area onscreen discussed in the step or task.

Pointer Arrow:
Highlights an item on the screen you need to point to or focus on in the step or task.

INTRODUCTION TO *EASY COMPUTER BASICS*

Computers don't have to be scary or difficult. Computers can be easy—if you know what to do.

That's where this book comes in. *Easy Computer Basics* is an illustrated, step-by-step guide to setting up and using your new computer. You'll learn how computers work, how to connect all the pieces and parts together, and how to start using them. All you have to do is look at the pictures and follow the instructions. Pretty easy.

Once you learn the basics, I'll show you how to do lots of useful stuff with your new PC. You'll learn how to write letters and memos, send and receive email messages, and search for information on the Internet. We'll even cover some fun stuff, including listening to music and working with digital photographs.

If you're worried about how to keep your PC up and running, we'll cover some basic system maintenance, too. And, just to be safe, I'll show you how to protect your computer when you're online—against viruses, spam, spyware, and computer attacks. It's not hard to do.

To help you find the information you need, I've organized *Easy Computer Basics* into 13 parts.

Part 1, "Understanding How Your Computer Works," describes all the pieces and parts of a typical computer system. Read this section to find out all about hard drives, keyboards, sound cards, and the like.

Part 2, "Setting Up Your Computer," shows you how to connect all those pieces and parts together and get your new computer system up and running.

Part 3, "Using Microsoft Windows XP," introduces the backbone of your entire system—the Microsoft Windows operating system—including how it works and how to use it.

Part 4, "Working with Files and Folders," shows you how to manage all the computer files you create—by moving, copying, renaming, and deleting them.

Part 5, "Using Microsoft Works," walks you through the popular program included free with most new PCs.

Part 6, "Using Microsoft Word," shows you how to use this popular word processor to create letters and other documents.

Part 7, "Connecting to the Internet," is all about getting online and doing stuff when you get there. You'll learn how to set up a new Internet connection, surf the Web, send and receive emails, and use instant messaging programs. You'll even learn how to search for information on the Internet, shop online, and bid on eBay auctions!

Part 8, "Playing Music and Movies," shows you how to download and play digital music files, how to listen to CDs on your PC, how to burn your own audio CDs, and how to watch DVDs on your computer screen.

Part 9, "Working with Pictures," helps you connect a digital camera to your PC and edit your digital photos.

Part 10, "Adding New Devices to Your System," shows you how to upgrade your computer system with new internal and external peripherals.

Part 11, "Setting Up a Wireless Home Network," helps you connect all the computers in your house into a wireless network and share a broadband Internet connection.

Part 12, "Protecting Your Computer," is all about stopping spam, viruses, spyware, and the like.

Part 13, "Taking Care of Your Computer," shows you how to keep your PC running smoothly and how to recover from serious crashes. And that's not all. At the back of the book you'll find a glossary of common computer terms—so you can understand what all the techie types are talking about!

So, is using a computer really this easy? You bet—just follow the simple step-by-step instructions, and you'll be computing like a pro!

UNDERSTANDING HOW YOUR COMPUTER WORKS

Chances are you're reading this book because you have a new computer. At this point you might not be totally sure what it is you've gotten yourself into. Just what is this mess of boxes and cables—how does it all go together, and how does it work?

We'll start by looking at the physical components of your system—the stuff we call computer *hardware*. A lot of different pieces and parts make up a typical computer system. You should note, however, that no two computer systems are identical because you can always add new components to your system—or disconnect other pieces you don't have any use for.

THE PARTS OF YOUR COMPUTER SYSTEM

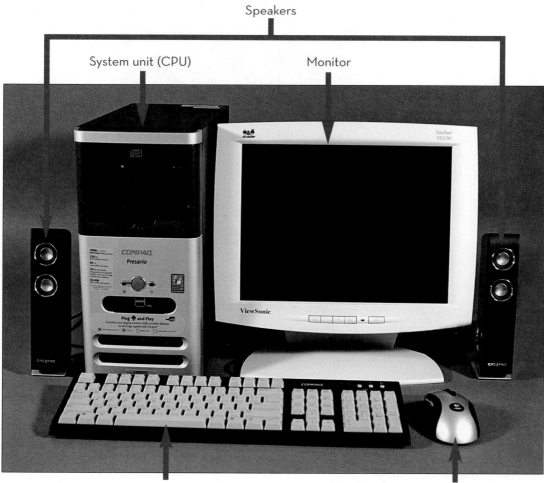

Speakers

System unit (CPU)

Monitor

Keyboard

Mouse

GETTING TO KNOW YOUR SYSTEM UNIT

The system unit is the most important piece of hardware in your computer system. It houses your computer's brain, disk drives, and many other components—which makes it the "mother ship" of your system.

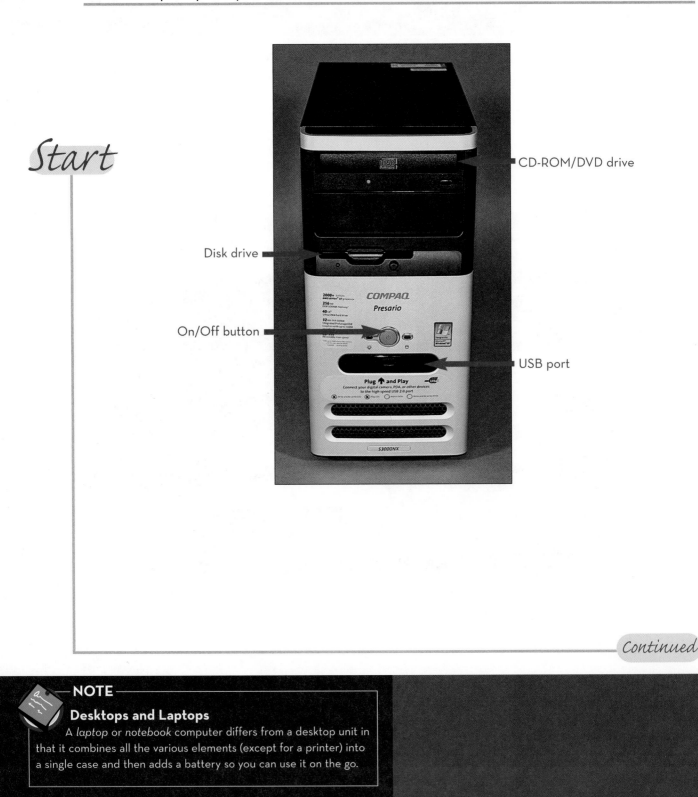

Start

Disk drive

On/Off button

CD-ROM/DVD drive

USB port

Continued

NOTE

Desktops and Laptops

A *laptop* or *notebook* computer differs from a desktop unit in that it combines all the various elements (except for a printer) into a single case and then adds a battery so you can use it on the go.

Power connection

Connections for peripherals

Slots for add-in cards

End

NOTE

Front and Back

The front of the system unit is where you insert CDs, DVDs, and other types of storage media. The back of the system unit is where all the other parts of your computer system connect.

NOTE

Connecting Ports

Every component you plug into your system unit has its own unique type of connector, so you have an assortment of different jacks—called *ports* in the computer world.

INSIDE THE CASE

Of all the components inside your system unit, the most important is the *motherboard*, which hosts your microprocessor, memory chips, and other components. This motherboard also contains several slots, into which you can plug additional *boards* (also called *cards*) that perform specific functions.

Power supply

Drive bays

Start

Motherboard

Card slots

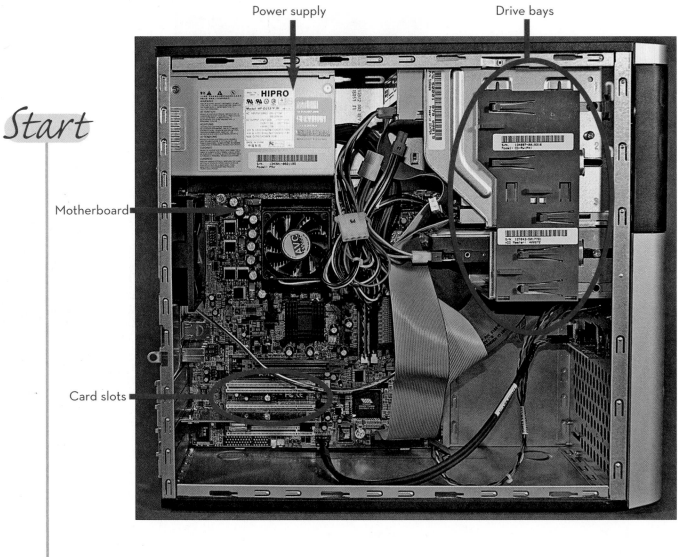

End

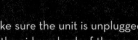TIP

Open the Case

To remove your system unit's case, make sure the unit is unplugged; then loosen the big screws or thumbscrews on either the side or back of the case. You should then be able to either slide off the entire case or pop open the top or back.

HARD DISK DRIVES: LONG-TERM STORAGE

The hard disk drive inside your system unit stores all your important data—up to 400GB worth. A hard disk consists of metallic platters that store data magnetically. Special read/write heads realign magnetic particles on the platters, much like a recording head records data onto magnetic recording tape.

Start

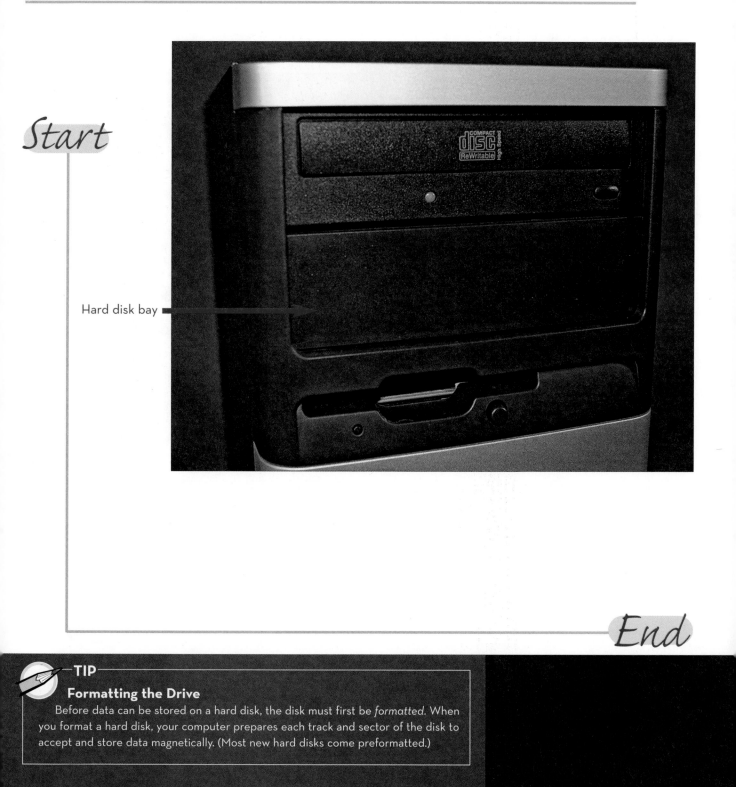

Hard disk bay

End

CD AND DVD DRIVES

CD-ROM discs look just like the compact discs you play on your audio system. Data is encoded in microscopic pits below the disc's surface and is read from the CD-ROM via a drive that uses a consumer-grade laser. The laser beam follows the tracks of the disc and reads the pits, translating the data into a form your computer can understand.

Start

Disc tray

End

KEYBOARD

A computer keyboard looks and functions just like a typewriter keyboard, except that computer keyboards have a few more keys (for navigation and special program functions). When you press a key on your keyboard, it sends an electronic signal to your system unit that tells your machine what you want it to do.

Start

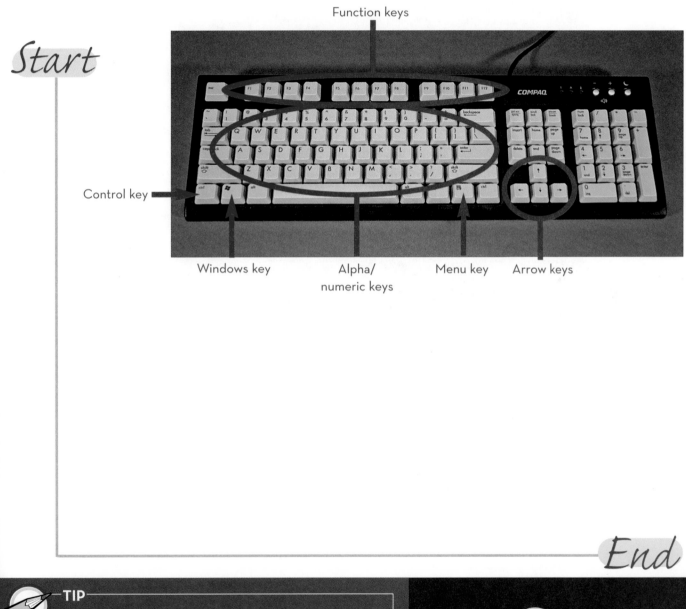

Function keys

Control key

Windows key

Alpha/ numeric keys

Menu key

Arrow keys

End

TIP
Wireless Keyboards
If you want to cut the cord, consider a wireless keyboard or mouse. These wireless devices work via radio frequency signals and let you work several feet away from your system unit, with no cables necessary.

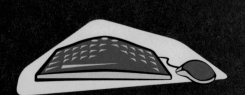

MOUSE

A *mouse* is a small, handheld input device for your computer. When you move the mouse along a flat surface, an onscreen pointer (called a *cursor*) moves in response. When you click (press and release) a mouse button, this motion initiates an action in your program.

Left button   Scroll wheel

Start

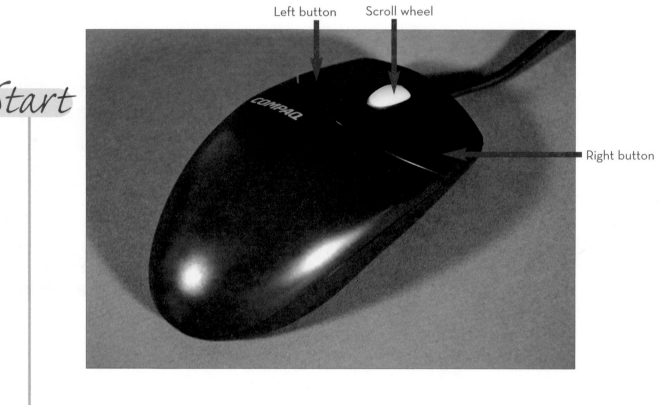

Right button

 End

TIP

Mouse Alternatives

A mouse is just one type of input device you can hook up to your PC. You can also control your computer with trackballs, joysticks, game controllers, and pen pads.

SOUND CARDS AND SPEAKERS

Most computers today come with separate right and left speakers, sometimes accompanied by a subwoofer for better bass. All speaker systems are driven by a sound card or chipset installed inside the system unit.

Left speaker

Right speaker

Subwoofer

End

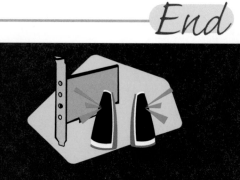

NOTE

Surround Sound

So-called 5.1 surround sound speaker systems come with five satellite speakers (three front and two rear) and the ".1" subwoofer—great for listening to movie soundtracks or playing explosive-laden videogames.

VIDEO CARDS AND MONITORS

Your computer electronically transmits words and pictures to your monitor. These images are created by a *video card* installed inside your system unit. Settings in Windows tell the video card and the monitor how to work together to display the images you see on the screen.

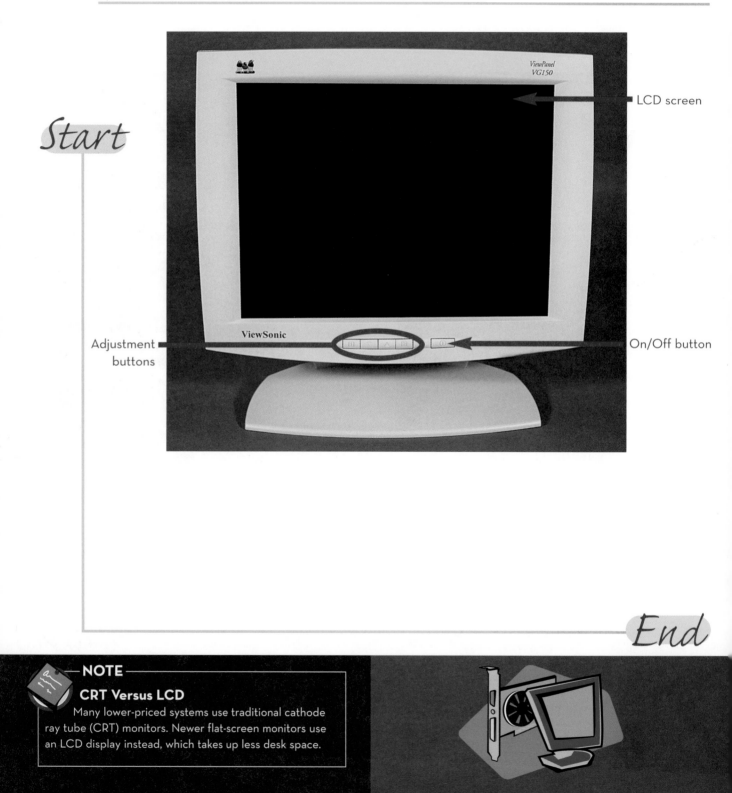

Start

End

LCD screen

Adjustment buttons

On/Off button

ViewPanel VG150

ViewSonic

NOTE

CRT Versus LCD

Many lower-priced systems use traditional cathode ray tube (CRT) monitors. Newer flat-screen monitors use an LCD display instead, which takes up less desk space.

PRINTERS

For permanent records of your work, you must add a printer to your system. The two most common types are *laser* printers and *inkjet* printers. Laser printers work much like copy machines, applying toner (powdered ink) to paper by using a small laser. Inkjet printers shoot jets of ink onto the paper's surface to create the printed image.

Start

Paper tray

Operating buttons

Paper output

End

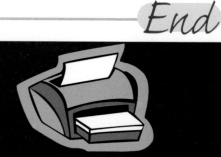

TIP

Black and White Versus Color

Black-and-white printers are faster than color printers and better if you're printing memos, letters, and other single-color documents. Color printers are essential if you want to print pictures taken with a digital camera.

SETTING UP YOUR COMPUTER

Now it's time to get connected. Position your system unit so you easily can access all the connections on the back, and carefully run the cables from each of the other components so that they're hanging freely at the rear of the system unit.

When you plug in a cable, you should make sure that it's *firmly* connected—both to the system unit and to the specific piece of hardware. Loose cables can cause all sorts of weird problems, so be sure they're plugged in really good.

TYPICAL CONNECTIONS

Power cable

Keyboard

Monitor

USB device

Mouse

Printer

Network

Speakers

Modem

CONNECTING THE MOUSE AND KEYBOARD

The first items you connect should be your mouse and keyboard. Most mice connect to a dedicated mouse port on your system unit. Most keyboards connect to a similar dedicated keyboard port on your system unit. Know, however, that many new mice and keyboards also connect via USB ports, so you should use whatever connection is appropriate.

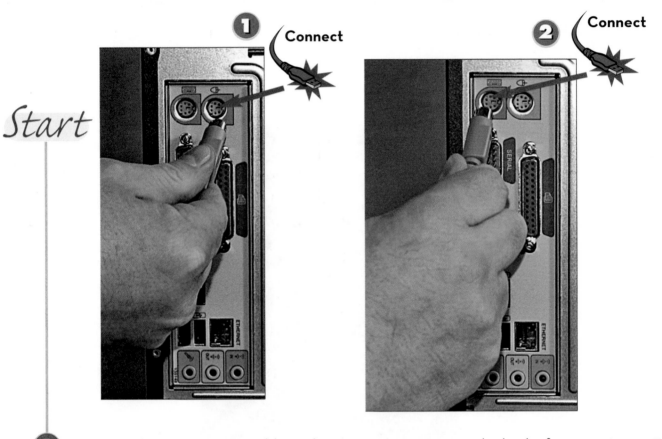

Start

Connect

Connect

End

1. Connect the green mouse cable to the green mouse port on the back of your system unit.

2. Connect the purple keyboard cable to the purple keyboard port on the back of your system unit.

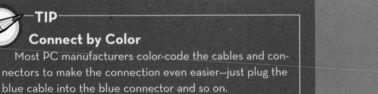

TIP

Connect by Color

Most PC manufacturers color-code the cables and connectors to make the connection even easier—just plug the blue cable into the blue connector and so on.

CONNECTING THE MONITOR

You have to connect your video monitor to your system unit and then connect it to a power source. Do not turn on the monitor until you're ready to power on your entire system.

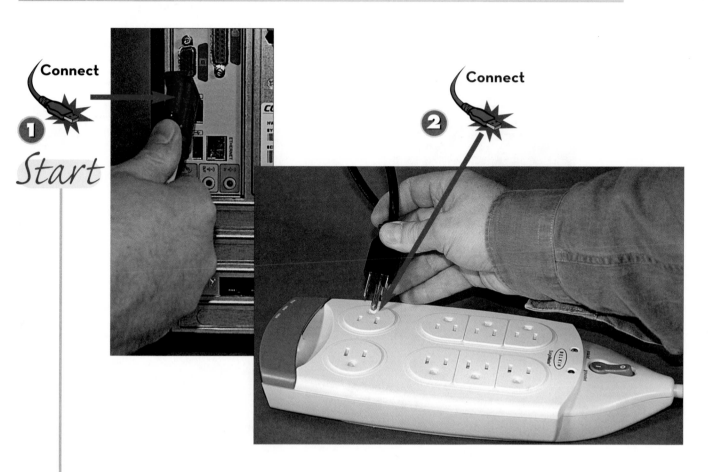

Connect

Start

Connect

1 Connect the blue monitor cable to the blue monitor port on the back of your system unit.

2 Connect the monitor's power cable to a power outlet.

End

TIP
Digital Connections
Some newer LCD monitors use a digital DVI connection instead of the older VGA-type connection. If you have a choice, a DVI connection delivers a crisper picture than the older analog connection.

CONNECTING THE AUDIO SYSTEM

To connect your audio system, connect the phono jack from your speaker system to the audio out or sound out connector on your system unit. You'll also have to connect your left and right speakers together—and connect them to your subwoofer, if you have one.

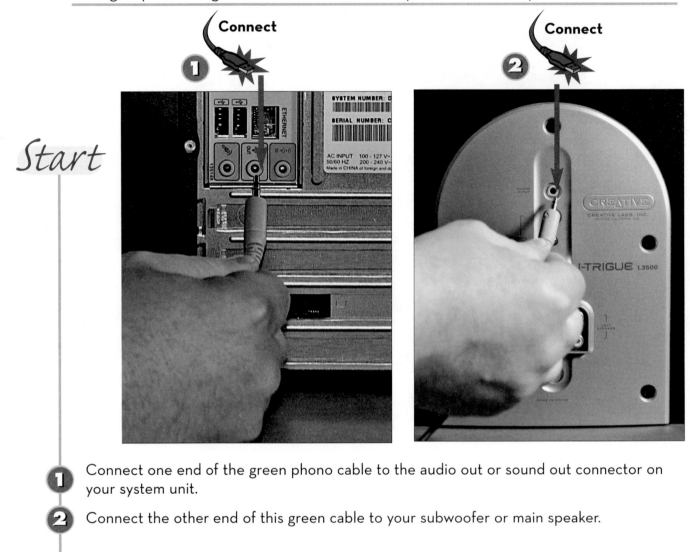

Start

1 Connect one end of the green phono cable to the audio out or sound out connector on your system unit.

2 Connect the other end of this green cable to your subwoofer or main speaker.

Continued

TIP
Your Connection Might Vary
Not all speaker systems connect the same way. Many surround systems use a separate box with various controls (like volume) that connects to both your PC and speakers. Make sure you read your manufacturer's instructions before you connect your speaker system.

Connect

③

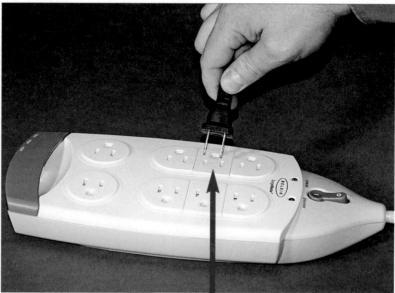

Connect

④

③ Connect your left and right speakers to your subwoofer, or to each other, as per the manufacturer's instructions.

④ Connect the power cable on your main speaker to a power source.

End

NOTE

Powered Speakers

Your PC doesn't include an audio power amplifier, so your computer speakers must be self-powered. This is why they must be connected to a power source to work.

TIP

Digital Speaker Systems

Some high-end speaker systems use a digital audio connector instead of the traditional analog audio out jack. If you have a digital speaker system, follow the manufacturer's instructions.

CONNECTING A PARALLEL PRINTER

If you have a printer with a parallel cable connection, connect it to the parallel port on the back of the system unit. This connector is sometimes labeled "printer" or "LPT1."

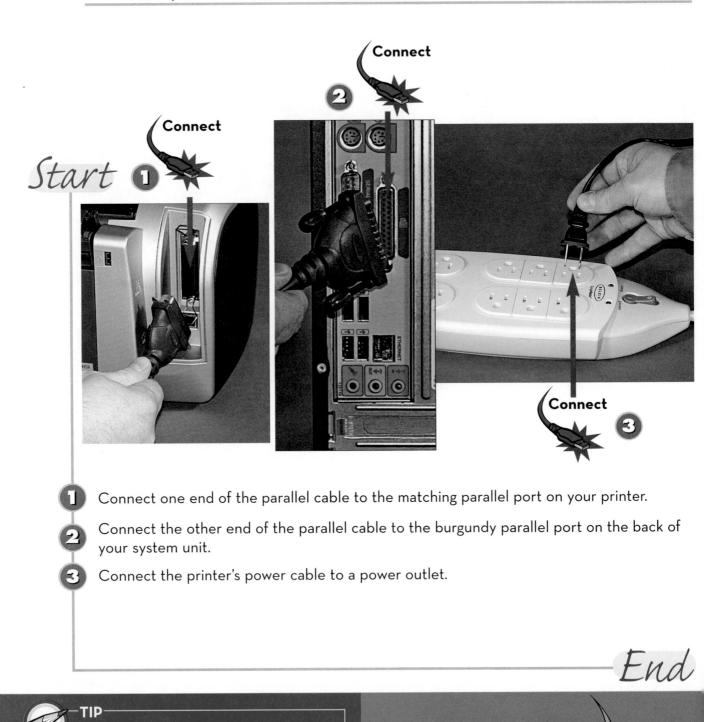

1 Connect one end of the parallel cable to the matching parallel port on your printer.

2 Connect the other end of the parallel cable to the burgundy parallel port on the back of your system unit.

3 Connect the printer's power cable to a power outlet.

End

TIP
USB Versus Parallel
Many newer printers connect to a USB port instead of the parallel port. If you have a USB printer, skip ahead to "Connecting a USB Printer," on the next page.

CONNECTING A USB PRINTER

Many newer printers connect via a USB cable. This type of connection is often easier to configure than the older parallel connection.

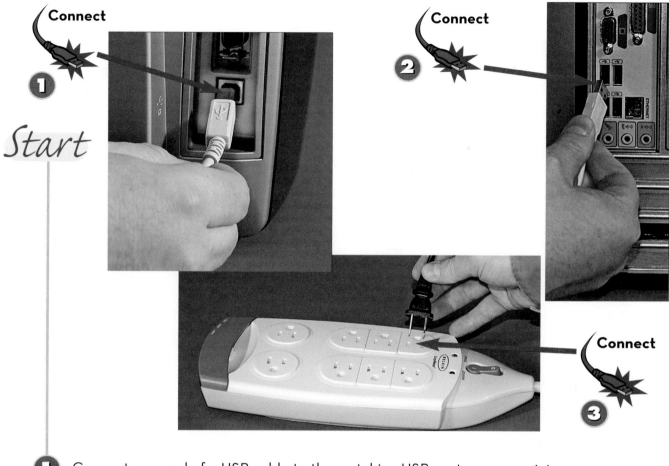

1. Connect one end of a USB cable to the matching USB port on your printer.

2. Connect the other end of the USB cable to a USB port on the back of your system unit.

3. Connect the printer's power cable to a power outlet.

TIP

Advantages of USB

Because they can be connected without powering down your PC, USB printers can be moved between computers more easily than printers that use the older parallel connection. In addition, USB cables are a lot thinner than parallel cables, so if your space is tight, this is the way to go.

CONNECTING THE MODEM

If you're connecting to the Internet via a dial-up connection, connect a cable from your telephone line to the modem in connector on your system unit. Then connect another cable from the modem out connector on your PC to your telephone.

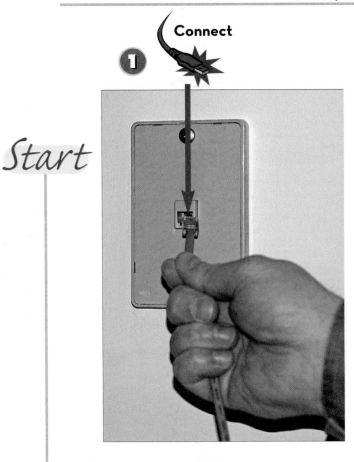

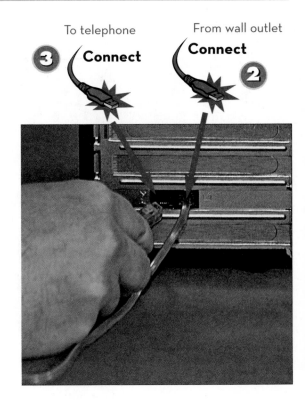

Start

End

1 Connect one end of a telephone cable to your wall phone outlet.

2 Connect the other end of this cable to the modem in connector on the back of your system unit.

3 Connect a second cable between the modem out connector on your system unit and your telephone (optional).

TIP

Broadband Modems

You can skip this step if you're using a cable modem or DSL modem to connect to the Internet. Wait until you have the rest of your system up and running; then follow the instructions you were given by your Internet service provider.

CONNECTING THE SYSTEM POWER CABLE

When all the other parts of your computer system are connected, you can then connect your system unit to a power source. Just make sure the power source is turned off before you connect!

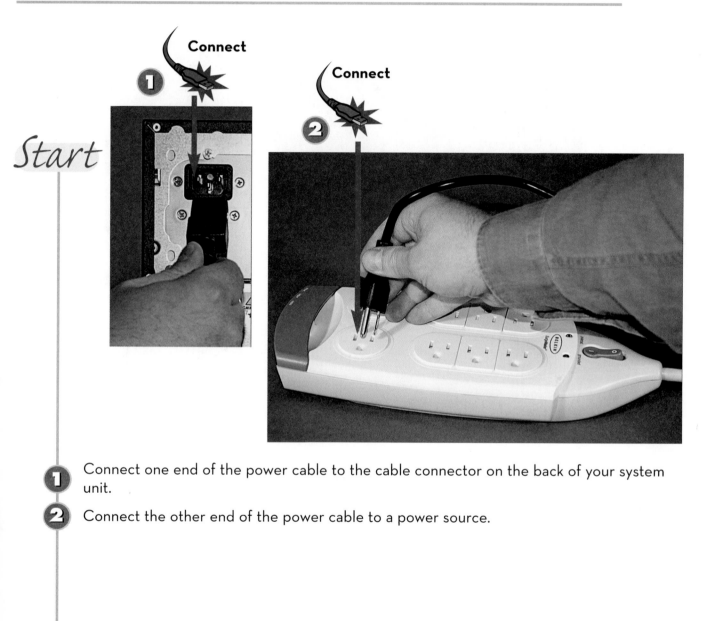

Start

① Connect

② Connect

End

① Connect one end of the power cable to the cable connector on the back of your system unit.

② Connect the other end of the power cable to a power source.

TIP

Use a Surge Suppressor

For extra protection, connect the power cable on your system unit to a surge suppressor rather than directly into an electrical outlet. This will protect your PC from power-line surges that could damage its delicate internal parts.

POWERING ON

Now that you have everything connected, sit back and rest for a minute. Next up is the big step—turning it all on!

Start

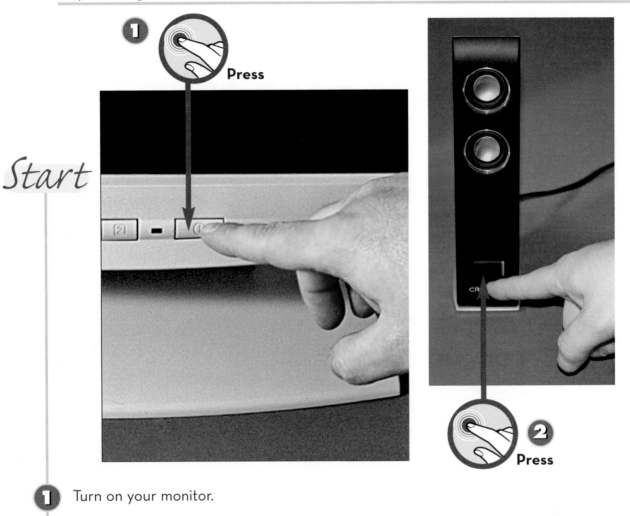

Press ①

Press ②

① Turn on your monitor.

② Turn on your speaker system—but make sure the speaker volume knob is turned down (toward the left).

Continued

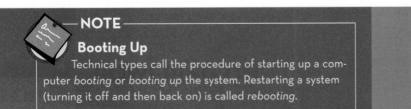

NOTE

Booting Up

Technical types call the procedure of starting up a computer *booting* or *booting up* the system. Restarting a system (turning it off and then back on) is called *rebooting*.

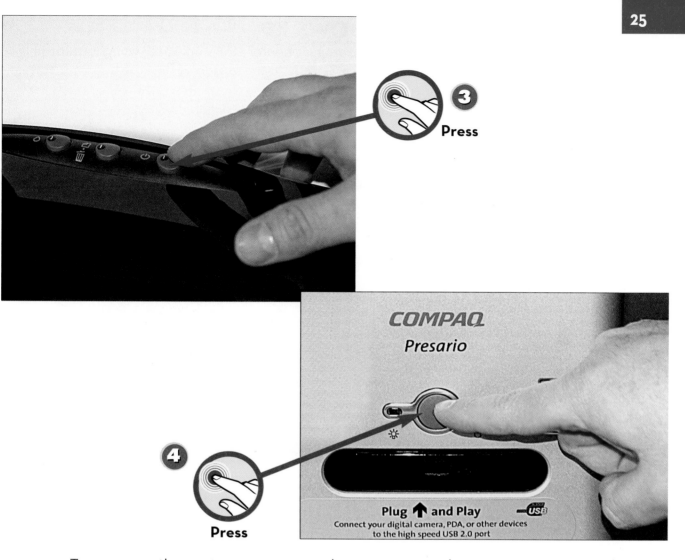

Press ③

④ **Press**

③ Turn on any other system components that are connected to your system unit, such as your printer, scanner, external modem, and so on.

④ Turn on your system unit.

End

CAUTION
Go in Order
Your system unit is the *last* thing you turn on. That's because when it powers on, it has to sense the other components of your system—which it can do only if the other components are plugged in and turned on.

TIP
Starting Up for the First Time
The first time you start your new PC, you're asked to do some basic setup operations, including activating and registering Windows.

LOGGING ON TO WINDOWS XP

Windows XP launches automatically as your computer starts up. After you get past the Windows Welcome screen, you're taken directly to the Windows desktop and your system is ready to run.

Start

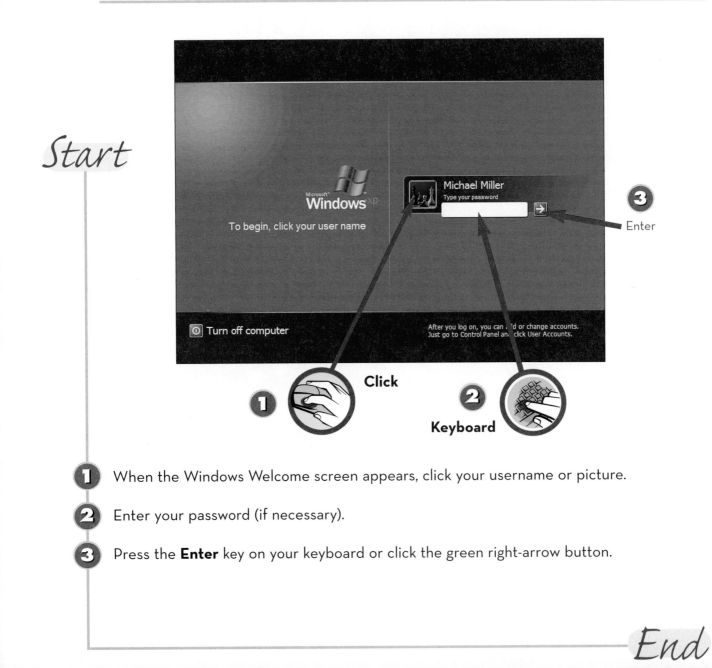

① When the Windows Welcome screen appears, click your username or picture.

② Enter your password (if necessary).

③ Press the **Enter** key on your keyboard or click the green right-arrow button.

End

TIP

Single-User Systems

If you have only a single user on your PC and that user doesn't have a password assigned, Windows moves past the Welcome screen with no action necessary on your part.

SHUTTING DOWN

When you want to turn off your computer, you do it through Windows. In fact, you don't want to turn off your computer any other way—you *always* want to turn things off through the official Windows procedure.

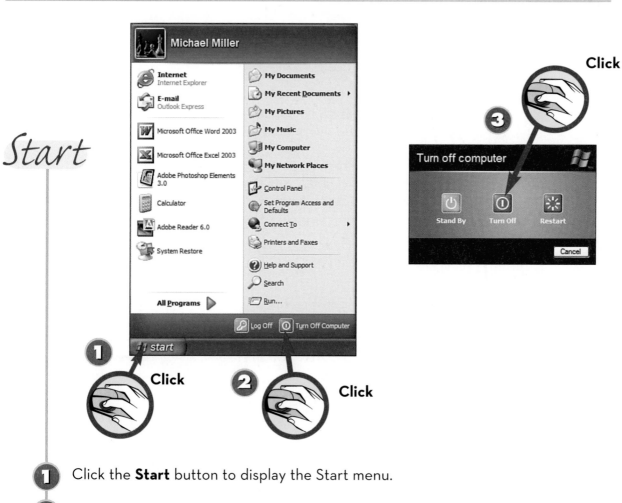

Start

Click

1 Click the **Start** button to display the Start menu.

2 Click **Turn Off Computer**.

3 When the Turn Off Computer dialog box appears, click **Turn Off**.

End

USING MICROSOFT WINDOWS XP

Microsoft Windows XP is a piece of software called an *operating system*. An operating system does what its name implies—it operates your computer system, working in the background every time you turn on your PC.

Equally important, Windows is what you see when you first turn on your computer, after everything turns on and boots up. The *desktop* that fills your screen is part of Windows, as is the taskbar at the bottom of the screen and the big menu that pops up when you click the Start button.

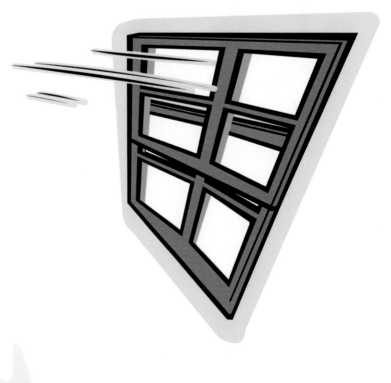

EXPLORING THE WINDOWS DESKTOP

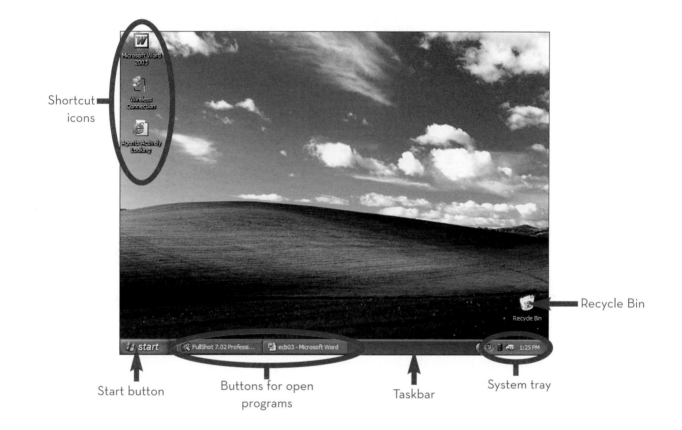

Shortcut icons

Recycle Bin

Start button

Buttons for open programs

Taskbar

System tray

POINTING AND CLICKING

To use Windows efficiently, you must master a few simple operations, all of which you perform with your mouse. The most common mouse operation is *pointing and clicking*. Simply move the mouse so the cursor is pointing to the object you want to select, and then click the left mouse button once.

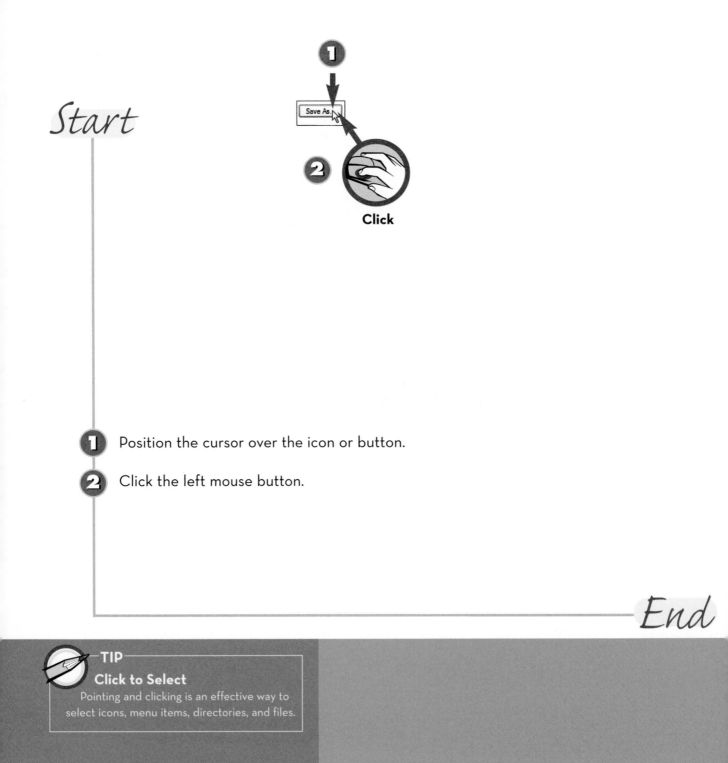

Start

Click

1 Position the cursor over the icon or button.

2 Click the left mouse button.

End

TIP
Click to Select
Pointing and clicking is an effective way to select icons, menu items, directories, and files.

DOUBLE-CLICKING

If you're using Windows XP's default operating mode, you'll need to *double-click* an item to activate an operation. This involves pointing at something onscreen with the cursor and then clicking the left mouse button twice in rapid succession. For example, to open a program, simply double-click a specific icon.

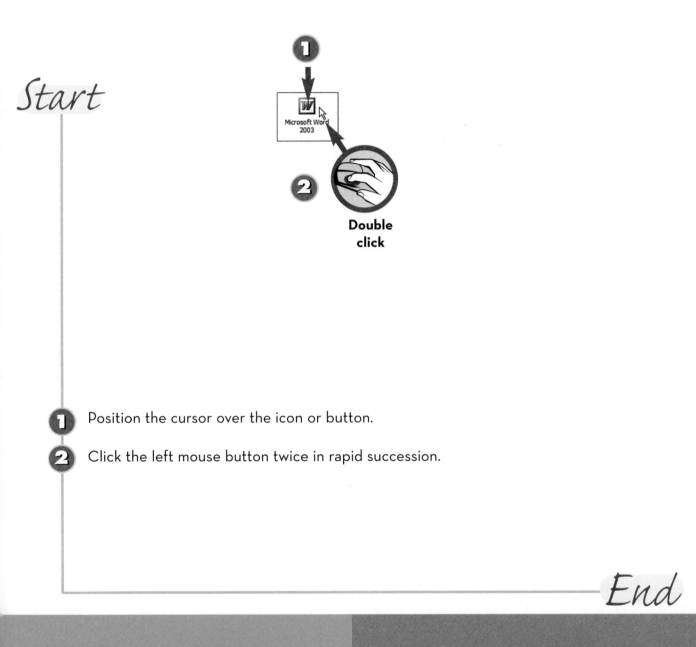

Start

Double click

1. Position the cursor over the icon or button.

2. Click the left mouse button twice in rapid succession.

End

RIGHT-CLICKING

When you select an item and then click the *right* mouse button, you'll often see a pop-up menu. This menu, when available, contains commands that directly relate to the selected object. Refer to your individual programs to see whether and how they use the right mouse button.

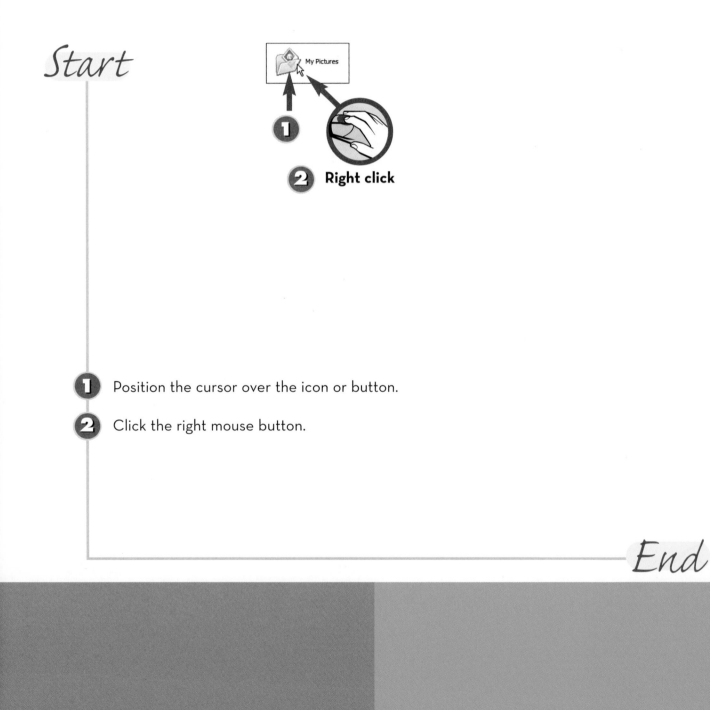

Start

My Pictures

① Right click

① Position the cursor over the icon or button.

② Click the right mouse button.

End

DRAGGING AND DROPPING

Dragging is a variation of clicking. To drag an object, point at it with the cursor and then press and hold down the left mouse button. Move the mouse without releasing the mouse button, and drag the object to a new location. When you're done moving the object, release the mouse button to *drop* the object onto the new location.

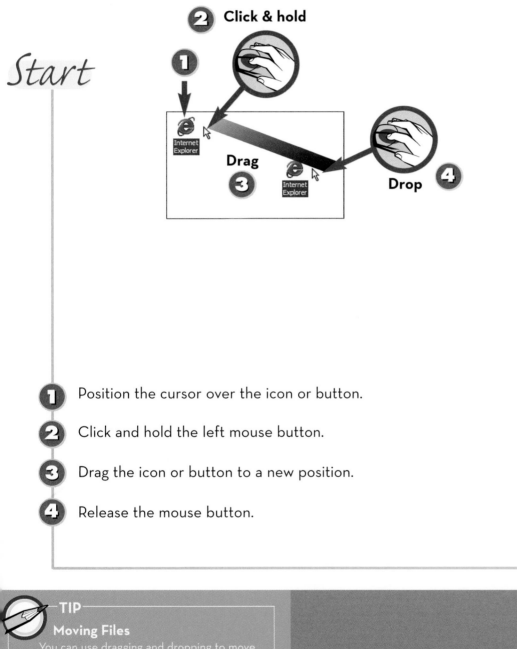

Start

End

1 Position the cursor over the icon or button.

2 Click and hold the left mouse button.

3 Drag the icon or button to a new position.

4 Release the mouse button.

HOVERING

When you position the cursor over an item without clicking, you're *hovering* over that item. Many operations require you to hover your cursor and then perform some other action.

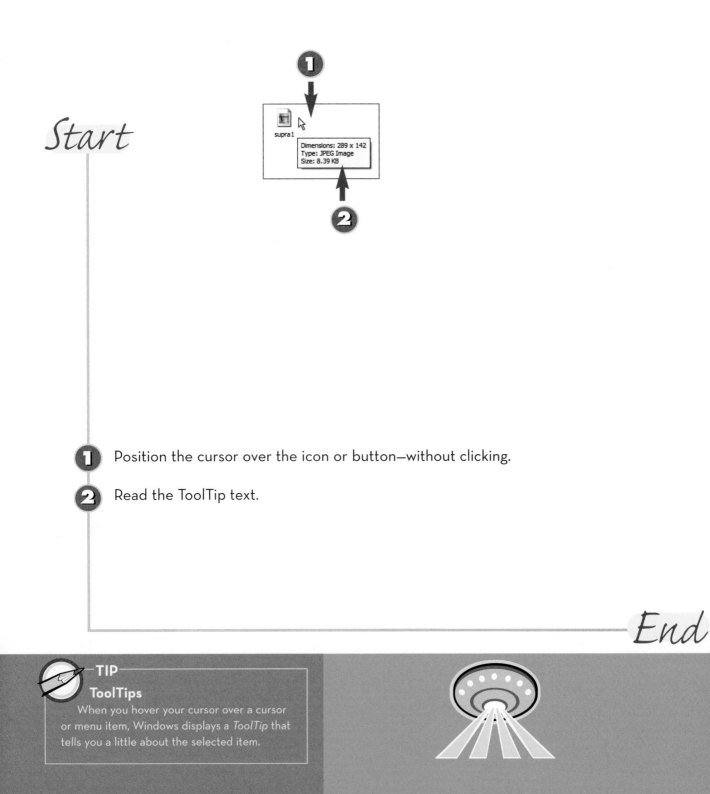

Start

supra1

Dimensions: 289 x 142
Type: JPEG Image
Size: 8.39 KB

1 Position the cursor over the icon or button—without clicking.

2 Read the ToolTip text.

End

TIP
ToolTips
When you hover your cursor over a cursor or menu item, Windows displays a *ToolTip* that tells you a little about the selected item.

MOVING A WINDOW

Every software program you launch (as explained later in this chapter in the task "Opening a Program") is displayed in a separate onscreen window. To move a window, click the window's title bar and drag the window anywhere on the desktop. When you release the mouse button, the window stays where you put it.

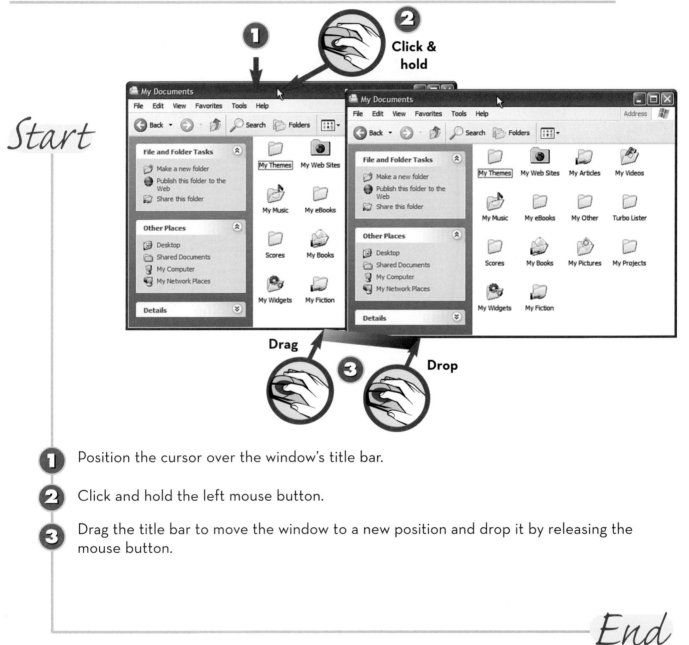

Start

End

1 Position the cursor over the window's title bar.

2 Click and hold the left mouse button.

3 Drag the title bar to move the window to a new position and drop it by releasing the mouse button.

SCROLLING A WINDOW

Many windows contain more information than can be displayed at once. When you have a long document or web page, only the first part of the document or page is displayed in the window. To view the rest of the document or page, you have to scroll down through the window, using the various parts of the scrollbar.

Start

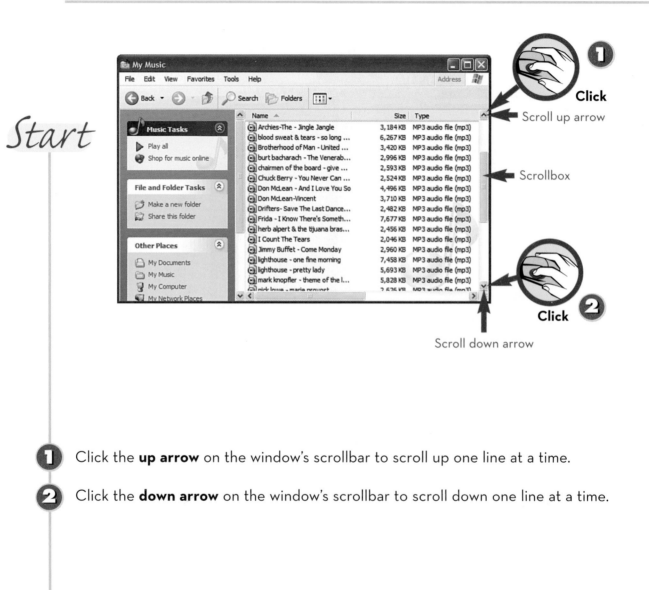

Click
Scroll up arrow

Scrollbox

Scroll down arrow
Click

1 Click the **up arrow** on the window's scrollbar to scroll up one line at a time.

2 Click the **down arrow** on the window's scrollbar to scroll down one line at a time.

End

TIP
Other Ways to Scroll
To move to a specific place in a long document, use your mouse to grab the scrollbox and drag it to a new position. You can also click the scrollbar between the scrollbox and the end arrow, which scrolls you one screen at a time.

RESIZING A WINDOW

You can change the size of most windows by dragging any edge of the window with your mouse. If you drag either side of the window, you resize the width. If you drag the top or bottom edge, you resize the height. And if you drag a corner, you resize the width and height at the same time.

Start

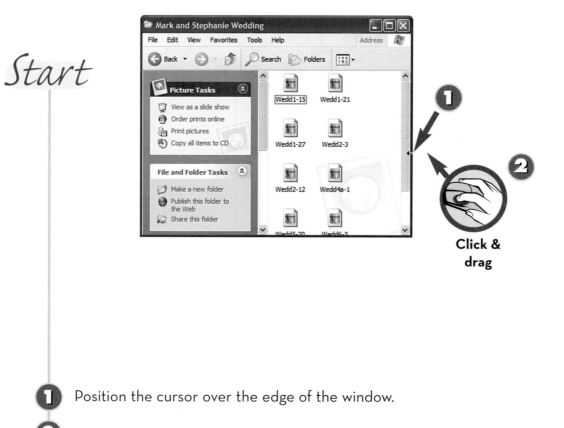

Click & drag

1 Position the cursor over the edge of the window.

2 Click and drag the edge of the window to a new position.

End

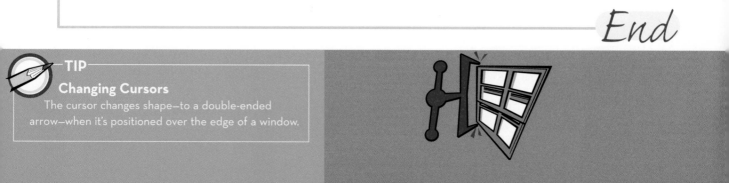

TIP

Changing Cursors

The cursor changes shape—to a double-ended arrow—when it's positioned over the edge of a window.

MAXIMIZING, MINIMIZING, AND CLOSING A WINDOW

After you've opened a window, you can maximize it to display full-screen. You can also minimize it so that it disappears from the desktop and resides as a button on the Windows Taskbar, and you can close it completely.

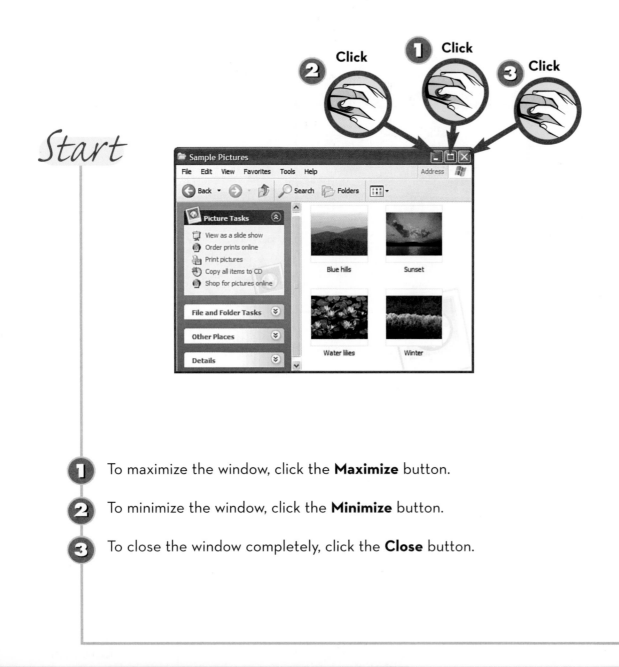

Start

1. To maximize the window, click the **Maximize** button.

2. To minimize the window, click the **Minimize** button.

3. To close the window completely, click the **Close** button.

End

TIP

Restoring a Window

If a window is already maximized, the Maximize button changes to a Restore Down button. When you click the Restore Down button, the window resumes its previous (premaximized) dimensions.

USING THE WINDOWS START MENU

All the software programs and utilities on your computer are accessed via Windows's Start menu, which consists of two columns of icons. Your most frequently used programs are listed in the left column; basic Windows utilities and folders are listed in the right column. To open a specific program or folder, just click the menu icon.

Start

Windows utilities and folders

2

Click

Michael Miller

Internet
Internet Explorer

E-mail
Outlook Express

Microsoft Office Word 2003

Microsoft Office Excel 2003

Adobe Photoshop Elements 3.0

Calculator

Adobe Reader 6.0

System Restore

My Documents

My Recent Documents ▶

My Pictures

My Music

My Computer

My Network Places

Control Panel

Set Program Access and Defaults

Connect To ▶

Printers and Faxes

Help and Support

Search

Run...

Frequently used programs

All Programs arrow ➡ **All Programs** ▷

Log Off   Turn Off Computer

start

1

Click

1 Click the green **Start** button to open the Start menu.

2 Click any menu item to launch a program or open a folder.

End

40

OPENING A PROGRAM

To view all the programs installed on your PC, open the Start menu and click the All Programs arrow. This displays a new menu called the Programs menu. From here, you can access various programs, sorted by type and title or manufacturer.

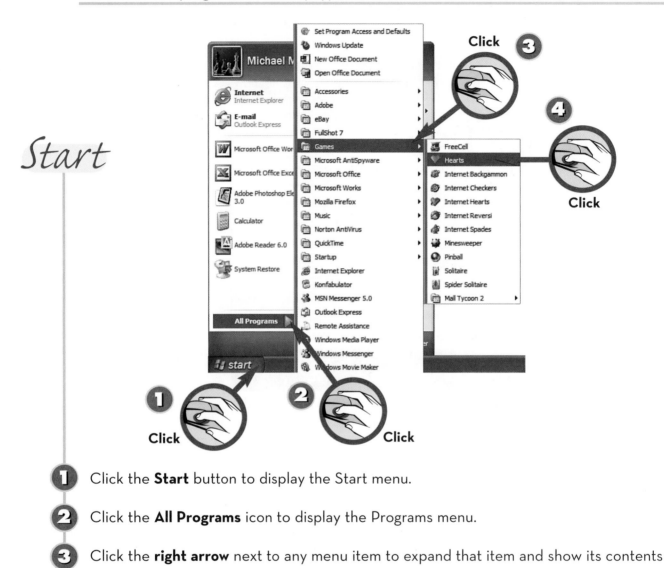

Start

1 Click the **Start** button to display the Start menu.

2 Click the **All Programs** icon to display the Programs menu.

3 Click the **right arrow** next to any menu item to expand that item and show its contents

4 Click the icon for the program you want to launch.

End

TIP

More Programs in the Folder

When more programs are contained within a master folder, you'll see an arrow to the right of the title. Click this arrow to display additional choices.

CREATING A NEW SHORTCUT ON THE DESKTOP

Desktop icons—those little pictures on your desktop—function as shortcuts for opening programs and documents. Placing a shortcut on your desktop is an alternative to launching items from the Start menu.

Start

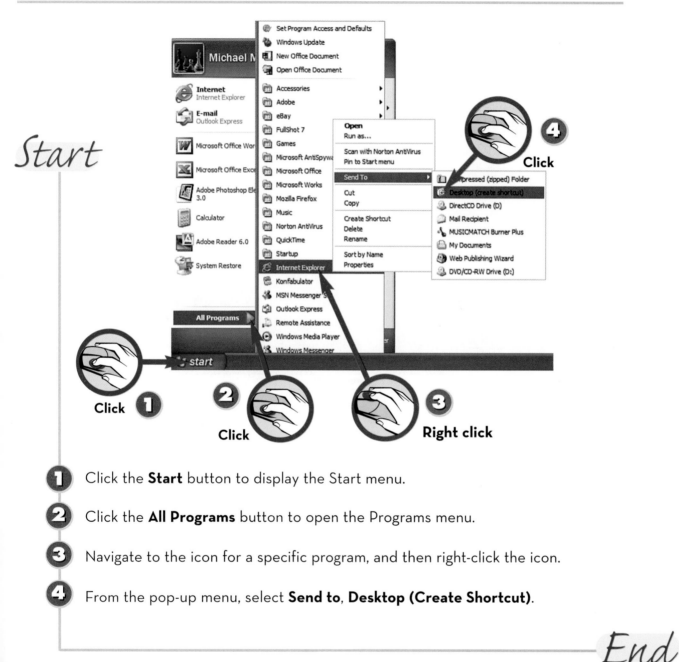

1. Click the **Start** button to display the Start menu.

2. Click the **All Programs** button to open the Programs menu.

3. Navigate to the icon for a specific program, and then right-click the icon.

4. From the pop-up menu, select **Send to, Desktop (Create Shortcut)**.

End

TIP
Alternative Methods
You can also create a shortcut by right-dragging a file icon directly to the desktop or by right-clicking the desktop and selecting **New, Shortcut** from the pop-up menu.

SWITCHING BETWEEN PROGRAMS

After you've launched a few programs, you can easily switch between one open program and another by clicking the buttons located at the bottom of the Windows desktop.

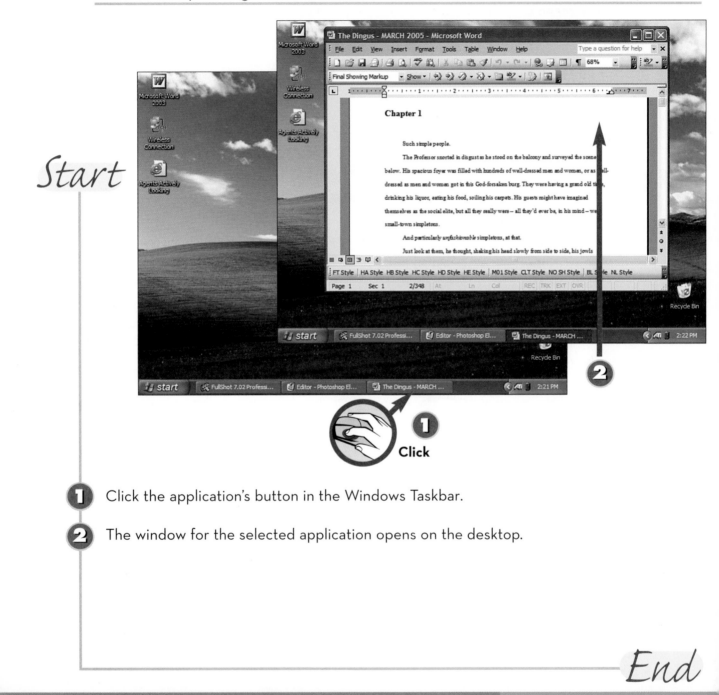

Start

Click

1. Click the application's button in the Windows Taskbar.

2. The window for the selected application opens on the desktop.

End

TIP

Keyboard Switching

You can also switch between programs. Hold down the **Alt** key and then press the **Tab** key repeatedly until the application window you want is selected. (This cycles through all open windows.) When you're at the window you want, release the **Alt** key.

USING MENUS

Most windows use a set of pull-down menus to store all the commands and operations you can perform. The menus are aligned across the top of the window, just below the title bar, in what is called a *menu bar*. You open (or pull down) a menu by clicking the menu's name; you select a menu item by clicking it with your mouse.

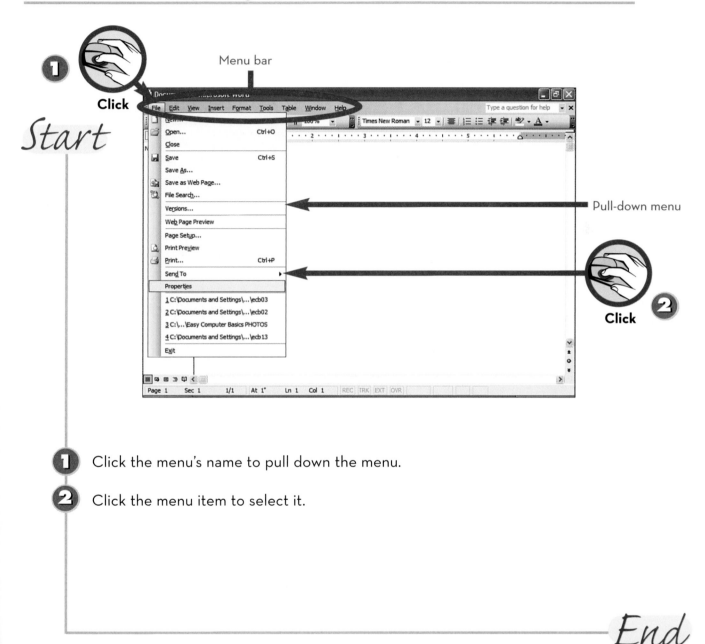

1 Click the menu's name to pull down the menu.

2 Click the menu item to select it.

End

USING TOOLBARS

Some Windows programs put the most frequently used operations on one or more *toolbars*, typically located just below the menu bar. A toolbar looks like a row of buttons, each with a small picture (called an *icon*) and maybe a bit of text. You activate the associated command or operation by clicking the button with your mouse.

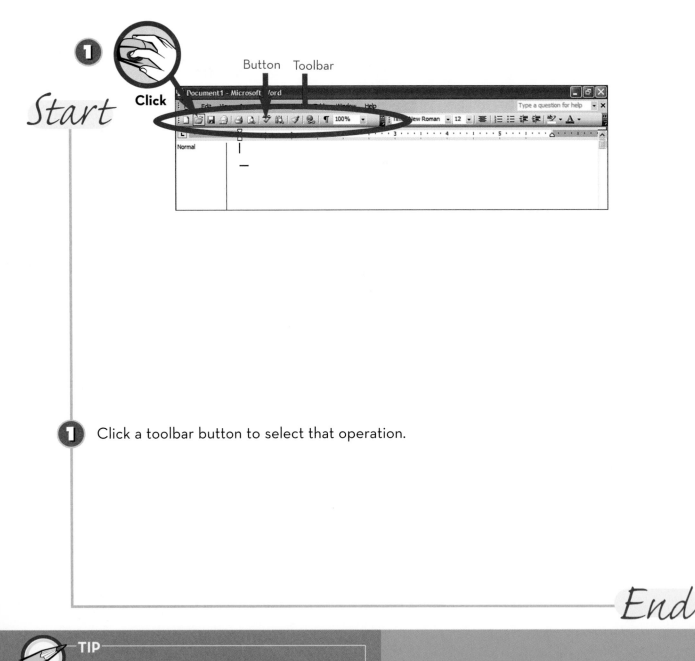

Button   Toolbar

Start   **Click**

Start

1 Click a toolbar button to select that operation.

End

MANAGING PC RESOURCES WITH MY COMPUTER

Windows's My Computer utility lets you access each major component of your system and perform basic maintenance functions. For example, you can use My Computer to "open" the contents of your hard disk and then copy, move, and delete individual files.

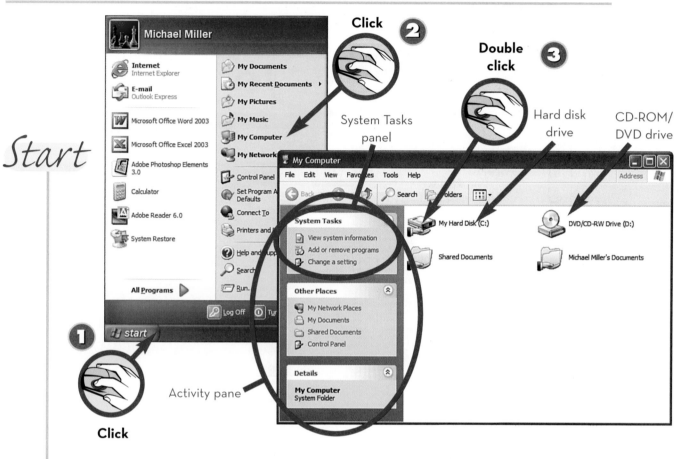

Start

End

1 Click the **Start** button to display the Start menu.

2 Click the **My Computer** icon.

3 Double-click any icon to view its contents.

TIP
View Drive Contents
To view the contents of a specific drive, double-click the drive's icon. You'll see a list of folders and files located on that drive; to view the contents of any folder, double-click the icon for that folder.

MANAGING WINDOWS WITH THE CONTROL PANEL

The Windows Control Panel is used to manage most (but not all) of Windows's configuration settings. The Control Panel is actually a system folder (like My Computer and My Documents) that contains several individual utilities that let you adjust and configure various system properties.

Start

1 Click the **Start** button to display the Start menu.

2 Click the **Control Panel** icon to open the Control Panel.

3 Click the icon for the category you want to configure.

Continued

TIP

Control Panel Categories

Individual settings within the Control Panel are organized by category. You first have to select a specific category to access all its related settings.

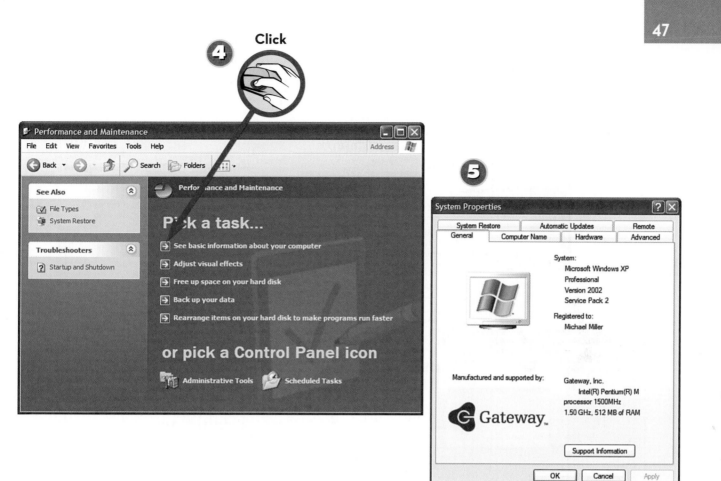

4   Click the task you want to perform.

5   Configure the settings for that task using the selected utility's dialog box.

End

NOTE

Configuring Individual Settings

When you open a configuration utility, you'll see a dialog box for that particular item. You can then change the individual settings within that dialog box; click the **OK** button to register your new settings.

CHANGING THE SIZE OF YOUR DESKTOP

You can configure your computer's display so that the desktop is larger or smaller than normal, by changing Windows's screen resolution. A larger desktop lets you view more things onscreen at the same time—even though each item is smaller than before. A smaller desktop displays fewer items, but they're larger.

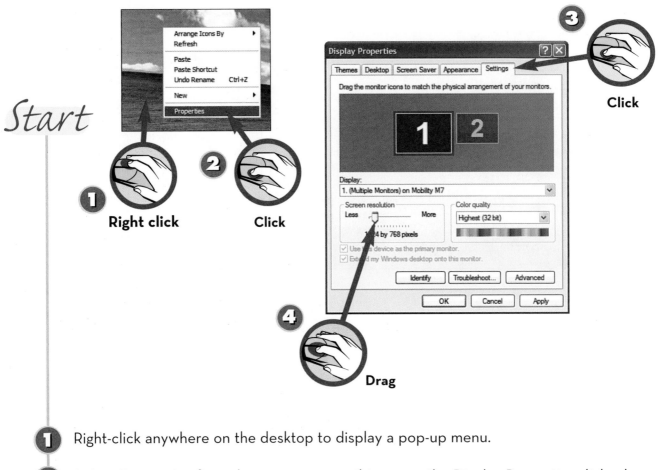

Start

Right click

Click

Click

Drag

① Right-click anywhere on the desktop to display a pop-up menu.

② Select **Properties** from the pop-up menu; this opens the Display Properties dialog box.

③ Click the **Settings** tab.

④ Adjust the **Screen Resolution** slider, and click **OK** when done.

End

NOTE

Resolution and Pixels

Resolution is measured in pixels, each of which is a single dot on your screen. You have to select both a horizontal and vertical resolution, such as 1024 (horizontal) by 768 (vertical) pixels.

SELECTING A NEW DESKTOP THEME

Desktop *themes* are specific combinations of background wallpaper, colors, fonts, cursors, sounds, and screensavers—all arranged around a specific look or topic. When you choose a new theme, the look and feel of your entire desktop changes. Windows's default theme is called Windows XP.

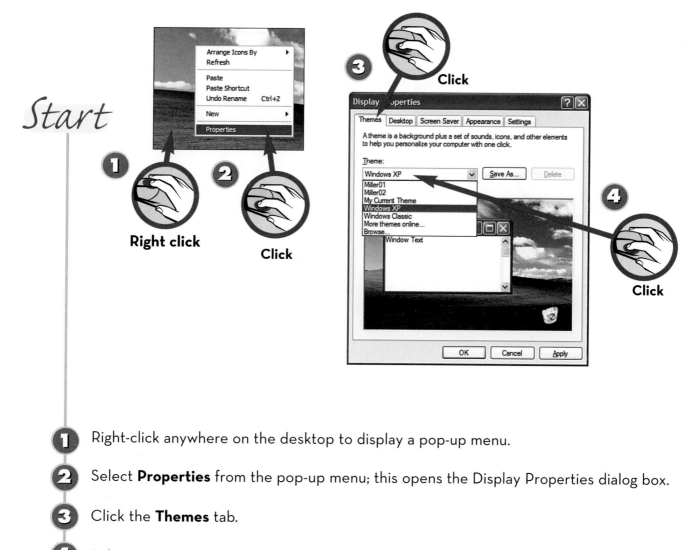

Start

Right click

Click

Click

Click

End

1 Right-click anywhere on the desktop to display a pop-up menu.

2 Select **Properties** from the pop-up menu; this opens the Display Properties dialog box.

3 Click the **Themes** tab.

4 Select a new theme from the **Theme** drop-down list; click **OK** when you're done.

TIP
More Themes
You can find additional themes in the Microsoft Plus! SuperPack add-on pack. Learn more at the Microsoft Plus! website (www.microsoft.com/windows/plus/).

PERSONALIZING THE DESKTOP BACKGROUND

Although changing themes is the fastest way to change the look of all your desktop elements, you can also change each element separately. For example, you can easily change your desktop's background pattern or wallpaper. You can choose from the many patterns and wallpapers included with Windows or select a graphic of your own choosing.

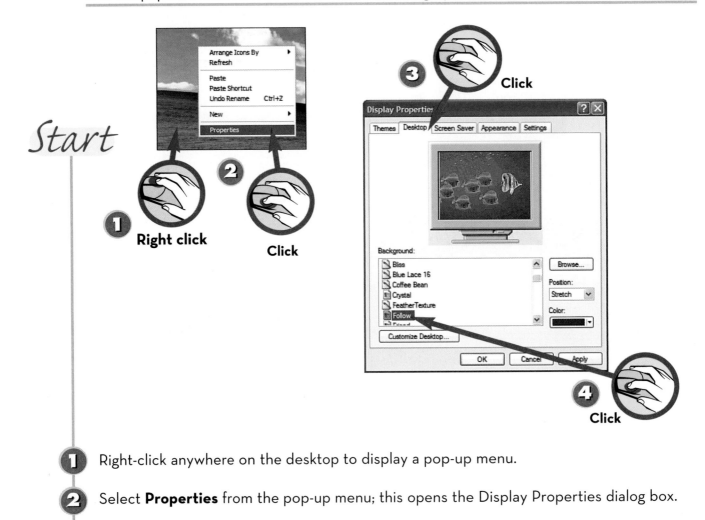

Start

1 Right-click anywhere on the desktop to display a pop-up menu.

2 Select **Properties** from the pop-up menu; this opens the Display Properties dialog box.

3 Click the **Desktop** tab.

4 Select one of Windows's built-in backgrounds from the **Background** list; then click **OK**.

End

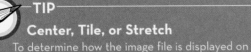
TIP
Center, Tile, or Stretch
To determine how the image file is displayed on your desktop, select one of the items from the **Position** pull-down list: Center, Tile, or Stretch.

CHANGING THE COLOR SCHEME

The default Windows XP desktop uses a predefined combination of colors and fonts. If you don't like this combination, you can choose from several other predefined schemes.

Start

Right click

Click

③ **Click**

Display Properties

Themes | Desktop | Screen Saver | Appearance | Settings

Inactive Window
Active Window
Window Text

Message Box

OK

Windows and buttons:
Windows XP style

Color scheme:
Olive Green
Default (blue)
Olive Green
Silver

Effects...
Advanced

OK | Cancel | Apply

④ **Click**

① Right-click anywhere on the desktop to display a pop-up menu.

② Select **Properties** from the pop-up menu; this opens the Display Properties dialog box.

③ Click the **Appearance** tab.

④ Pull down the **Color Scheme** list, and select a new theme. Click **OK** when done. Default (Blue) is the standard Windows XP color scheme.

End

SETTING UP ADDITIONAL USERS

If you have multiple people using your PC, you should assign each user in your household his or her own password-protected user account. Anyone trying to access another user's account and files without the password will then be denied access.

Start

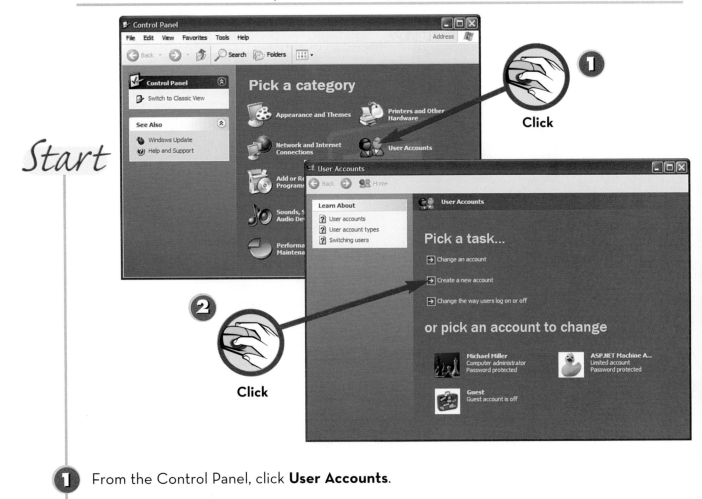

Click

Click

① From the Control Panel, click **User Accounts**.

② Click **Create a New Account**.

Continued

TIP

Different Users

You can create three types of user accounts—computer administrator, limited, and guest. You should set yourself up as an administrator because only this account can make systemwide changes to your PC.

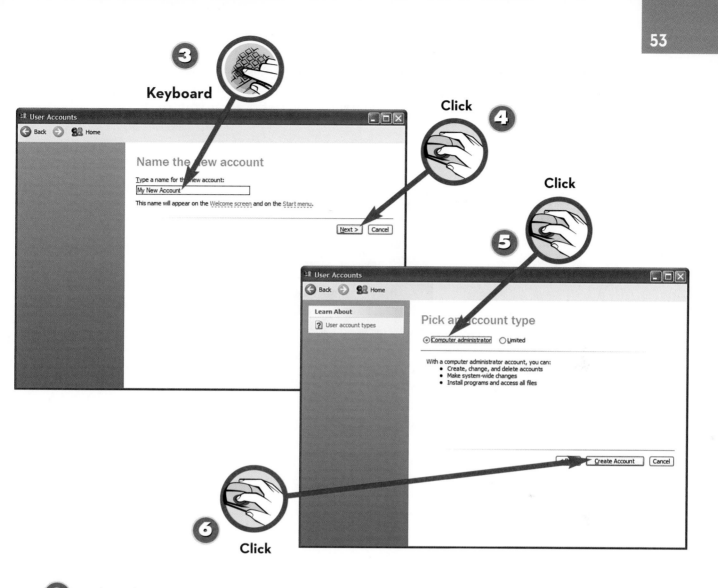

Keyboard

Click 4

Click 5

6 **Click**

3 When the **User Accounts** screen appears, enter a name for the account.

4 Click **Next**.

5 On the Pick an Account Type screen, check either the **Computer Administrator** or **Limited** option.

6 Click the **Create Account** button. Windows XP now creates the new account and randomly assigns a picture that will appear next to the username.

End

TIP
Change Your Picture
You can change an account picture by returning to the User Accounts utility, selecting the account, and then selecting the Change My Picture option.

TIP
Create a Password
By default, no password is assigned to the new account. You can assign a password by returning to the User Accounts utility, selecting the account, and then selecting the Create a Password option.

USING A SCREENSAVER

Screensavers display moving designs on your computer screen when you haven't typed or moved the mouse for a while. This prevents static images from burning into your screen and provides some small degree of entertainment if you're bored at your desk.

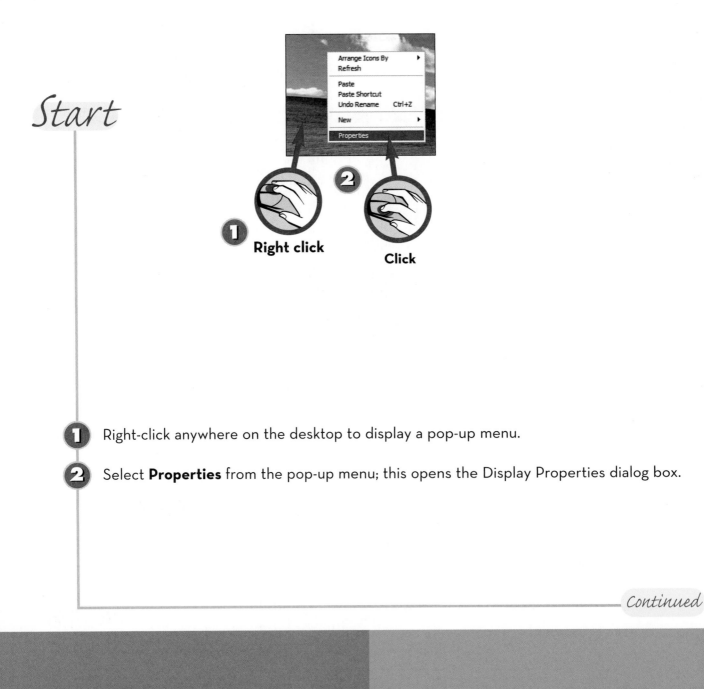

Start

Right click

Click

1 Right-click anywhere on the desktop to display a pop-up menu.

2 Select **Properties** from the pop-up menu; this opens the Display Properties dialog box.

Continued

Click

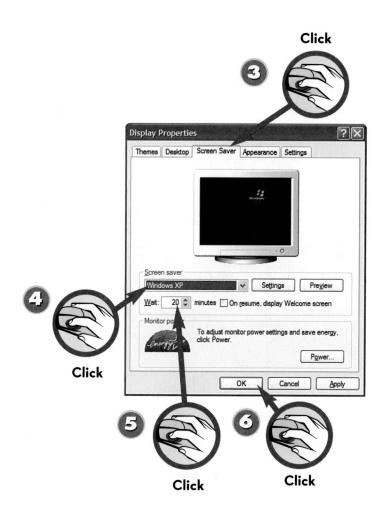

Click

Click **Click**

3 Click the **Screen Saver** tab.

4 Select a screensaver from the **Screen Saver** drop-down list.

5 Select the number of minutes you want the screen to be idle before the screensaver activates.

6 Click **OK** when you're done.

End

TIP
Configure the Screensaver
Click the Settings button to configure settings
specific to an individual screensaver (if available).

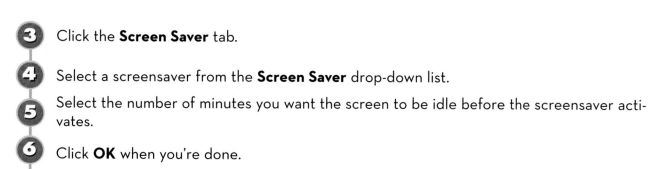

GETTING HELP IN WINDOWS

When you can't figure out how to perform a particular task, it's time to ask for help. In Windows XP, this is done through the Help and Support Center.

Start

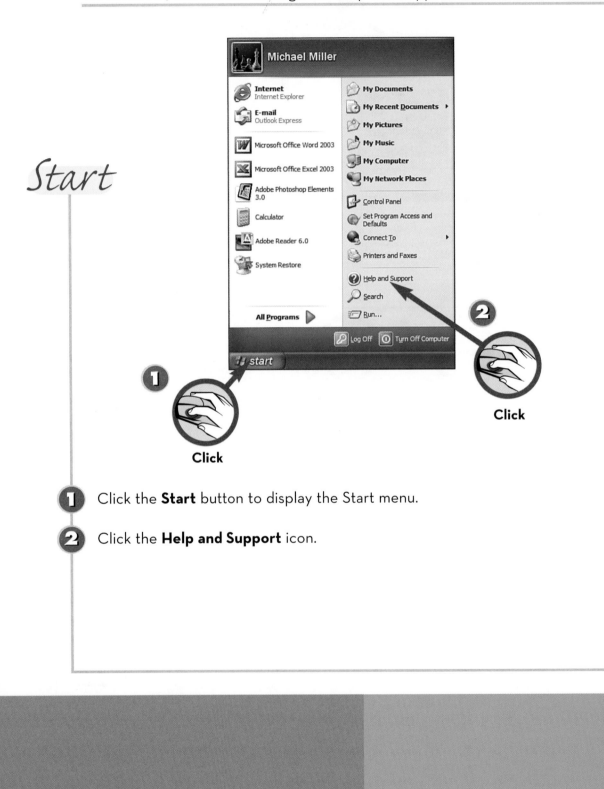

Click

Click

1 Click the **Start** button to display the Start menu.

2 Click the **Help and Support** icon.

Continued

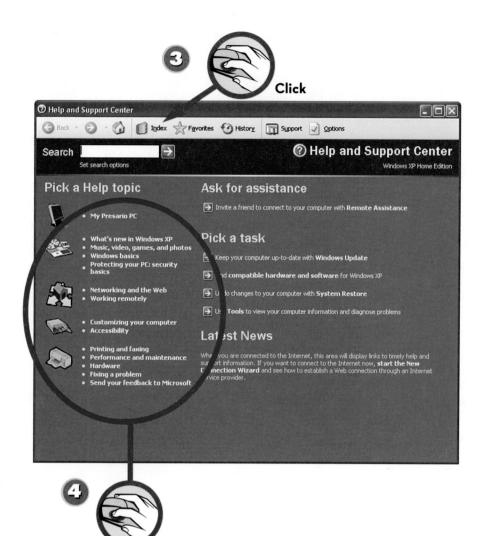

Click

Click

③ Click the **Index** button to display a list of help topics.

④ Click a topic to display information about that topic.

End

TIP

Search for Help

You can also use the Search box to search for specific help topics. If you're connected to the Internet, Windows will search Microsoft's online Knowledge Base for more answers.

WORKING WITH FILES AND FOLDERS

All the data for documents and programs on your computer are stored in electronic files. These files are then arranged into a series of folders and subfolders—just as you'd arrange paper files in a series of file folders in a filing cabinet.

In Windows XP you can use either My Computer or My Documents (both accessible from the Windows Start menu) to view and manage the folders and files on your system. Both of these tools work similarly and enable you to customize the way they display their contents.

The My Documents folder contains not only individual files, but also other folders—called *subfolders*—that themselves contain other files. Most of the file-related operations you'll want to undertake are accessible directly from the File and Folder Tasks section in the Tasks pane, located at the left of the My Documents window.

THE MY DOCUMENTS FOLDER

View the parent folder

View the last-viewed folder

Folder

Change the folder view

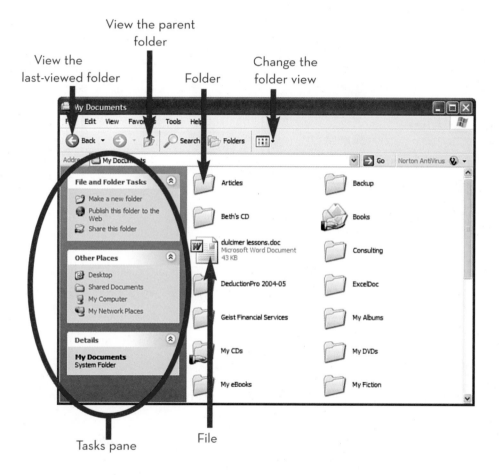

Tasks pane

File

CHANGING THE WAY FILES ARE DISPLAYED

You can choose to view the contents of a folder in a variety of ways. The default view is the Tiles view; you can experiment with each view to determine which you like best.

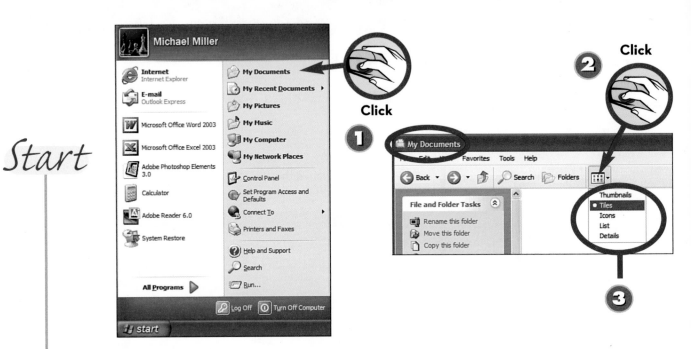

Start

Click

Click

1   Open the **Start** menu and click **My Documents**.

2   Double-click any folder to view the folder's contents; then click the **Views** button on the toolbar.

3   Select from the **Thumbnails**, **Tiles**, **Icons**, **List**, and **Details** views.

End

TIP

Which View Is Best?

Thumbnails view is best for working with graphics files. Details view is best if you're looking for files by date or size.

SORTING FILES AND FOLDERS

When viewing files in My Computer or My Documents, you can sort your files and folders in a number of ways. To view your files in alphabetical order, choose to sort by Name. To see all similar files grouped together, choose to sort by Type. To sort your files by the date and time they were last edited, choose the Modified option.

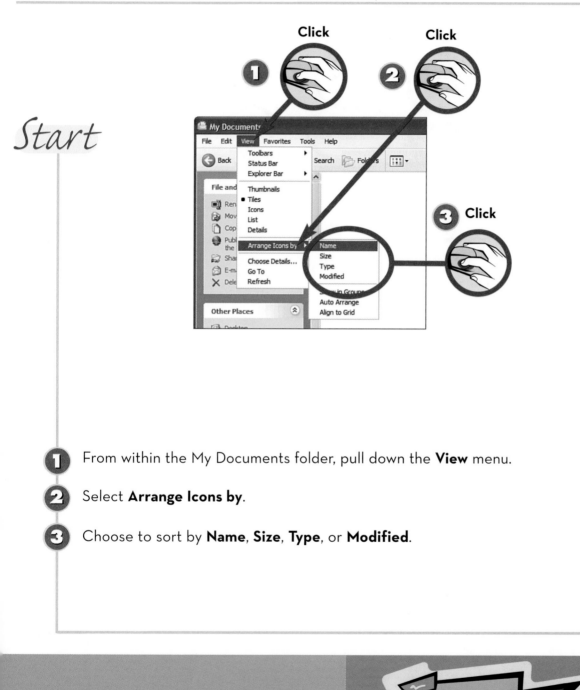

Start

Click

Click

Click

End

1 From within the My Documents folder, pull down the **View** menu.

2 Select **Arrange Icons by**.

3 Choose to sort by **Name**, **Size**, **Type**, or **Modified**.

NAVIGATING FOLDERS

You can navigate through the folders and subfolders in My Computer, My Documents, and other folders in several ways.

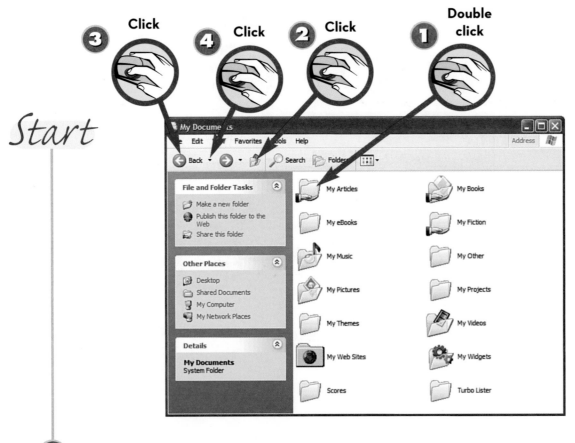

1 To view the contents of a disk or folder, double-click an icon.

2 To move up the hierarchy of folders and subfolders to the next highest item, click the **Up** button on the toolbar.

3 To move back to the disk or folder previously selected, click the **Back** button on the toolbar.

4 To choose from the history of disks and folders previously viewed, click the down arrow on the **Back** button and select a disk or folder.

TIP

Moving Forward

If you've moved back through multiple disks or folders, you can move forward to the next folder by clicking the Forward button.

NAVIGATING WITH THE FOLDERS PANE

Another way to navigate your files and folders is to use the Folders pane, which displays a hierarchical folder tree.

Start

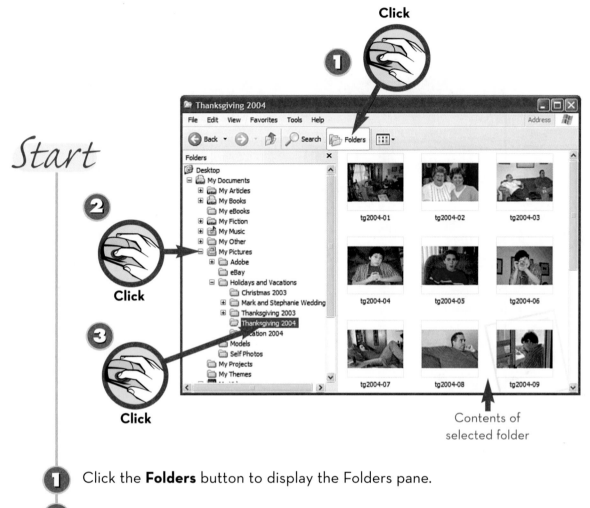

Contents of
selected folder

1 Click the **Folders** button to display the Folders pane.

2 Click the plus icon next to a folder to display all the subfolders it contains.

3 Click a folder to display its contents.

End

NOTE

Windows Explorer

Windows XP's Folders pane is similar to the Windows Explorer utility found in previous versions of Windows.

CREATING A NEW FOLDER

The more files you create, the harder it is to organize and find things on your hard disk. When the number of files you have becomes unmanageable, you need to create more folders—and subfolders—to better categorize your files.

Start

Click

Keyboard

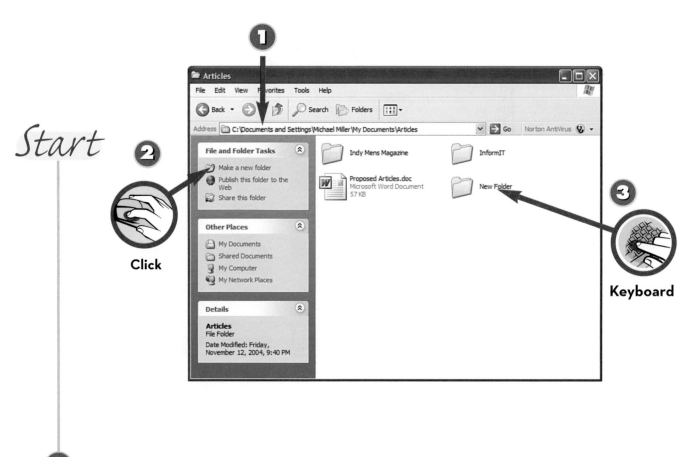

1. Navigate to the drive or folder where you want to place the new folder.

2. Select **Make a New Folder** from the File and Folder Tasks panel.

3. A new, empty folder now appears with the filename **New Folder** highlighted. Type a name for your folder and press **Enter**.

End

CAUTION

Illegal Characters

Folder names and filenames can include up to 255 characters—including many special characters. You *can't*, however, use the following "illegal" characters: \ / : * ? " < > |.

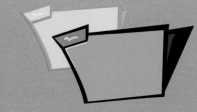

RENAMING A FILE OR FOLDER

When you create a new file or folder, it helps to give it a name that describes its contents. Sometimes, however, you might need to change a file's name. Fortunately, Windows makes renaming an item relatively easy.

Start

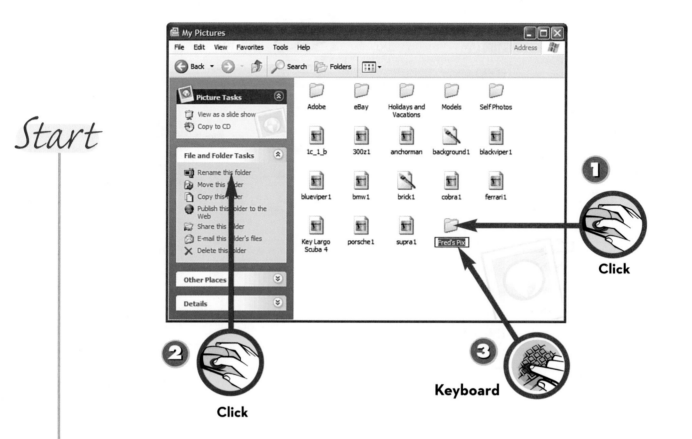

1. Click the file or folder you want to rename.

2. Click **Rename This File** from the File Tasks list, or press **F2**; this highlights the filename.

3. Type a new name for your folder (which overwrites the current name), and press **Enter**.

End

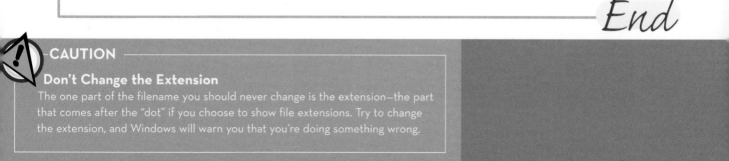

-CAUTION

Don't Change the Extension

The one part of the filename you should never change is the extension—the part that comes after the "dot" if you choose to show file extensions. Try to change the extension, and Windows will warn you that you're doing something wrong.

COPYING A FILE OR FOLDER

There are many ways to copy a file in Windows XP. The easiest method is to use the Task pane in the My Documents folder.

Start

End

1. Click the item you want to copy.

2. Click **Copy This File** in the File Tasks list; this opens the Copy Items dialog box.

3. Navigate to and select the new location for the item.

4. Click the **Copy** button.

TIP

Copy to a New Folder

If you want to copy the item to a new folder, click the New Folder button before you click the Copy button.

MOVING A FILE OR FOLDER

Moving a file (or folder) is different from copying it. Moving cuts the item from its previous location and places it in a new location. Copying leaves the original item where it was *and* creates a copy of the item elsewhere.

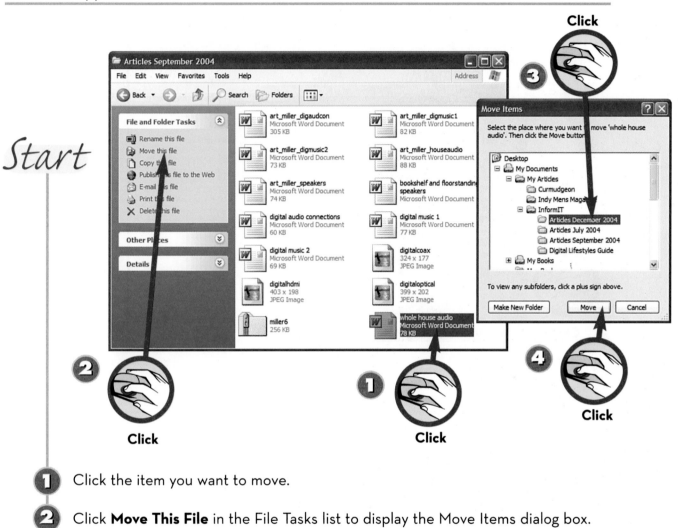

Start

Click

Click

Click

Click

1. Click the item you want to move.

2. Click **Move This File** in the File Tasks list to display the Move Items dialog box.

3. Navigate to and select the new location for the item.

4. Click the **Move** button.

End

TIP
Move to a New Folder
If you want to move the item to a new folder, click the New Folder button before you click the Move button.

DELETING A FILE OR FOLDER

Too many files eat up too much hard disk space—which is a bad thing. Because you don't want to waste disk space, you should periodically delete those files (and folders) you no longer need. When you delete a file, you send it to the Windows Recycle Bin, which is kind of a trash can for deleted files.

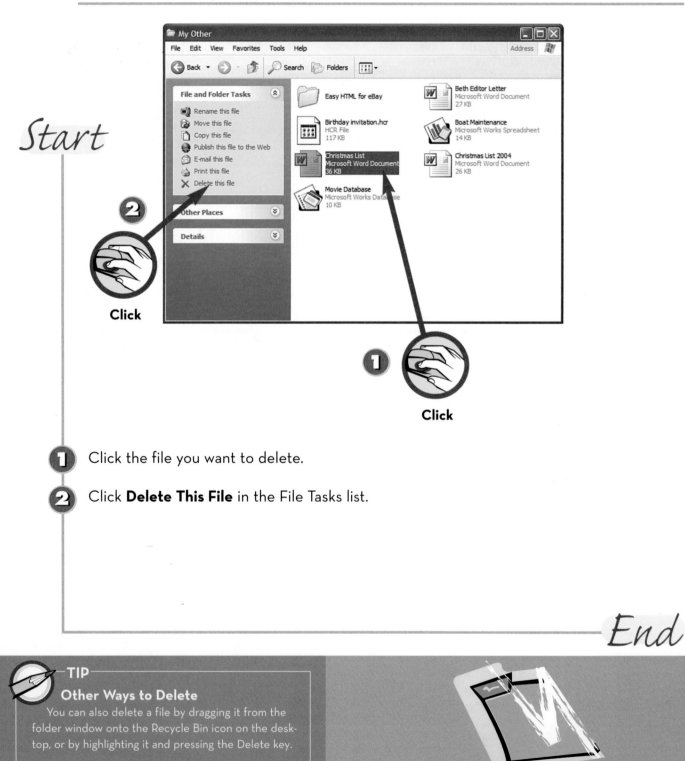

Start

Click

Click

1️⃣ Click the file you want to delete.

2️⃣ Click **Delete This File** in the File Tasks list.

End

TIP

Other Ways to Delete

You can also delete a file by dragging it from the folder window onto the Recycle Bin icon on the desktop, or by highlighting it and pressing the Delete key.

RESTORING DELETED FILES

Have you ever accidentally deleted the wrong file? If so, you're in luck. Windows stores the files you delete in the Recycle Bin, which is actually a special folder on your hard disk. For a short period of time, you can "undelete" files from the Recycle Bin back to their original locations.

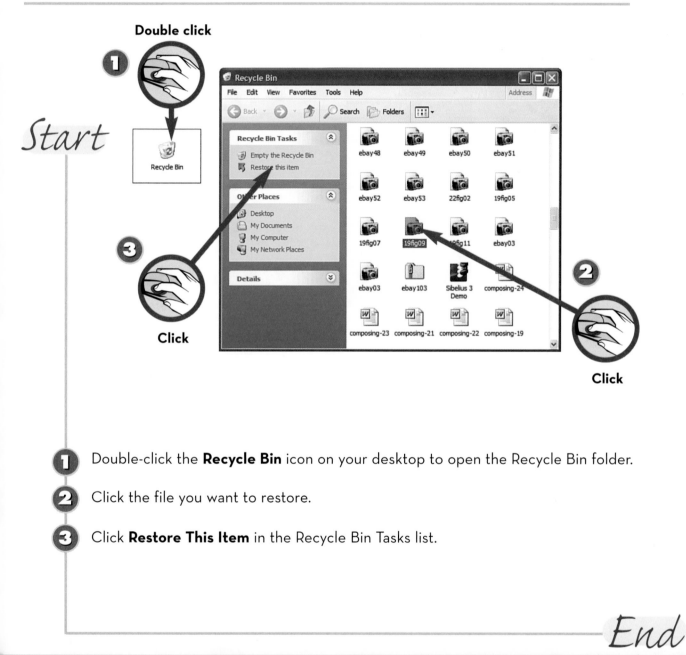

Double click

Start

Click

Click

1. Double-click the **Recycle Bin** icon on your desktop to open the Recycle Bin folder.

2. Click the file you want to restore.

3. Click **Restore This Item** in the Recycle Bin Tasks list.

End

EMPTYING THE RECYCLE BIN

By default, the deleted files in the Recycle Bin can occupy 10% of your hard disk space. When you've deleted enough files to exceed this 10%, the oldest files in the Recycle Bin are automatically and permanently deleted from your hard disk. You can also manually empty the Recycle Bin, and thus free up some hard disk space.

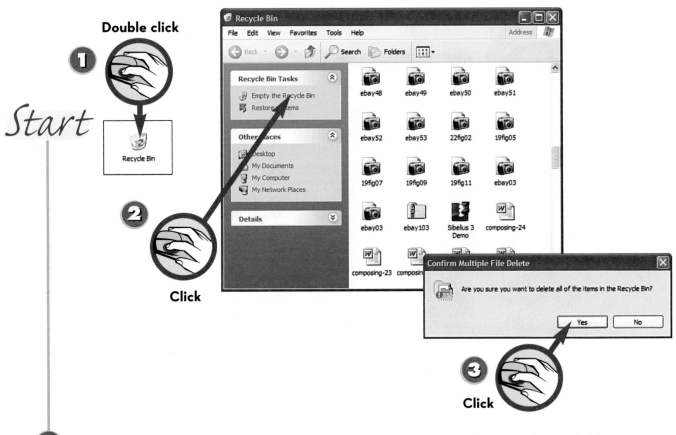

Double click

Start

Click

Click

1. Double-click the **Recycle Bin** icon on your desktop to open the Recycle Bin folder.

2. Click **Empty the Recycle Bin** in the Recycle Bin Tasks list.

3. When the Confirm File Delete dialog box appears, click **Yes** to completely erase the file.

End

TIP

Fast Empty

You can also empty the Recycle Bin by right-clicking its icon on the Windows desktop and selecting Empty Recycle Bin from the pop-up menu.

COMPRESSING A FILE

Really big files can be difficult to copy or share. Fortunately, Windows XP lets you create *compressed* folders, which take big files and compress them down in size. After the file has been transferred, you can then uncompress the file back to its original state.

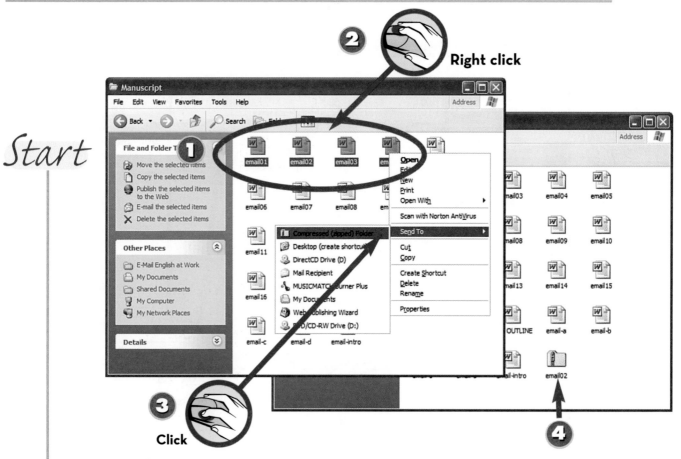

Right click

Start

Click

1 Select the file(s) you want to compress. (To select more than one file, hold down the **Ctrl** key when clicking.)

2 Right-click the selected file(s) to display the pop-up menu.

3 Select **Send to, Compressed (Zipped) Folder**.

4 Windows creates a new zipped folder in this same folder that contains copies of the selected files.

End

NOTE

Zip Files
The compressed folder is actually a file with a **.zip** extension, so it can be used with other compression/decompression programs, such as WinZip.

EXTRACTING FILES FROM A COMPRESSED FOLDER

The process of decompressing a file is actually an *extraction* process. That's because you extract the original file(s) from the compressed folder. In Windows XP, this process is eased by the use of the Extraction Wizard.

Start

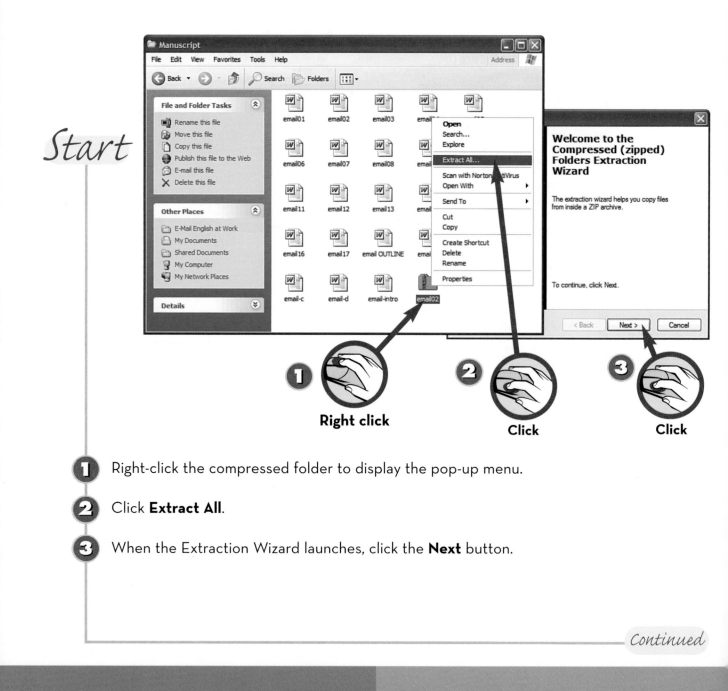

Right click

Click

Click

1 Right-click the compressed folder to display the pop-up menu.

2 Click **Extract All**.

3 When the Extraction Wizard launches, click the **Next** button.

Continued

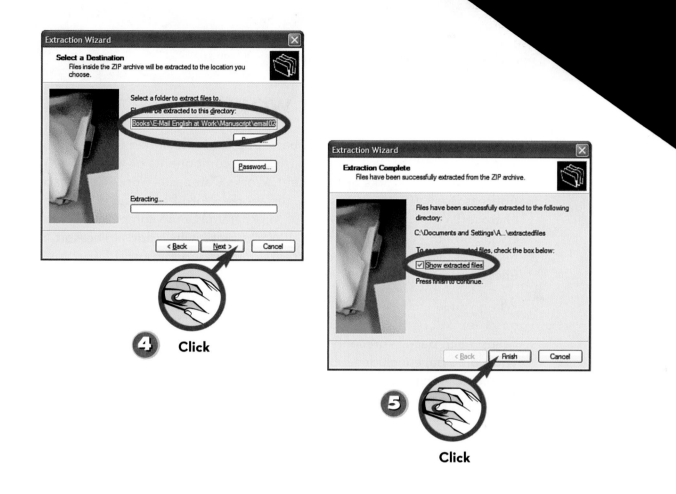

4 Select to which folder you want to extract the files and click **Next**.

5 The wizard now extracts the files and displays the Extraction Complete page. Click the **Finish** button to view the files you've just extracted.

End

TIP

Zipper Icon
Compressed folders are distinguished by the little zipper on the folder icon.

MICROSOFT WORKS

Works is a suite of five basic applications, all tied together by an application called the Task Launcher. The key components of Works are Works Word Processor, Works Spreadsheet, Works Database, Works Calendar, and Works Address Book. (On many systems, the Works Word Processor is replaced by Microsoft Word, a more fully featured program.) Some computer manufacturers include the complete Microsoft Works Suite, which adds Microsoft Money, Microsoft Picture It!, Microsoft Streets & Trips, and Microsoft Encarta Encyclopedia.

When you launch Microsoft Works, the Works Task Launcher appears onscreen. Along the top of the Task Launcher are buttons that link to five pages; each page represents a different way to enter a program or document. The Home page includes tabs to view your Calendar and Contacts, as well as a Quick Launch bar that lets you launch any application directly. The Templates page helps you create particular types of documents. The Programs page lets you launch specific Works programs, whereas the Projects page helps you create large-scale projects. And the History page lets you reload any document you've recently edited with any Works application.

When Task Launcher is launched, select a page, select a program or task, and then you're ready to work!

THE WORKS TASK LAUNCHER

Home page Templates page Programs page Projects page History page

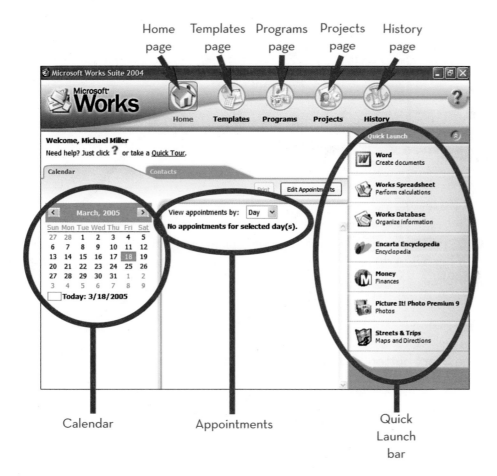

Calendar Appointments Quick Launch bar

LAUNCHING A PROGRAM

You use the Programs page to launch individual Works applications. After you select a program and task, the Task Launcher opens the program you selected with the appropriate task-based template or wizard loaded.

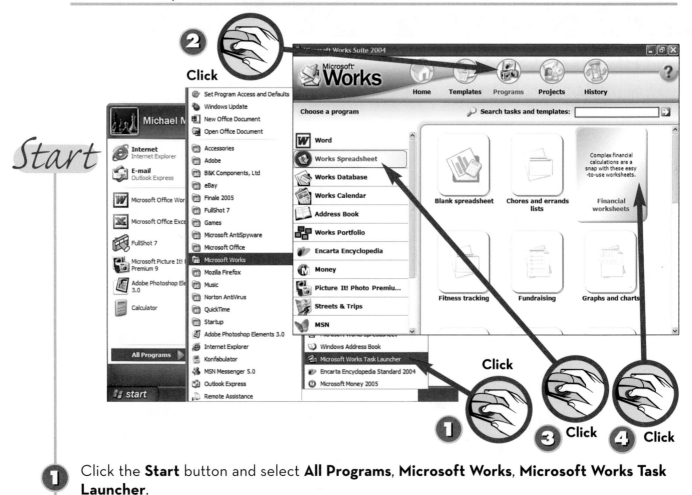

1. Click the **Start** button and select **All Programs**, **Microsoft Works**, **Microsoft Works Task Launcher**.

2. From the Works Task Launcher, click the **Programs** page.

3. From the **Choose a Program** list, click a program icon.

4. From the tasks displayed for that program, click a task.

STARTING A NEW TASK

To create a specific type of document—and have Works automatically load the right program for that task—you use the Templates page. Select a task, and Works will launch the appropriate program with the selected template already loaded.

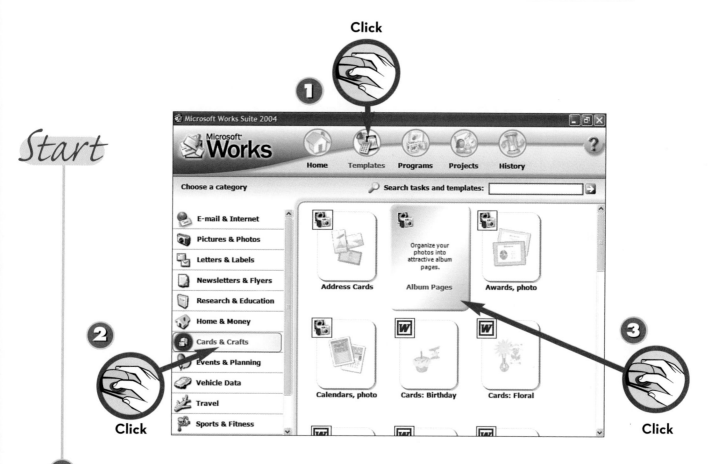

Start

Click

Click

Click

1. From the Works Task Launcher, click the **Templates** page.

2. From the **Choose a Category** list, click the type of task you want to start.

3. From the templates displayed for that category, click a specific template.

End

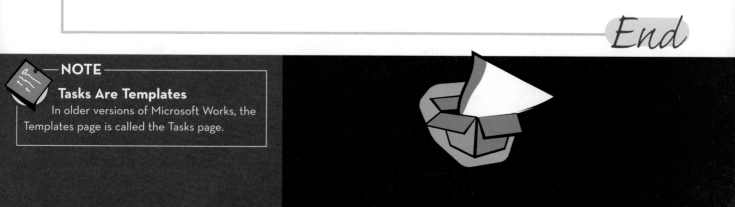

NOTE

Tasks Are Templates

In older versions of Microsoft Works, the Templates page is called the Tasks page.

OPENING AN EXISTING DOCUMENT

If you've been working with Works for awhile, you can use the History page to reopen documents you previously created. The History page lists all your recently used files, newest files first.

1 Click

Start

Microsoft Works Suite 2004

Microsoft® Works

Home   Templates   Programs   Projects   History   ?

Clear History

Use the History list

To open a document, click its name.

To sort by name, date, template, or program, click a heading.

If you do not see the file you are looking for in this History list, you can search your computer for files and folders by clicking the link below.

Find files and folders

Name	Date	Template	Program
Coach a Sports Team	2/25/2005	N/A	My Projects O...
Coach a Sports Team	2/25/2005	N/A	My Projects O...
Do Well in School	2/25/2005	N/A	My Projects O...
Topic List	N/A	N/A	Word
august	N/A	N/A	Word
6130-30	5/11/2001	N/A	Word
6130-32	5/17/2001	N/A	Word
SE Using the Internet Outline	10/1/2004	N/A	Word
july	N/A	N/A	Word
december	N/A	N/A	Word
september	N/A	N/A	Word
Tricks11	N/A	N/A	Word
may	N/A	N/A	Word

2 Click

1 From the Works Task Launcher, click the **History** page.

2 Click the name of the file you want to open.

End

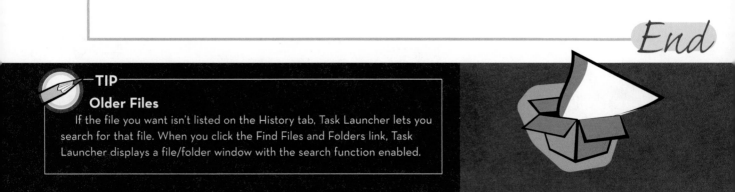

TIP
Older Files
If the file you want isn't listed on the History tab, Task Launcher lets you search for that file. When you click the Find Files and Folders link, Task Launcher displays a file/folder window with the search function enabled.

MANAGING A BIG PROJECT

Moving? Planning a party? Getting ready for the holidays? Microsoft Works helps you with many big projects by offering a ready-made project planner, complete with suggested tasks for each project.

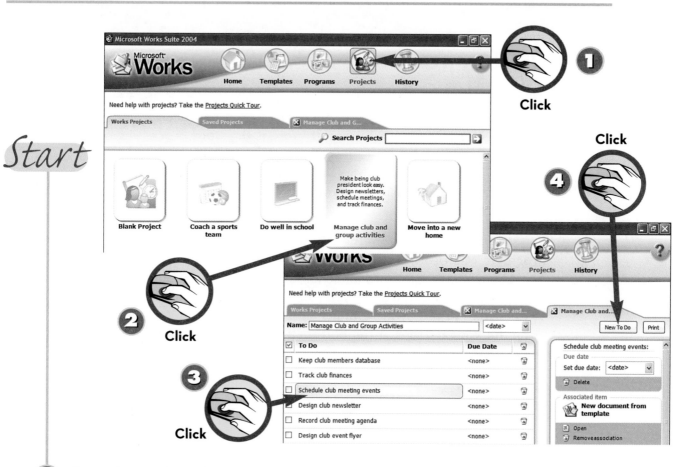

Start

End

1. From the Works Task Launcher, click the **Projects** page.

2. Click the button for the project you want to start.

3. Click an item in the **To Do** list to set a Due Date.

4. Click the **New to Do** button to add new items to the To Do list.

TIP

Build Your Own

If a specific project isn't listed on the Projects page, click the Blank Project button to build your own custom project and To Do list.

6

USING MICROSOFT WORD

When you want to write a letter, fire off a quick memo, create a report, or create a newsletter, you use a type of software program called a *word processor*. For most computer users, Microsoft Word is the word processing program of choice. Word is a full-featured word processor, and it's included with both Microsoft Works Suite and Microsoft Office. You can use Word for all your writing needs—from basic letters to fancy newsletters, and everything in between.

You start Word either from the Windows Start menu (by selecting Start, All Programs, Microsoft Word) or, if you're using Microsoft Works, from the Works Task Launcher. When Word launches, a blank document appears in the Word workspace. Word can display your document in one of five views: Normal, Web Layout, Print Layout, Outline, and Reading Layout. You select a view by using the View buttons at the bottom left of the Word window or by making a selection from the View menu.

THE MICROSOFT WORD WORKSPACE

Title bar   Menu bar

Toolbars

Ruler

View buttons

Status bar

Document   Scroll bars   Task pane

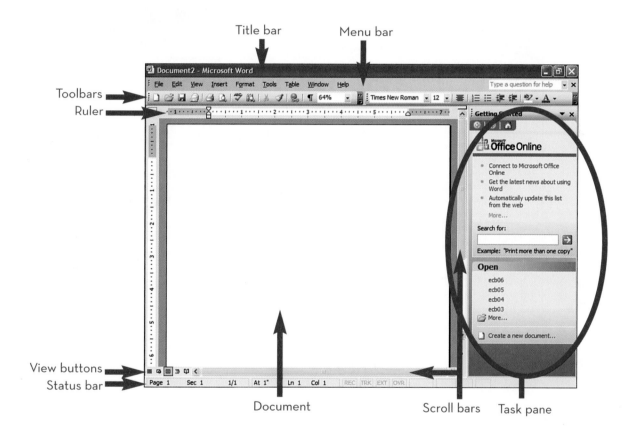

CREATING A NEW DOCUMENT

Any new Word document you create is based on what Word calls a *template*. A template combines selected styles and document settings—and, in some cases, prewritten text or calculated fields—to create the building blocks for a specific type of document. You use templates to give yourself a head start on specific types of documents.

Click

Start

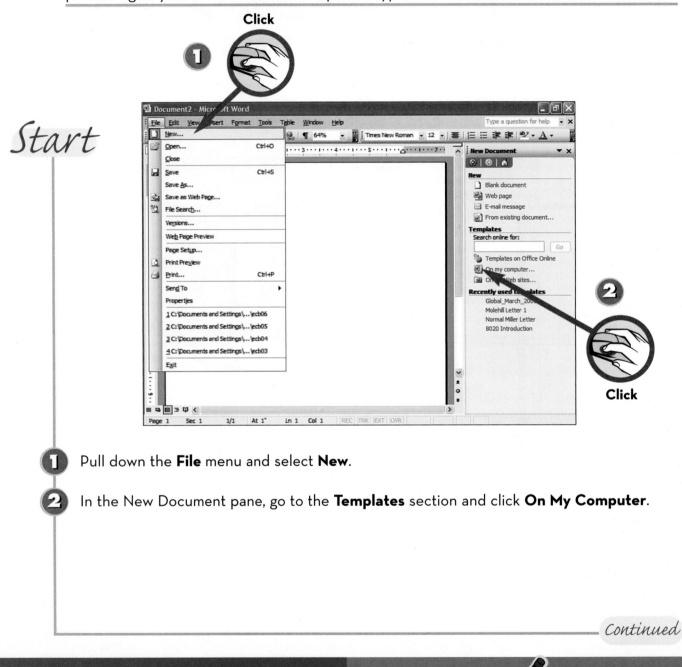

Click

1 Pull down the **File** menu and select **New**.

2 In the New Document pane, go to the **Templates** section and click **On My Computer**.

Continued

Click

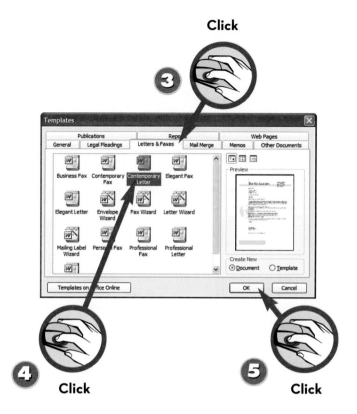

3

4 **Click**

5 **Click**

3 In the Templates dialog box, click the tab for a certain type of document.

4 Click the icon for the template you want.

5 Click **OK** to create a new document based on this template.

End

NOTE

Working with Documents

Anything you create with Word—a letter, memo, newsletter, and so on—is called a *document*. A document is nothing more than a computer file that can be copied, moved, deleted, or edited from within Word.

TIP

Favorite Templates

To select a recently used template, go to the Recently Used Templates section of the New Document pane and click a template name.

SAVING A DOCUMENT

Every document you create that you want to keep must be saved to a new file. The first time you save a file, you have to specify a filename and location.

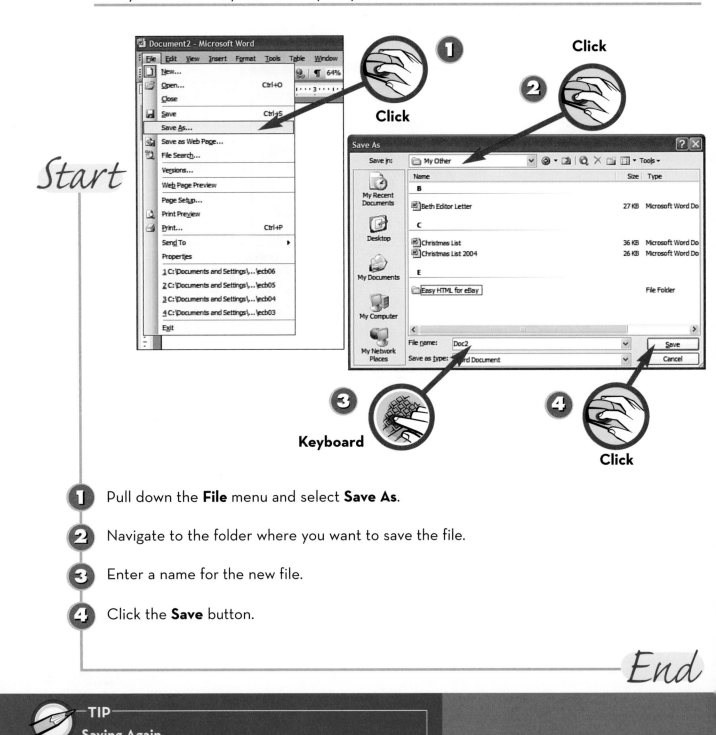

Start

Click

Click

Click

Keyboard

Click

End

1. Pull down the **File** menu and select **Save As**.

2. Navigate to the folder where you want to save the file.

3. Enter a name for the new file.

4. Click the **Save** button.

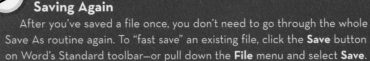

TIP

Saving Again

After you've saved a file once, you don't need to go through the whole Save As routine again. To "fast save" an existing file, click the **Save** button on Word's Standard toolbar—or pull down the **File** menu and select **Save**.

OPENING AN EXISTING DOCUMENT

After you've created a document, you can reopen it at any time for additional editing.

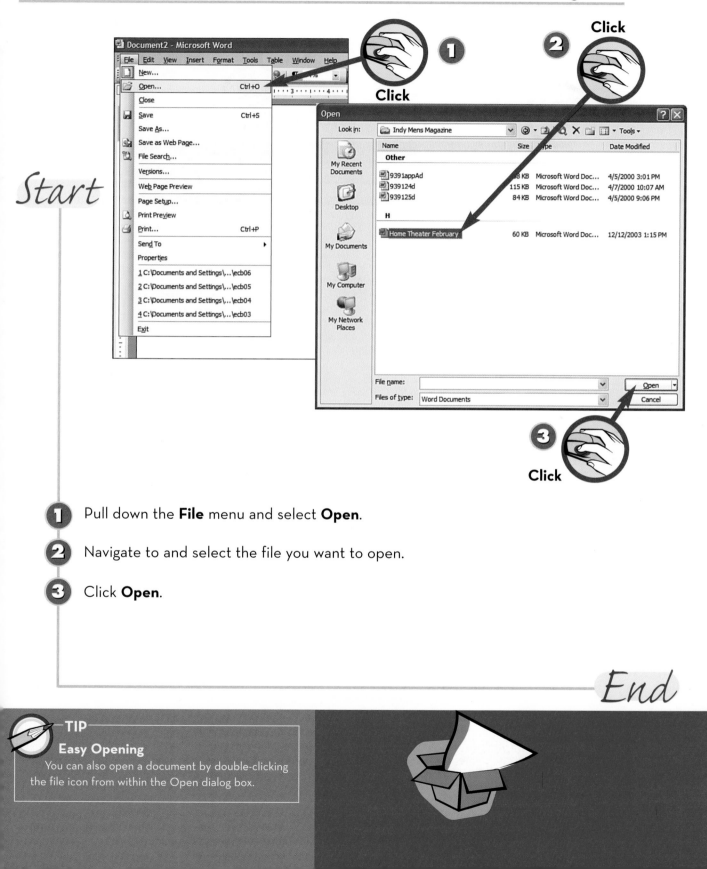

Start

1 Pull down the **File** menu and select **Open**.

2 Navigate to and select the file you want to open.

3 Click **Open**.

End

TIP
Easy Opening
You can also open a document by double-clicking
the file icon from within the Open dialog box.

ENTERING TEXT

You enter text in a Word document at the *insertion point,* which appears onscreen as a blinking cursor. When you start typing on your keyboard, the new text is added at the insertion point.

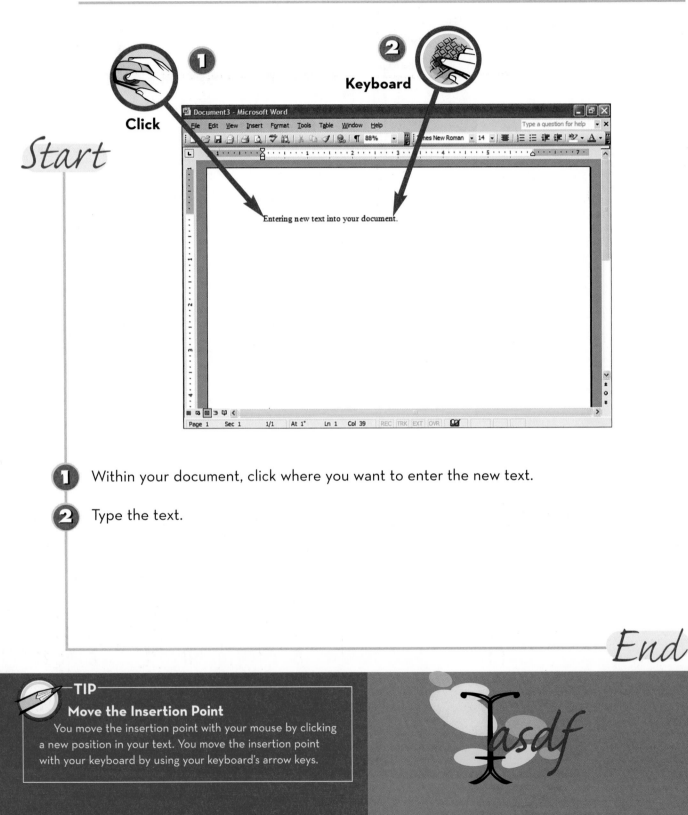

Start

1 Within your document, click where you want to enter the new text.

2 Type the text.

End

TIP

Move the Insertion Point

You move the insertion point with your mouse by clicking a new position in your text. You move the insertion point with your keyboard by using your keyboard's arrow keys.

EDITING TEXT

Word lets you cut, copy, and paste text—or graphics—to and from anywhere in your document or between documents. Use your mouse to select the text you want to edit and then select the appropriate command from the Edit menu or the toolbar.

Start

Click

2

1

Click & drag

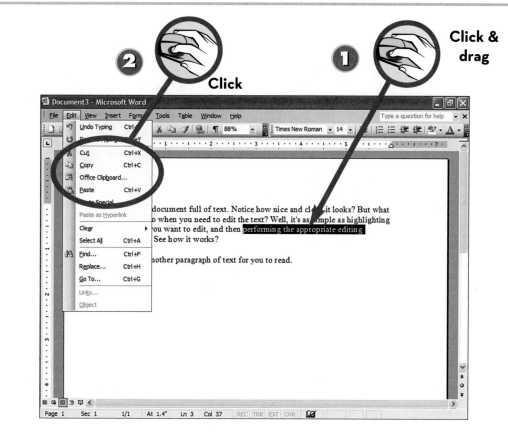

1 Click and drag the cursor to select the text you want to edit.

2 Pull down the **Edit** menu and select **Copy** to copy the text, **Cut** to cut the text, or **Paste** to paste any text you've copied or cut.

End

TIP
Keyboard Shortcuts
You also can select text using your keyboard; use the Shift key—in combination with other keys—to highlight blocks of text. For example, Shift+Left arrow selects one character to the left.

FORMATTING TEXT

After your text is entered and edited, you can use Word's numerous formatting options to add some pizzazz to your document.

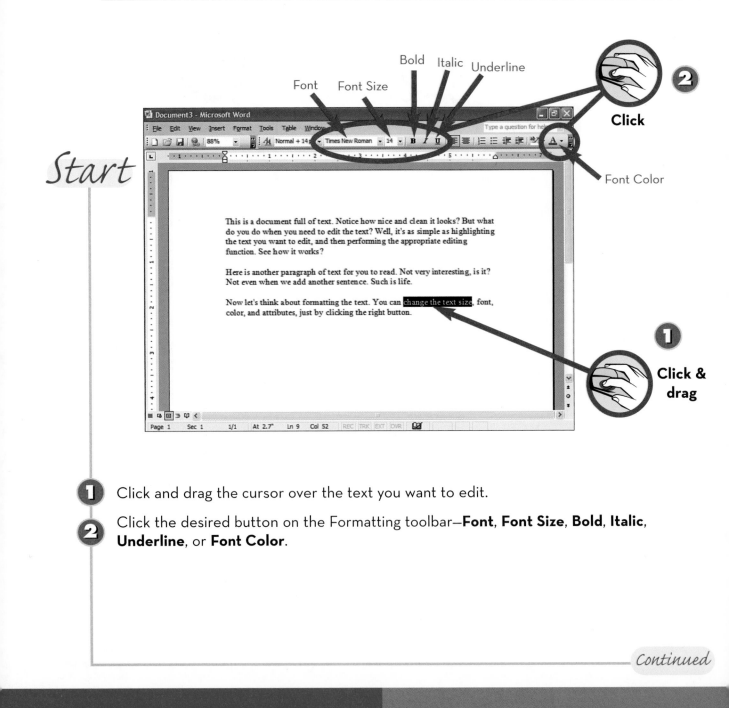

1. Click and drag the cursor over the text you want to edit.

2. Click the desired button on the Formatting toolbar—**Font**, **Font Size**, **Bold**, **Italic**, **Underline**, or **Font Color**.

Continued

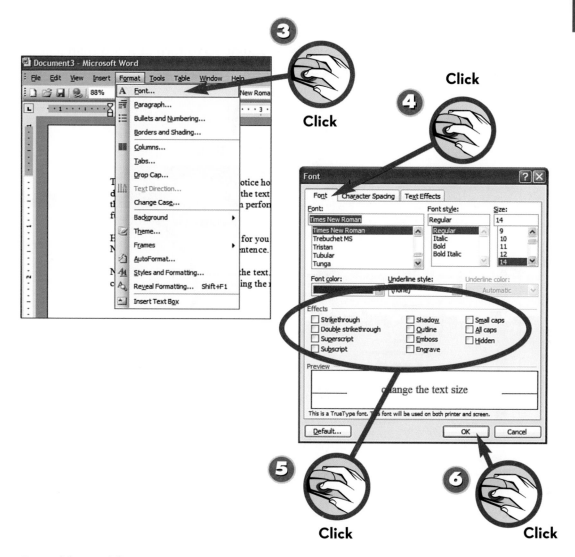

Click

Click

Click

Click

Click

3 For additional formatting options, pull down the **Format** menu and select **Font** to display the Font dialog box.

4 Click the **Font** tab.

5 Select the formatting you want—including Strikethrough, Double Strikethrough, Superscript, Subscript, Shadow, Outline, Emboss, Engrave, Small Caps, All Caps, and Hidden.

6 Click **OK** when done.

End

TIP

See Your Formatting

It's easiest to format text when you're working in Print Layout view because this displays your document as it will look when printed. To switch to this view, pull down the **View** menu and select **Print Layout**.

FORMATTING PARAGRAPHS

When you're creating a complex document, you need to format more than just a few words here and there. To format complete paragraphs, use Word's Paragraph dialog box.

Start

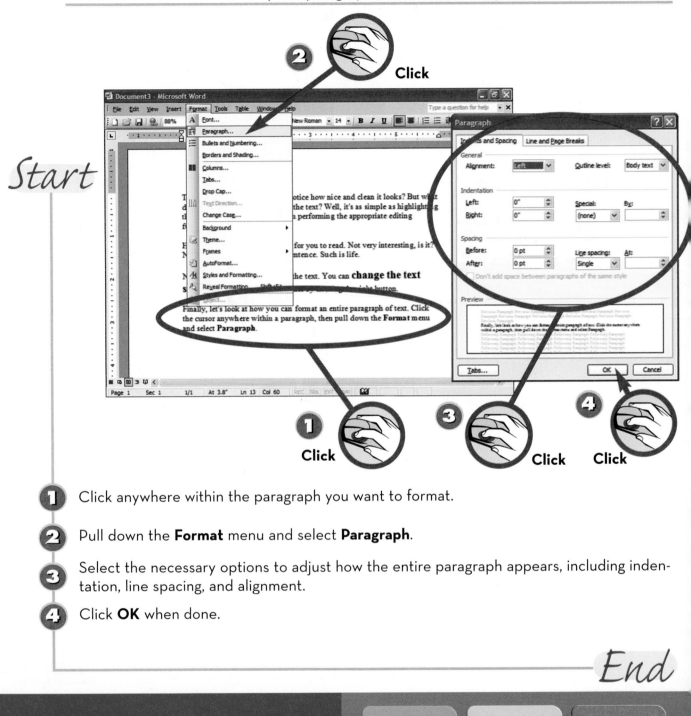

2 Click

1 Click

3 Click

4 Click

1 Click anywhere within the paragraph you want to format.

2 Pull down the **Format** menu and select **Paragraph**.

3 Select the necessary options to adjust how the entire paragraph appears, including indentation, line spacing, and alignment.

4 Click **OK** when done.

End

APPLYING STYLES

If you have a preferred paragraph formatting you use repeatedly, you don't have to format each paragraph individually. Instead, you can assign all your formatting to a paragraph *style* and then assign that style to specific paragraphs throughout your document.

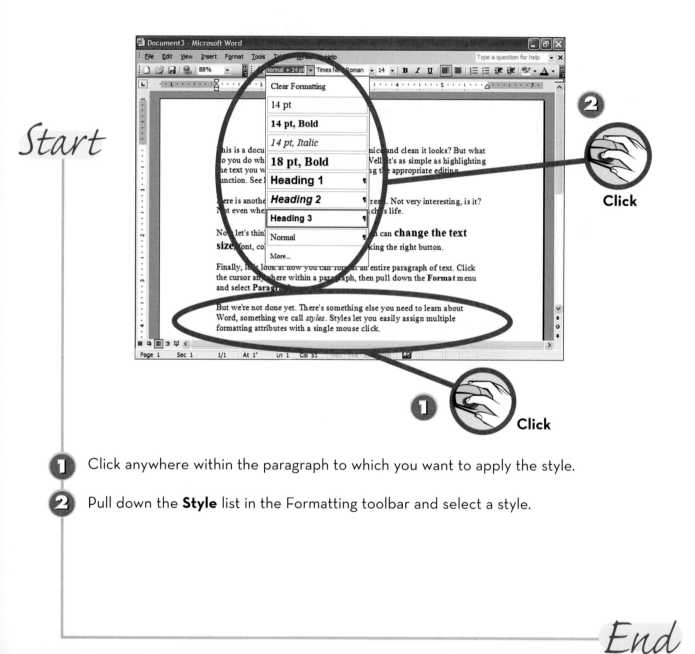

Start

Click

Click

1. Click anywhere within the paragraph to which you want to apply the style.

2. Pull down the **Style** list in the Formatting toolbar and select a style.

End

NOTE

Style Elements

Styles include formatting for fonts, paragraphs, tabs, borders, numbering, and more.

CHECKING YOUR SPELLING

If you're not a great speller, you'll appreciate Word's automatic spell checking. You can see it right onscreen; just deliberately misspell a word, and you'll see a squiggly red line under the misspelling. That's Word telling you you've made a spelling error!

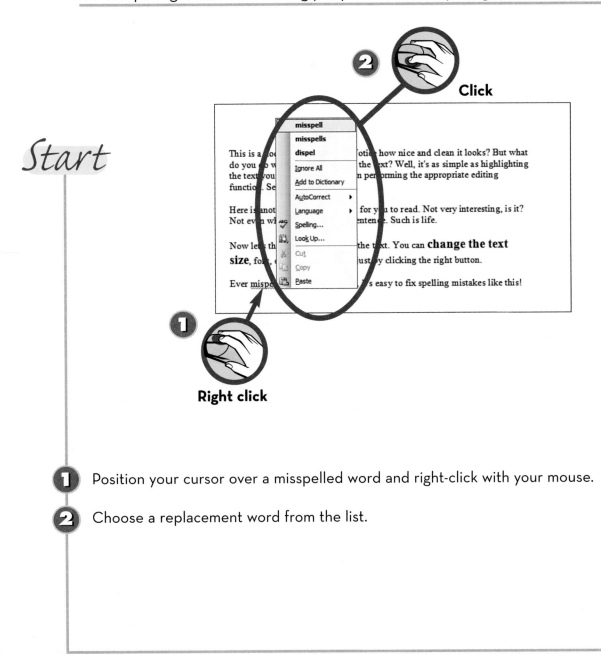

Start

2 **Click**

1 **Right click**

1 Position your cursor over a misspelled word and right-click with your mouse.

2 Choose a replacement word from the list.

End

spelling ✓

PRINTING A DOCUMENT

When you've finished editing your document, you can instruct Word to send a copy to your printer. When you want to print multiple copies, print only selected pages, or print to a different (nondefault) printer, use Word's Print dialog box.

Start

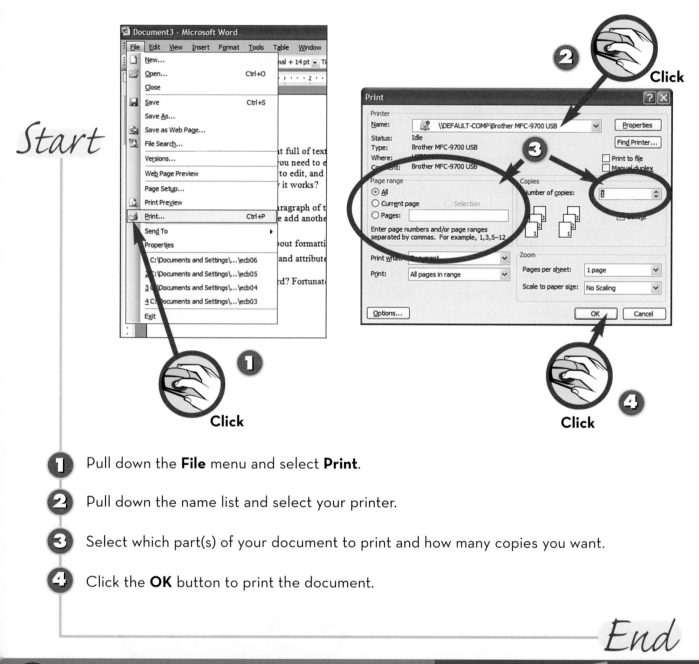

Click

Click

1. Pull down the **File** menu and select **Print**.

2. Pull down the name list and select your printer.

3. Select which part(s) of your document to print and how many copies you want.

4. Click the **OK** button to print the document.

End

 TIP
Fast Print
The fastest way to print a document is with Word's fast print option. You activate a fast print by clicking the Print button on Word's Standard toolbar. This bypasses the Print dialog box and all other configuration options.

CONNECTING TO THE INTERNET

It used to be that most people bought personal computers to do work—word processing, spreadsheets, databases, the sort of programs that still make up the core of Microsoft Works and Microsoft Office. But today, most people also buy PCs to access the Internet—to send and receive email, surf the Web, and chat with other users.

The first step in going online is establishing a connection between your computer and the Internet. To do this, you have to sign up with an Internet service provider (ISP), which, as the name implies, provides your computer with a connection to the Internet.

Depending on what's available in your area, you can choose from two primary types of connections: dial-up or broadband. Dial-up is slower than broadband, but it's also cheaper. If you do a lot of web surfing, it's probably worth a few extra dollars a month to get the faster broadband connection.

INTERNET EXPLORER

Toolbar—click these buttons to perform common functions

Address box—enter web addresses here

Go button—click to go to the selected web page

Web page hyperlink

SETTING UP A NEW INTERNET CONNECTION

After you sign up for Internet service, you need to configure your computer to work with your ISP. All you have to do is connect your PC's modem to your telephone line (or your computer to the broadband modem) and use Windows XP's New Connection Wizard.

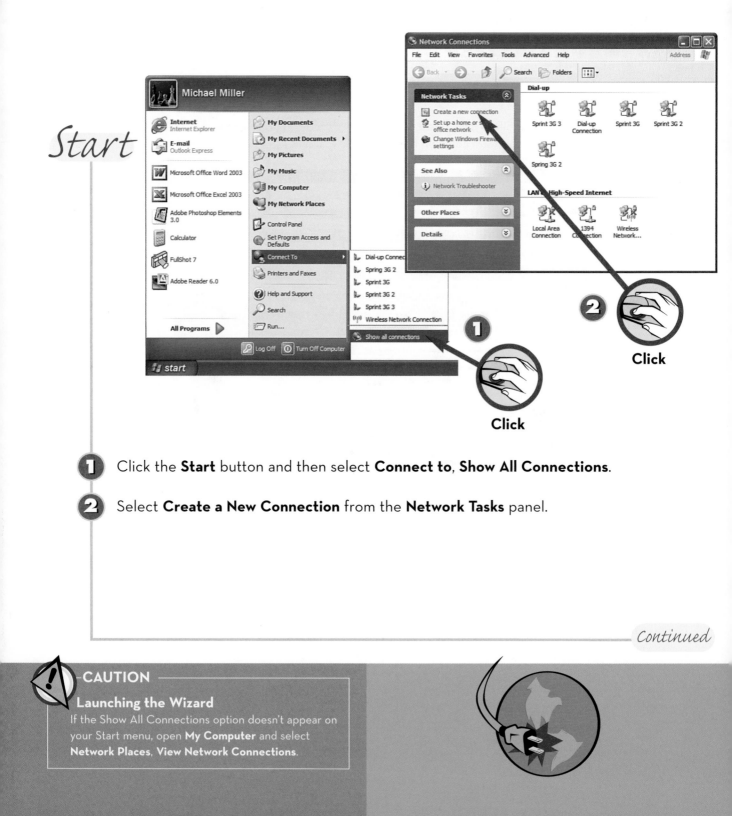

Start

Click

Click

1. Click the **Start** button and then select **Connect to, Show All Connections**.

2. Select **Create a New Connection** from the **Network Tasks** panel.

Continued

Continued

CAUTION

Launching the Wizard

If the Show All Connections option doesn't appear on your Start menu, open **My Computer** and select **Network Places, View Network Connections**.

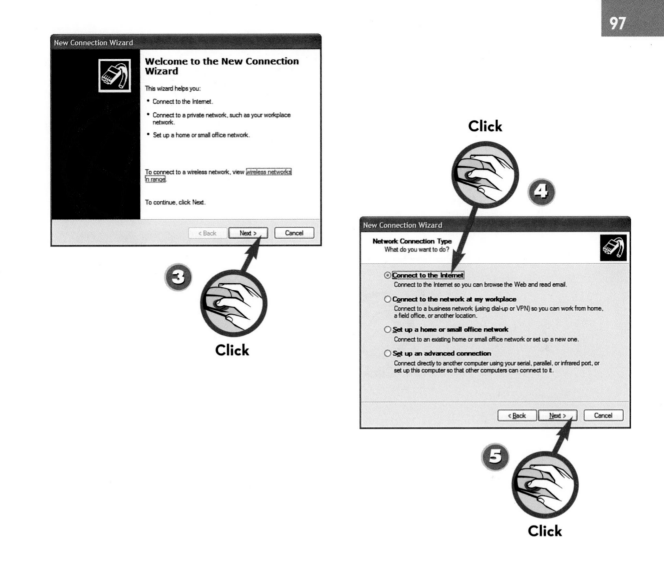

Click

Click

Click

Click

3 When the New Connection Wizard appears, click **Next**.

4 When the Network Connection Type screen appears, select **Connect to the Internet**.

5 Click **Next**.

Continued

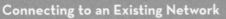

TIP
Connecting to an Existing Network
If you've already set up a home network with its own Internet connection, select **Set Up a Home or Small Office Network** from the Network Connections window and follow the instructions from there.

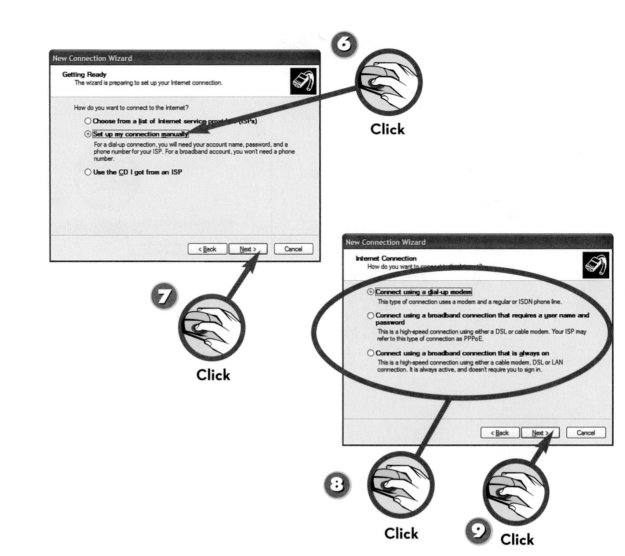

6 Select **Set Up My Connection Manually**.

7 Click **Next**.

8 Select which type of connection you have—dial-up, broadband with username and password, or always-on broadband.

9 Click **Next**.

Continued

TIP

Choosing a New Provider

If you haven't yet signed up for Internet service, select **Choose from a List of Internet Service Providers** and follow the instructions from there. You can subscribe to Microsoft's own MSN service or select from a list of other available ISPs.

Keyboard

New Connection Wizard

Connection Name
What is the name of the service that provides your Internet connection?

Type the name of your ISP in the following box.

ISP Name

The name you type here will be the name of the connection you are creating.

< Back   Next >   Cancel

Click

Keyboard

New Connection Wizard

Phone Number to Dial
What is your ISP's phone number?

Type the phone number below.

Phone number:

You might need to include a "1" or the area code, or both. If you are not sure you need the extra numbers, dial the phone number on your telephone. If you hear a modem sound, the number dialed is correct.

< Back   Next >   Cancel

Click

10 If prompted, enter the name of your Internet service provider.

11 Click **Next**.

12 If you have a dial-up ISP, enter the provider's dial-up phone number.

13 Click **Next**.

Continued

TIP
Broadband Connections
If you selected the always-on broadband connection option, you won't be prompted for any information about your ISP, username, or password. Go directly to step 18, instead.

Keyboard

Keyboard

New Connection Wizard

Internet Account Information
You will need an account name and password to sign into your Internet account.

Type an ISP account name and password, then write down this information and store it in a safe place. (If you have forgotten an existing account name or password, contact your ISP.)

User name: |

Password:

Confirm password:

☑ Use this account name and password when anyone connects to the Internet from this computer

☑ Make this the default Internet connection

< Back   Next >   Cancel

Keyboard

Click

⑭ If prompted, enter the username provided by your ISP.

⑮ Enter the password provided by your ISP.

⑯ Reenter the password.

⑰ Click **Next**.

Continued

Click

 Click the **Finish** button.

End

SURFING THE WEB WITH INTERNET EXPLORER

Internet Explorer (IE) is a web browser that lets you quickly and easily browse the World Wide Web. When you enter a new web address in the Address box and press Enter (or click the Go button), IE loads the new page. You can also click any link on a web page to go to the new page. Let's demonstrate with a quick tour of the Web.

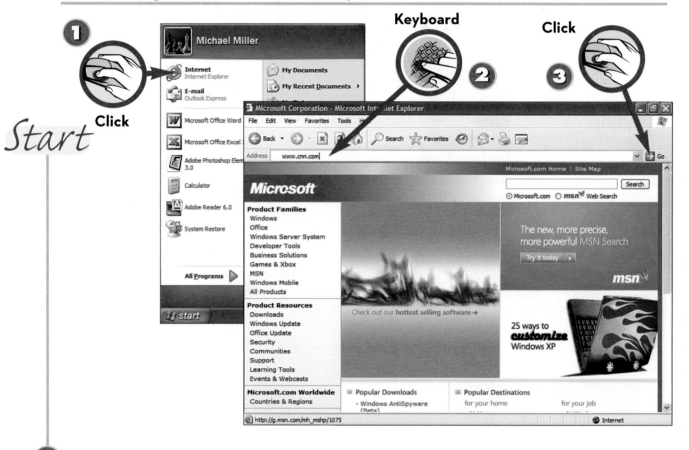

1 Connect to your ISP, and then launch Internet Explorer by selecting **Start**, **Internet**.

2 Let's find out what's happening out in the real world by heading over to one of the most popular news sites. Enter **www.cnn.com** in the **Address** box.

3 Click the **Go** button to go to the CNN.com site.

Continued

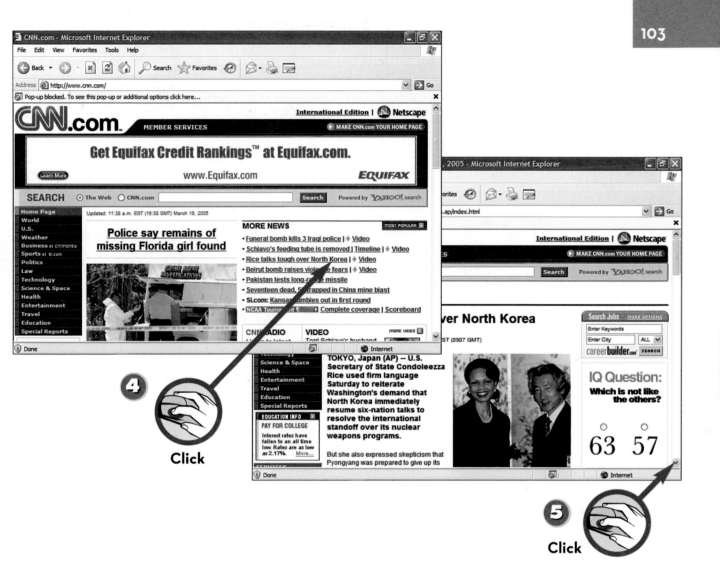

4 Click any headline or link to read the complete story.

5 Click the down scroll button to read more of the story.

Continued

TIP

Change IE's Home Page

When you first launch Internet Explorer, it loads your predefined home page. To change Internet Explorer's home page, drag a page's icon from Internet Explorer's Address box onto the Home button on the toolbar.

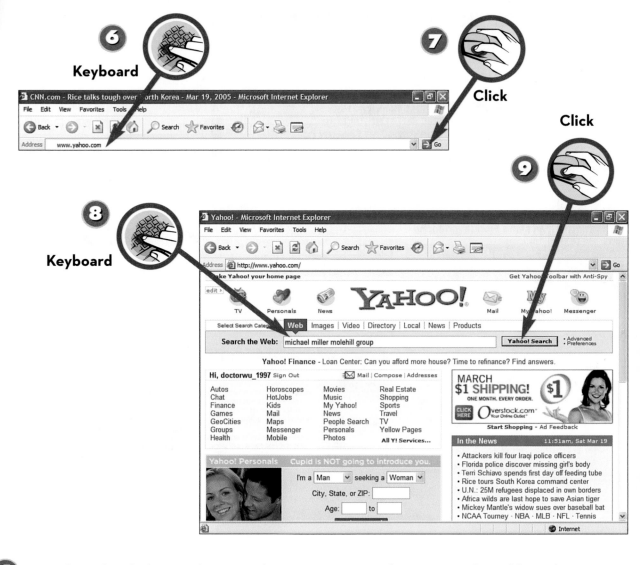

6 Keyboard

7 Click

Click

9

8 Keyboard

---

6 Now, let's do a little searching at Yahoo!. Enter **www.yahoo.com** in the **Address** box.

7 Click the **Go** button to go to Yahoo!.

8 Ready to search? Enter **michael miller molehill group** in the **Search the Web** box at the top of the page.

9 Click the **Yahoo! Search** button to begin the search.

Continued

TIP

Searching the Web

To find a particular page on the Web, you use a search site. These sites, such as Google and Yahoo!, let you enter a query and search for web pages that contain those keywords.

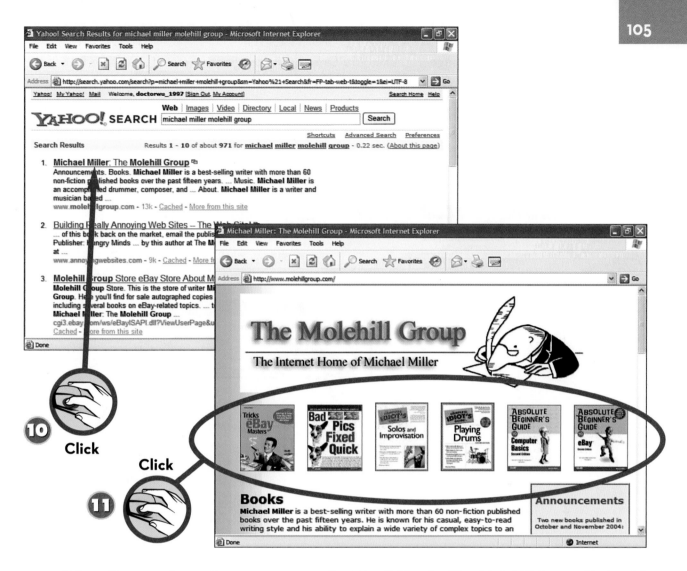

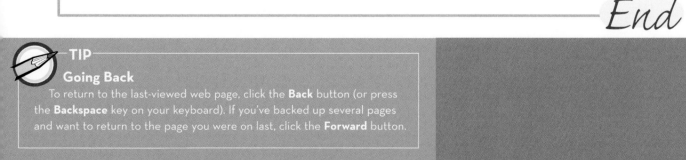

10 When the search results page appears, find the listing for The Molehill Group (it should be near the top) and click the link.

11 You're now taken to *my* website, The Molehill Group. Click one of the book pictures at the top of the page to read more about that book.

End

TIP

Going Back

To return to the last-viewed web page, click the **Back** button (or press the **Backspace** key on your keyboard). If you've backed up several pages and want to return to the page you were on last, click the **Forward** button.

SAVING YOUR FAVORITE PAGES

When you find a web page you like, you can add it to a list of Favorites within Internet Explorer. This way, you can easily access any of your favorite sites just by selecting them from the list.

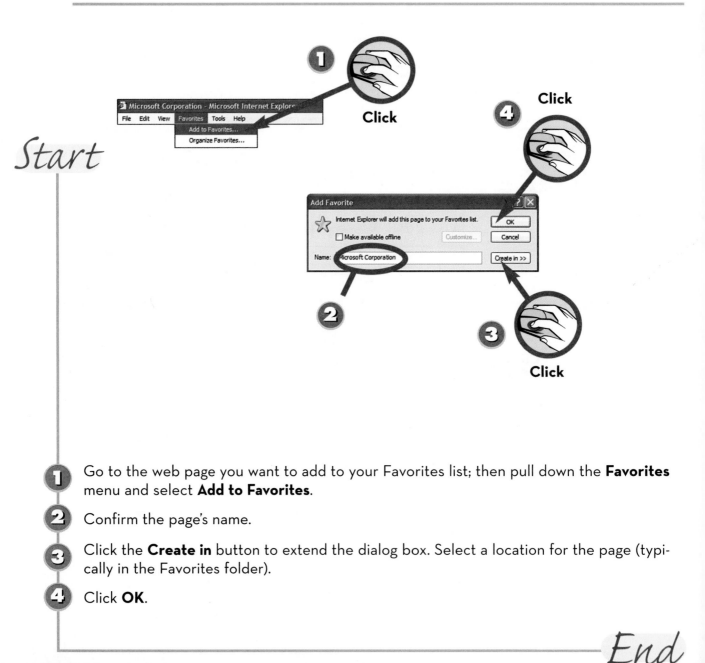

Start

Click

Click

Click

1. Go to the web page you want to add to your Favorites list; then pull down the **Favorites** menu and select **Add to Favorites**.

2. Confirm the page's name.

3. Click the **Create in** button to extend the dialog box. Select a location for the page (typically in the Favorites folder).

4. Click **OK**.

End

RETURNING TO A FAVORITE PAGE

After a web page is saved to your Favorites list, you can return to that page at any time by selecting it from the list—no need to reenter that page's web address.

Click

Click

① ② ③

Start

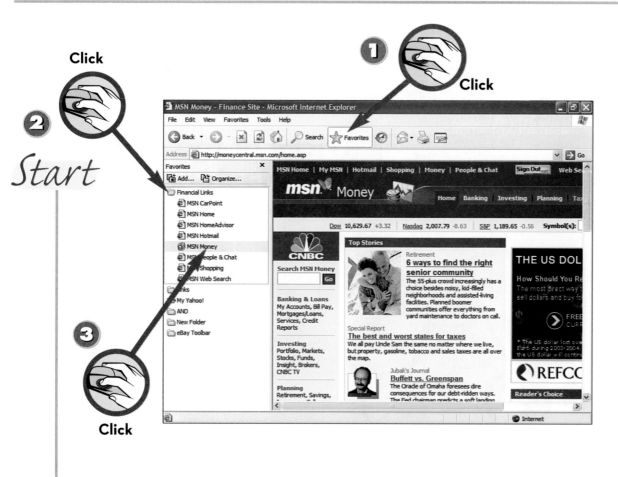

Click

① Click the **Favorites** button on the toolbar to display the Favorites pane.

② Click any folder in the Favorites pane to display the contents of that folder.

③ Click a favorite page, and IE goes to that page.

End

TIP

Hide the Favorites Pane

Click the **Favorites** button again to hide the Favorites pane.

REVISITING HISTORY

Internet Explorer keeps track of web pages you've recently visited so you can easily revisit them without having to reenter the web page address.

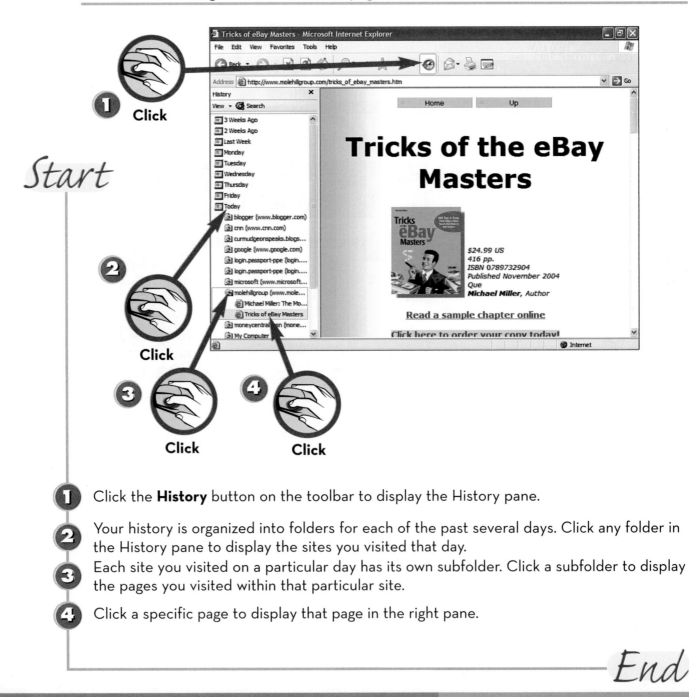

1. Click the **History** button on the toolbar to display the History pane.

2. Your history is organized into folders for each of the past several days. Click any folder in the History pane to display the sites you visited that day.

3. Each site you visited on a particular day has its own subfolder. Click a subfolder to display the pages you visited within that particular site.

4. Click a specific page to display that page in the right pane.

End

TIP

Recent History

To revisit one of the last half-dozen or so pages viewed in your current session, click the down arrow on the **Back** button. This drops down a menu containing the last nine pages you've visited. Click a page to return to it.

SEARCHING THE WEB WITH GOOGLE

A web search engine lets you search for virtually anything online. The most popular search engine today is Google (www.google.com), which indexes more than eight million web pages. Google is very easy to use and returns extremely accurate results.

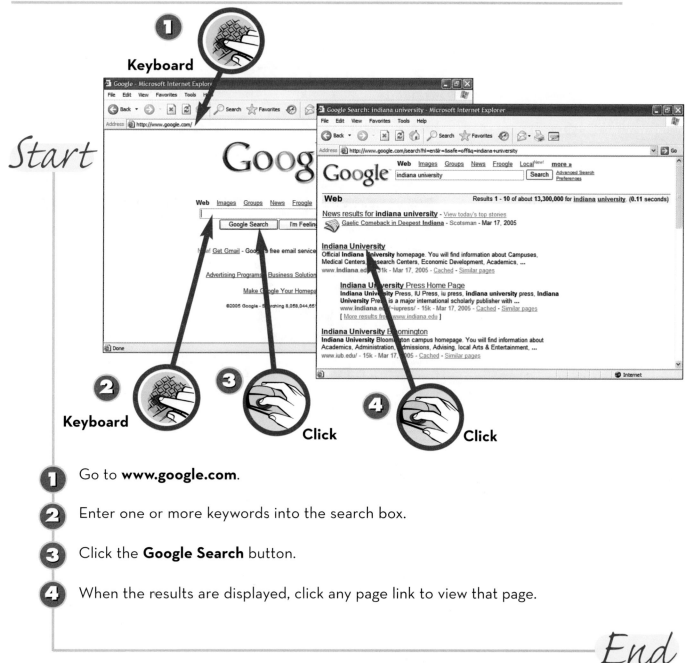

Start

1 Keyboard

2 Keyboard

3 Click

4 Click

End

1 Go to **www.google.com**.

2 Enter one or more keywords into the search box.

3 Click the **Google Search** button.

4 When the results are displayed, click any page link to view that page.

TIP

Advanced Searching

Google also offers a variety of advanced search options to help you fine-tune your search. Just click the **Advanced Search** link and choose the appropriate options.

FINDING NEWS AND OTHER INFORMATION ONLINE

The Web is a terrific source for all sorts of news and information. Let's take a quick look at some of the most popular news, weather, and sports sites—the best way to stay informed online!

Start

① For the top headlines from a variety of sources, go to Google News (news.google.com).

② For in-depth international news, go to BBC News (news.bbc.co.uk).

Continued

TIP

More News

Other full-service news sites include ABC News (abcnews.go.com), CBSNews.com (www.cbsnews.com), CNN.com (www.cnn.com), and MSNBC (www.msnbc.msn.com).

Keyboard

Keyboard

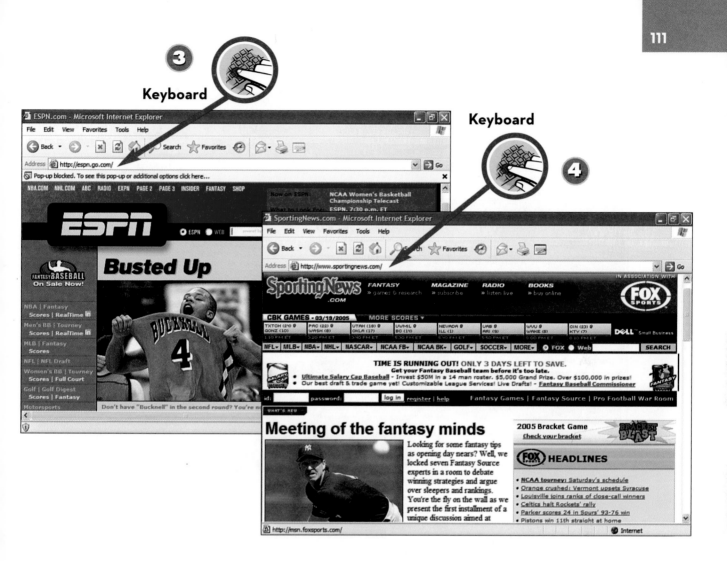

3 For comprehensive sports coverage, go to ESPN.com (espn.go.com).

4 For additional sports coverage, go to SportingNews.com (www.sportingnews.com).

Continued

NOTE

Sports on the Web

The best sports sites on the Web resemble the best news sites—they're actually portals to all sorts of content and services, including up-to-the-minute scores, post-game recaps, in-depth reporting, and much more.

TIP

Local Sports

If you follow a particular sports team, check out that team's local newspaper on the Web. Chances are you'll find a lot of in-depth coverage there that you won't find at other sites.

5 The online site for The Weather Channel is found at www.weather.com.

6 For additional weather forecasts and information, go to AccuWeather.com (www.accuweather.com).

Continued

TIP

Weather on the Web

Weather reports and forecasts are readily available on the Web; most of the major news portals and local websites offer some variety of weather-related services. There are also a number of dedicated weather sites on the Web, all of which offer local and national forecasts, weather radar, satellite maps, and more.

Keyboard

7

Keyboard

8

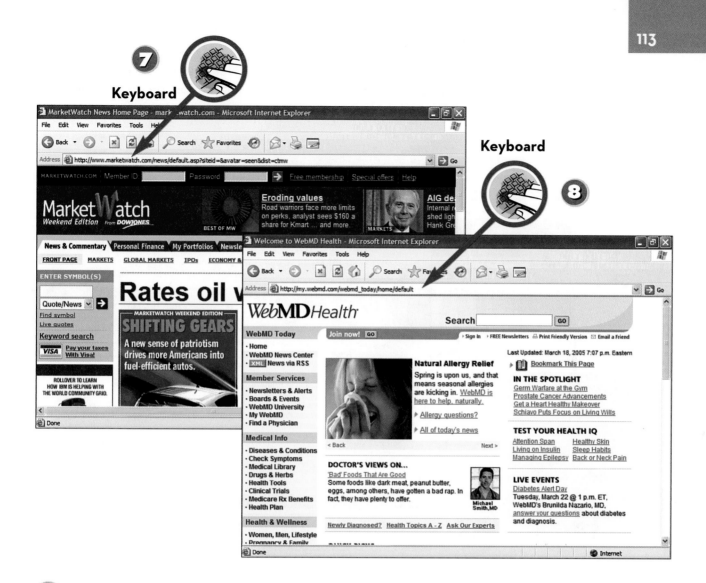

7 Find in-depth financial information at MarketWatch (www.marketwatch.com).

8 For health and medical information, go to WebMD Health (my.webmd.com).

End

TIP
More Financial Sites
Other popular financial sites include Motley Fool (www.fool.com), MSN Money (moneycentral.msn.com), and Yahoo! Finance (finance.yahoo.com).

CAUTION
Health Information Online
As useful as online health sites are, they should not and cannot serve as substitutes for a trained medical opinion.

SHOPPING FOR BARGAINS AT SHOPPING.COM

When you're shopping for bargains online, numerous sites let you perform automatic price comparisons. Search for the product you want, and then search for the lowest price—it's that easy. One of the most popular of these shopping comparison sites is Shopping.com (www.shopping.com).

Start

Keyboard

Click

Click

1 Go to www.shopping.com.

2 Click a category in the left column.

3 Fine-tune your search by product feature and brand.

Continued

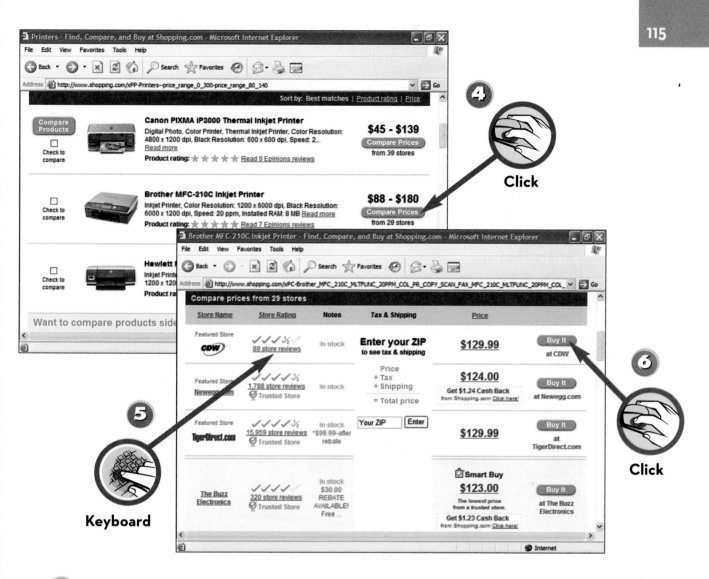

4 When you find the product you want, click the **Compare Prices** button.

5 Click a **Store Reviews** link to find out what other customers think of a particular retailer.

6 Click the **Buy It** button to go to a store and make a purchase.

End

TIP
Shipping Costs

Often the merchant with the lowest price also has the highest shipping costs. Enter your ZIP Code to calculate the total price for the item, including shipping costs. Base your decision on the total price you'll have to pay.

CAUTION
Merchant Reputation

Some online retailers might be bait-and-switch artists, or offer poor service, or take forever to ship items. Check the retailer ratings and read the customer reviews.

BIDDING FOR ITEMS ON EBAY

Some of the best bargains on the Web come from other consumers selling items via online auction at eBay (www.ebay.com). An eBay auction is a web-based version of a traditional auction. You find an item you'd like to own and then place a bid on the item. Other users also place bids, and at the end of the auction the highest bidder wins.

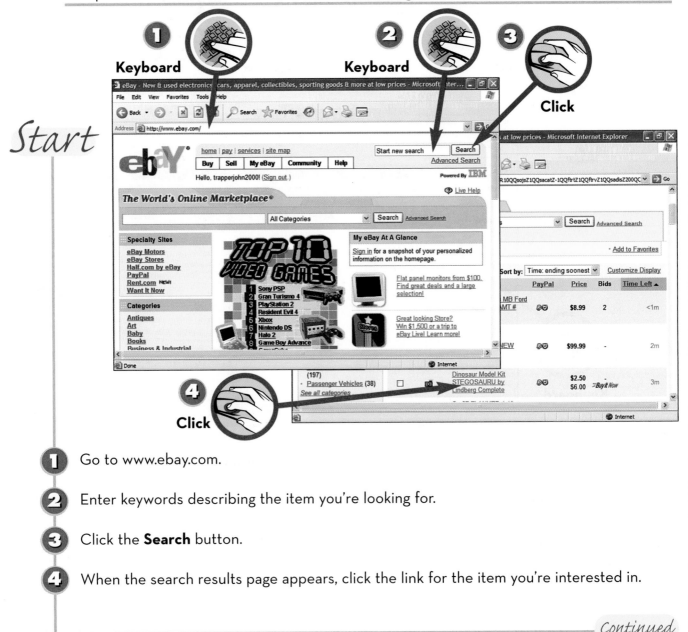

Start

Keyboard

Keyboard

Click

Click

1 Go to www.ebay.com.

2 Enter keywords describing the item you're looking for.

3 Click the **Search** button.

4 When the search results page appears, click the link for the item you're interested in.

Continued

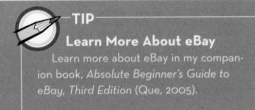

TIP

Learn More About eBay

Learn more about eBay in my companion book, *Absolute Beginner's Guide to eBay, Third Edition* (Que, 2005).

5

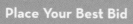

6

Keyboard

7

Click

5 Read the description of the item and check out the seller's feedback rating.

6 Scroll down to the Ready to Bid? section and enter the maximum amount you're willing to pay.

7 Click the **Place Bid** button.

Continued

Continued

TIP

Place Your Best Bid

Always bid the highest amount you're willing to pay. eBay's proxy software enters only the minimum bid necessary, without revealing your maximum bid amount.

TIP

Check the Feedback

Check the feedback rating of the seller, and avoid those sellers with low or negative feedback. Click the feedback number to read individual comments from other users.

eBay.com Review and Confirm Bid (Ends Mar-19-05 09:41:39 PST) 5962953103 - Microsoft Internet Explorer

File Edit View Favorites Tools Help

Back • • Search Favorites

Address http://offer.ebay.com/ws/eBayISAPI.dll?MfcISAPICommand=MakeBid&uiid=-73722509&co_partnerid=&item=5962953103&fb=1&user▾ Go

Review and Confirm Bid

Hello trapperjohn2000! (Not you?)

Important:

If you are in the market for toys, take a minute to educate yourself about products that have been recalled by the U.S. Consumer Product Safety Commission (CPSC) by clicking here. This information is provided for all listings in this category, and it in no way implies anything about the item you are currently bidding on.

Item title: Dinosaur Model Kit STEGOSAURU by Lindberg Complete
Your maximum bid: **US $4.01**

Shipping and handling: US $4.50 - Standard Flat Ra
Shipping insurance: US $1.30 (Optional)
Payment methods: PayPal, Personal check, Mc

By clicking on the button below, you commit to b

    Confirm Bid

You are agreeing to a contract -- You will enter into winning bidder. You are responsible for reading the full methods. Seller assumes all responsibility for listing th

9

eBay item 5962953103 (Ends Mar-19-05 09:41:39 PST) - Dinosaur Model Kit STEGOSAURU by Lindberg - Micro...

File Edit View Favorites Tools Help

Back • • Search Favorites

Address http://offer.ebay.com/ws/eBayISAPI.dll ▾ Go

Bid Confirmation   Item number: 5962953103

You are signed in   Email to a friend | This item is being tracked in My eBay

✓ **You are the current high bidder**

Important: Another user may still outbid you, especially during these final minutes. To see if you've been outbid, click the **Check your status** button.

How does bidding work? See example.

How do you keep track of this item? Use My eBay.

Title: Dinosaur Model Kit STEGOSAURU by Lindberg Complete

Time left: 2 mins 18 secs

Current bid: US $2.50

Your maximum bid: US $4.01

    Check Your Status
See if you're still the high bidder

What else can you do?

Done   Internet

8

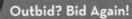

Click

8 When the Review and Confirm Bid page appears, click the **Confirm Bid** button.

9 Your bid is officially entered and the Bid Confirmation page is displayed, which shows your bid status.

Continued

TIP

Outbid? Bid Again!

If you get outbid during the course of the auction, eBay sends you an immediate email informing you of this. You can then return to the item listing bid and make a new, higher bid—or not.

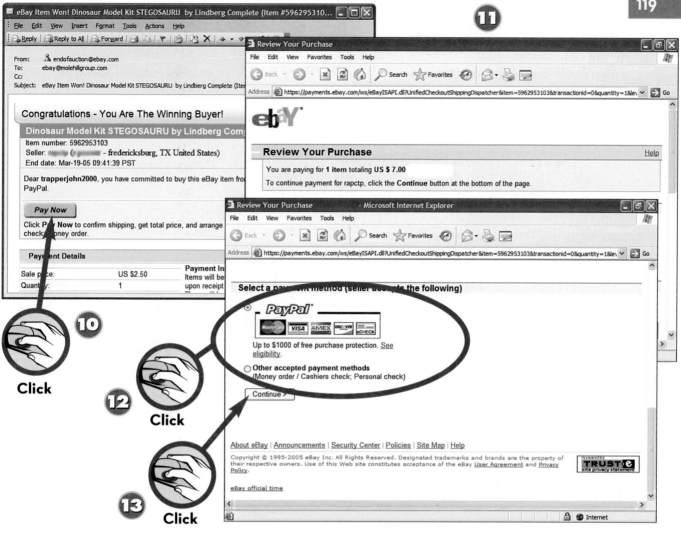

Click ⑩

Click ⑫

Click ⑬

⑩ If you're the high bidder at the end of the auction period, you win! When you receive the end-of-auction notification email from eBay, click the **Pay Now** button.

⑪ You're now taken to a Review Your Purchase page on the eBay site.

⑫ Scroll down to the bottom of the page and select a payment method.

⑬ Click the **Continue** button; then follow the onscreen instructions to make your payment and complete your purchase.

End

TIP
Win by Sniping
Experienced buyers don't place their bids until the final seconds of an auction—a process called *sniping*. When you place a high bid at the last second, other bidders don't have a chance to respond, which increases your odds of winning.

NOTE
Pay with Plastic
If the seller accepts PayPal payments, you can pay for your auction purchase with a credit card. If not, you'll have to send a check or money order via mail.

SETTING UP AN EMAIL ACCOUNT

An email message is like a regular letter, except that it's composed electronically and delivered almost immediately via the Internet. One of the most popular email programs is Microsoft Outlook Express, which is included as part of Windows XP. We'll look at how to set up Outlook Express to work with the email account you have with your Internet service provider.

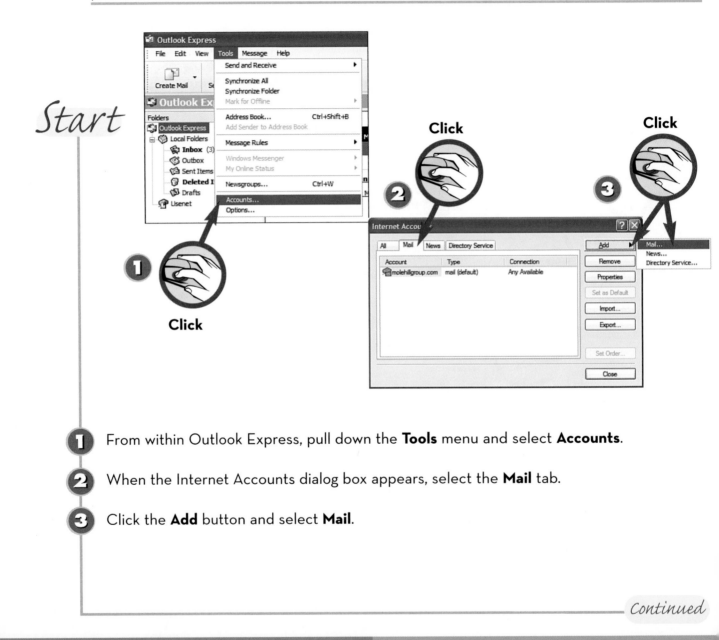

Start

Click

Click

Click

1 From within Outlook Express, pull down the **Tools** menu and select **Accounts**.

2 When the Internet Accounts dialog box appears, select the **Mail** tab.

3 Click the **Add** button and select **Mail**.

Continued

Keyboard

Internet Connection Wizard

Your Name

When you send e-mail, your name will appear in the From field of the outgoing message.
Type your name as you would like it to appear.

Display name: Mike Marvel

For example: John Smith

< Back   Next >   Cancel

Click

Keyboard

Internet Connection Wizard

Internet E-mail Address

Your e-mail address is the address other people use to send e-mail messages to you.

E-mail address: bob@isp.com

For example: someone@microsoft.com

< Back   Next >   Cancel

Click

④ Enter your name.

⑤ Click **Next**.

⑥ Enter your email address.

⑦ Click **Next**.

Continued

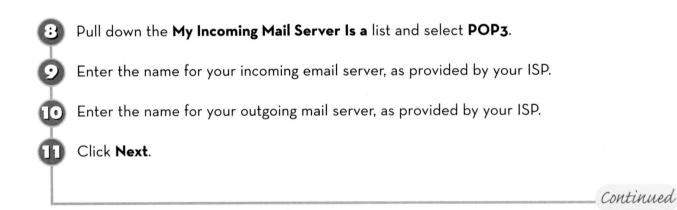

8 Pull down the **My Incoming Mail Server Is a** list and select **POP3**.

9 Enter the name for your incoming email server, as provided by your ISP.

10 Enter the name for your outgoing mail server, as provided by your ISP.

11 Click **Next**.

Continued

TIP

Server Names

Your Internet service provider should provide you with the server names you need to enter. Some providers might instruct you to use a server type other than POP3.

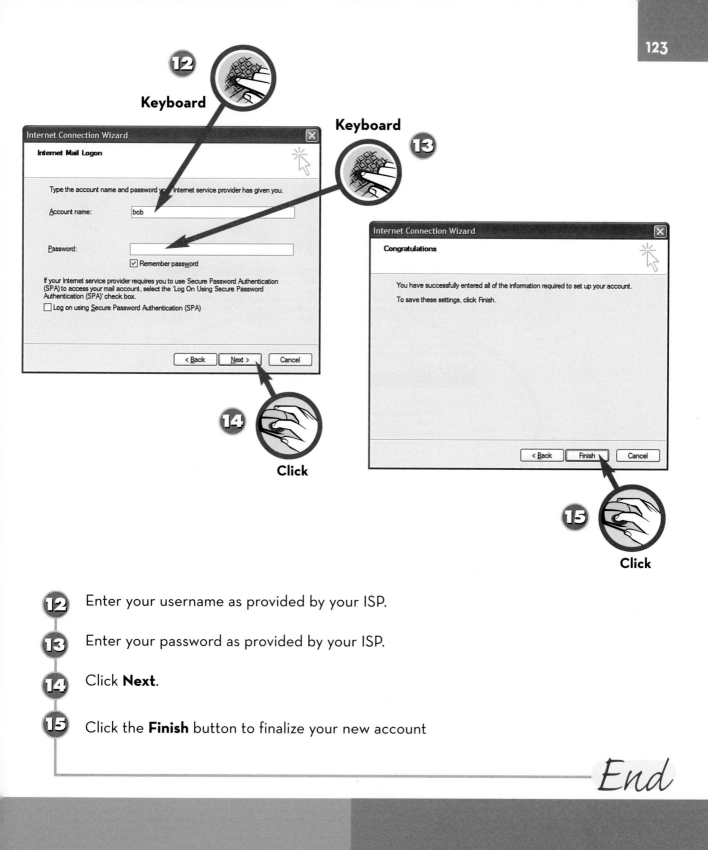

Keyboard

Keyboard

12 Enter your username as provided by your ISP.

13 Enter your password as provided by your ISP.

14 Click **Next**.

15 Click the **Finish** button to finalize your new account

End

READING AN EMAIL MESSAGE

When you receive new email messages, they're stored in the Outlook Express Inbox. To display all new messages, select the **Inbox** icon from the **Folders** list. All waiting messages now appear in the Message pane.

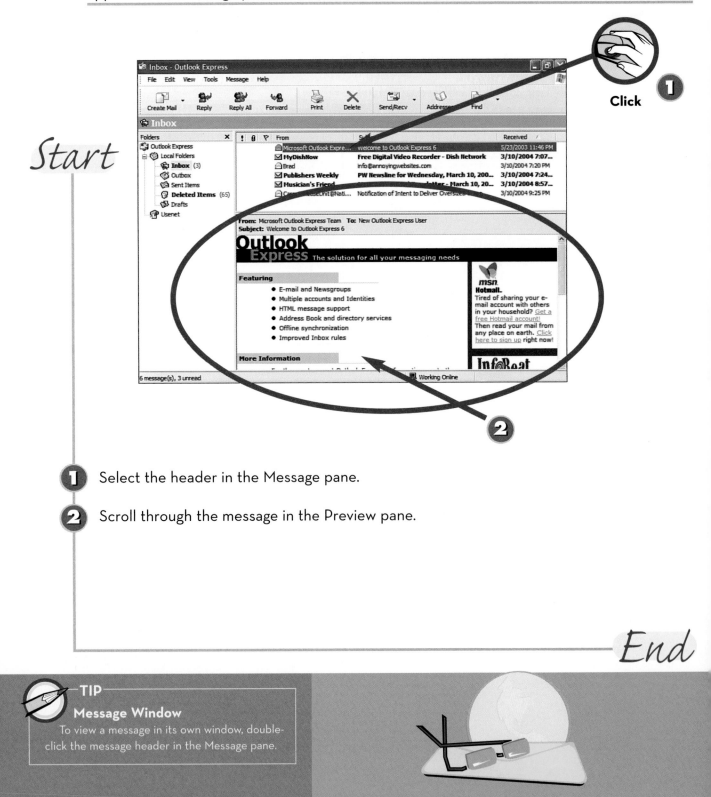

Start

Click

1 Select the header in the Message pane.

2 Scroll through the message in the Preview pane.

End

REPLYING TO AN EMAIL MESSAGE

It's easy to reply to any message you receive. And here's a neat trick: All the text from your original message is automatically "quoted" in your reply!

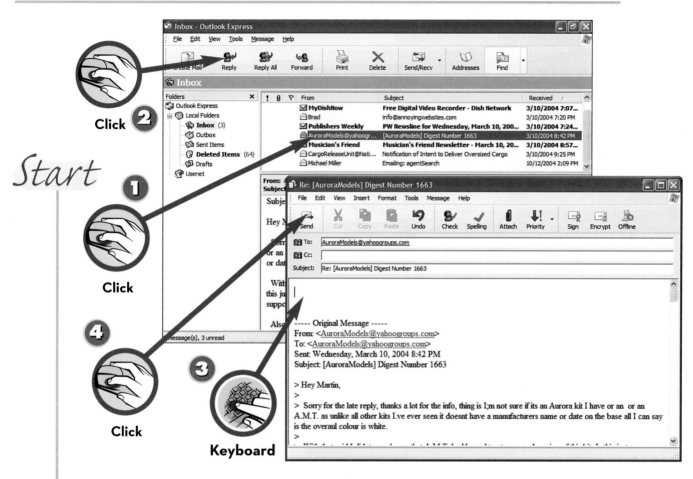

Start

Click ①

Click ②

Keyboard ③

Click ④

① Select the message header in the Message pane.

② Click the **Reply** button on the Outlook Express toolbar.

③ Enter your reply text in the message window.

④ Click the **Send** button to send your reply to the original sender.

End

COMPOSING A NEW EMAIL MESSAGE

Composing a new message is similar to replying to a message. The big difference is that you have to manually enter the recipient's email address.

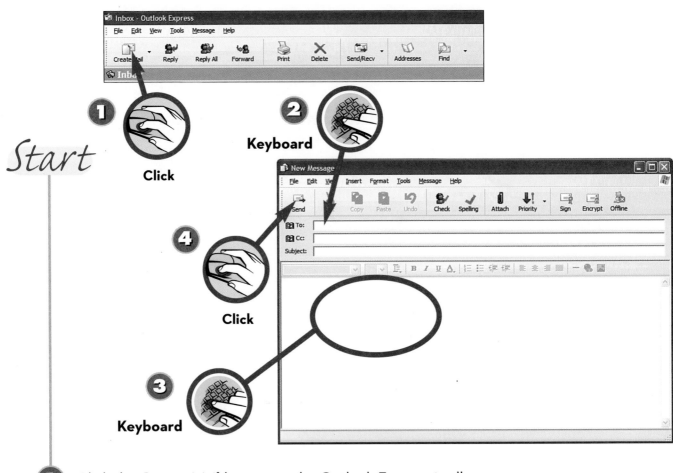

Start

Click

Keyboard

Click

Keyboard

End

1. Click the **Create Mail** button on the Outlook Express toolbar.

2. Enter the email address of the recipient(s) in the **To** field; then enter the address of anyone you want to receive a carbon copy in the **Cc** box.

3. Move your cursor to the main message area and type your message.

4. When your message is complete, send it to the Outbox by clicking the **Send** button.

TIP

Send to Multiple Recipients

You can enter multiple addresses in the To field, as long as you separate multiple addresses with a semicolon (;), like this: mmiller@molehillgroup.com; gjetson@sprockets.com.

SENDING A FILE VIA EMAIL

The easiest way to share a file with another user is via email, as an *attachment*. To send a file via email, you attach that file to a standard email message. When the message is sent, the file travels along with it; when the message is received, the file is right there, waiting to be opened.

Click (4)   **Click** (1)   **Click** (2)

Start

(3) **Click**

1. Start with a new message and then click the **Attach** button in the message's toolbar.

2. Navigate to and select the file you want to send.

3. Click **Attach**.

4. Send the message as normal by clicking the **Send** button.

End

CAUTION

Large Files

Be wary of sending extra-large files over the Internet. They can take a long time to upload if you're on a dial-up connection—and just as long for the recipient to download when received.

ADDING CONTACTS IN WINDOWS MESSENGER

Instant messaging lets you communicate one on one, in real-time, with your friends, family, and colleagues. One of the most popular IM programs is Windows Messenger (also known as MSN Messenger). But before you can send an instant message to another user, that person has to be on your Messenger contact list.

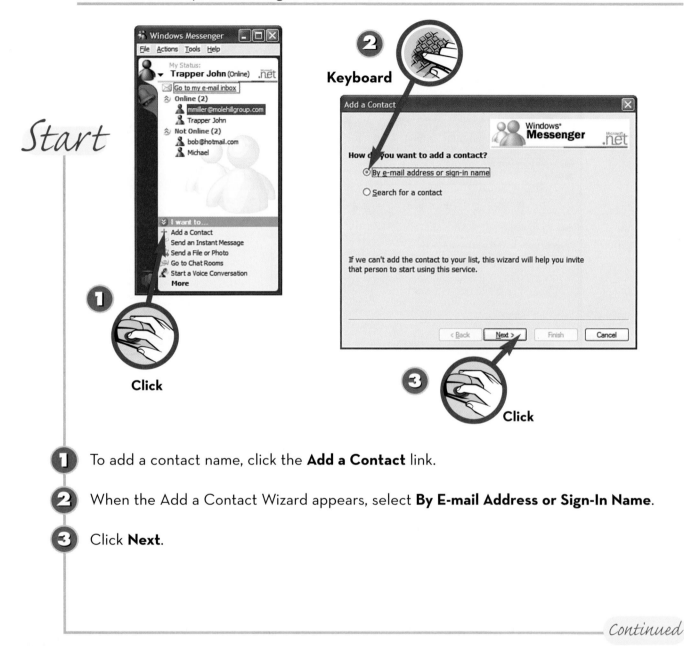

Start

Keyboard

Click

Click

1. To add a contact name, click the **Add a Contact** link.

2. When the Add a Contact Wizard appears, select **By E-mail Address or Sign-In Name**.

3. Click **Next**.

Continued

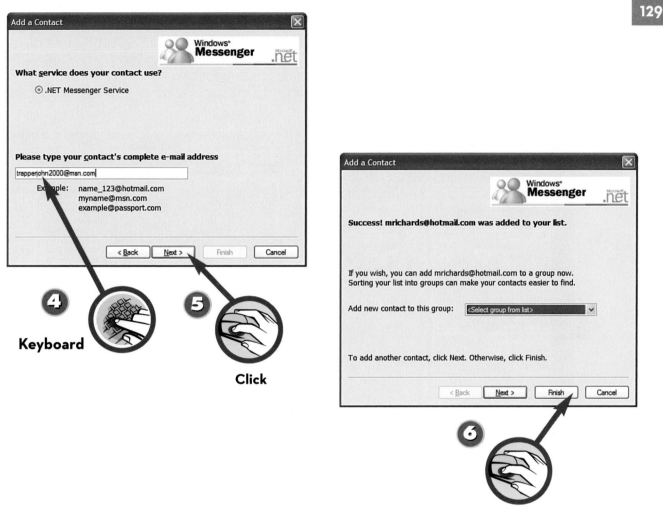

④ Enter the user's email address.

⑤ Click **Next**.

⑥ If the user you specified has a Microsoft Passport, that contact will be added to your contact list. Click **Finish**.

End

TIP
Search for Contacts
To search for a contact, launch the Add a Contact Wizard, select the **Search for a Contact** option, and then click **Next**. Follow the onscreen instructions to search by first name, last name, or country.

INSTANT MESSAGING WITH WINDOWS MESSENGER

To send an instant message to another user, both of you have to be online at the same time. If that person is on your contact list, he'll show up as being online in Windows Messenger; you'll also appear on his online list.

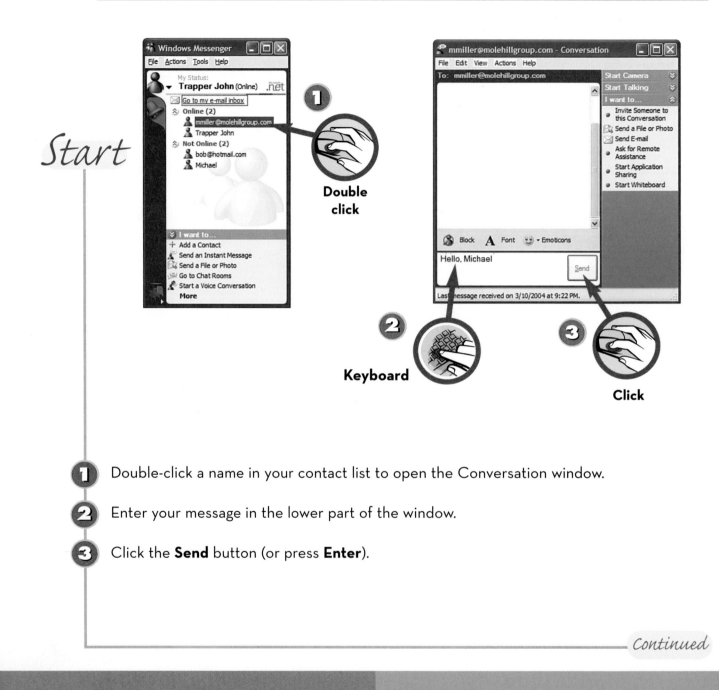

Start

Double click

Keyboard

Click

1 Double-click a name in your contact list to open the Conversation window.

2 Enter your message in the lower part of the window.

3 Click the **Send** button (or press **Enter**).

Continued

4 Your message text appears in your Conversation window—and in the Conversation window of your recipient.

5 Messages sent by your recipient also appear in your Conversation window.

End

PLAYING MUSIC AND MOVIES

Your personal computer can do more than just compute. It can also serve as a fully functional audio/video playback center!

That's right, you can use your PC to listen to your favorite audio CDs and to watch the latest movies on DVD. And you do all of this with a software program called Windows Media Player—included free with your new PC!

WINDOWS MEDIA PLAYER

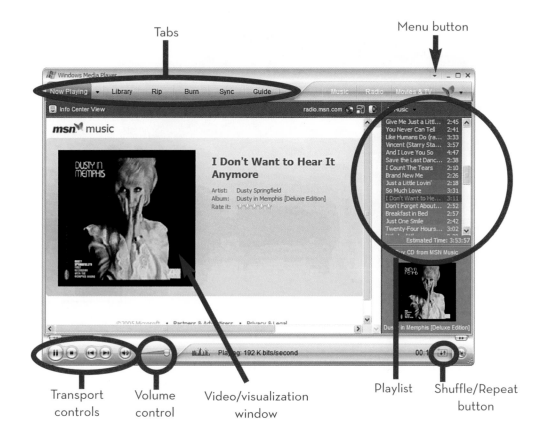

Tabs

Menu button

Transport controls

Volume control

Video/visualization window

Playlist

Shuffle/Repeat button

PLAYING A CD

You play audio CDs using your PC's CD-ROM drive and Windows Media Player (WMP).
You can also use WMP to play songs you've downloaded to your PC from the Internet and
(if your PC has a DVD drive) to play DVD movies.

Start

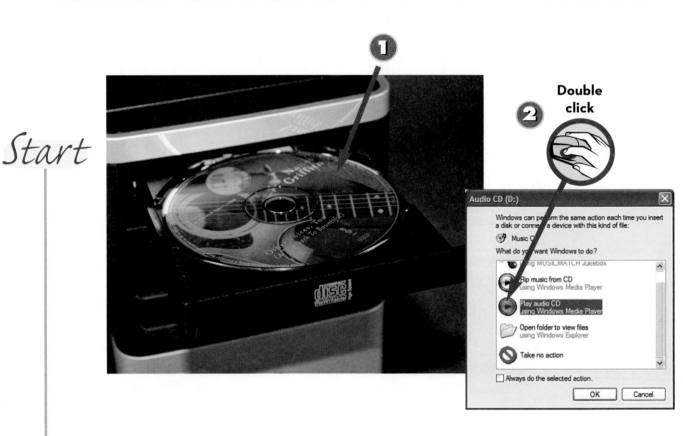

Double click

1 Insert a CD into your PC's CD-ROM drive.

2 Windows will ask what you want to do; double-click **Play Audio CD Using Windows Media Player**.

Continued

TIP

Online Music Stores

You can buy downloadable music at many online music stores, including the
iTunes Music Store (www.apple.com/itunes/store/), MSN Music (music.msn.com),
and Napster (www.napster.com). Most stores charge 99¢ per song.

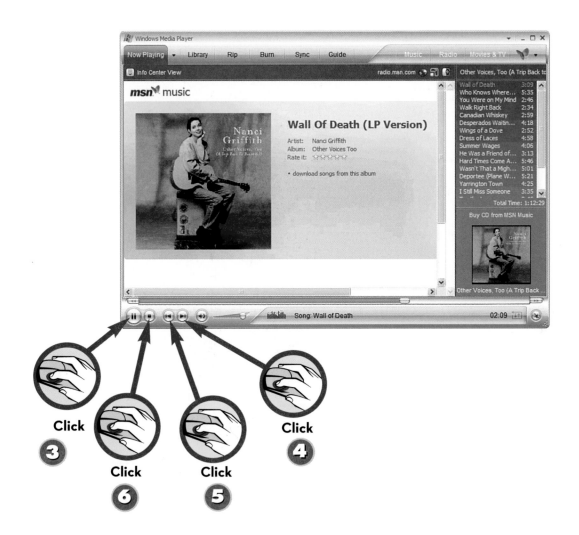

Click ③

Click ⑥

Click ⑤

Click ④

③ The CD should start playing automatically; to pause the CD, click the **Pause** button and then click **Play** to resume playback.

④ To skip to the next track, click the **Next** button.

⑤ To replay the last track, click the **Previous** button.

⑥ To stop playback completely, click the **Stop** button.

End

TIP

Download the Latest Version

This book covers Windows Media Player version 10. To download the latest version of Windows Media Player, go to www.microsoft.com/windows/windowsmedia/.

NOTE

Launching Windows Media Player

If WMP doesn't start automatically when you load a CD into your PC's CD-ROM drive, you can launch it manually from the Windows Start menu.

RIPPING A CD TO YOUR HARD DISK

Windows Media Player lets you copy music from your CDs to your PC's hard drive. You can then listen to these digital audio files on your computer, transfer the files to a portable music player, or burn your own custom mix CDs. This process of copying files from a CD to your hard disk is called *ripping*.

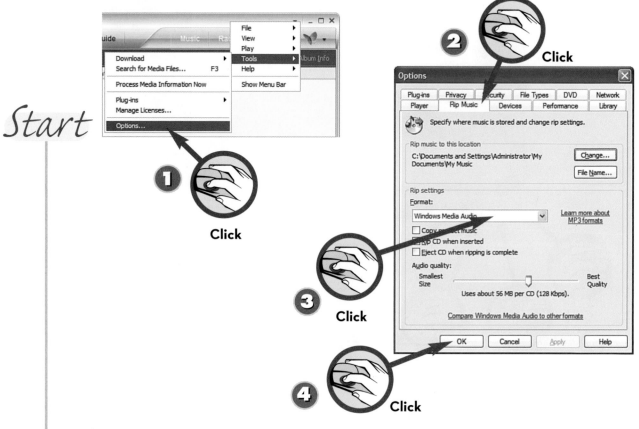

Start

Click

Click

Click

Click

1 Before you rip a CD, you have to set the recording quality level. Pull down the **Tools** menu and select **Options**.

2 When the Options dialog box appears, click the **Rip Music** tab.

3 Pull down the **Format** list and select the file format and recording quality you want.

4 Click **OK**.

Continued

Click

Click

Title	Length	Rip Status	Artist	Composer	Genre	Style	Data Provider
Wall of Death	3:09		Nanci Griffith	Richard Thompson	Country		AMG
Who Knows Where the Time Goes?	5:35		Nanci Griffith	Sandy Denny	Country		AMG
You Were on My Mind	2:46		Nanci Griffith	Sylvia Fricker	Country		AMG
Walk Right Back	2:34		Nanci Griffith	Sonny Curtis	Country		AMG
Canadian Whiskey	2:59		Nanci Griffith	Tom Russell	Country		AMG
Desperados Waiting for a Train	4:18		Nanci Griffith	Guy Clark	Country		AMG
Wings of a Dove	2:52		Nanci Griffith	Bob Ferguson	Country		AMG
Dress of Laces	4:58		Nanci Griffith	John Grimaudo; Saylor White	Country		AMG
Summer Wages	4:06		Nanci Griffith	Ian Tyson	Country		AMG
He Was a Friend of Mine	3:13		Nanci Griffith	Traditional	Country		AMG
Hard Times Come Again No More	5:46		Nanci Griffith	Stephen Foster	Country		AMG
Wasn't That a Mighty Storm	5:01		Nanci Griffith	Traditional	Country		AMG
Deportee (Plane Wreck at Los Gatos)	5:21		Nanci Griffith	Martin Hoffman; Woody Guthrie	Country		AMG
Yarrington Town	4:25		Nanci Griffith	Mickie Merkens	Country		AMG
I Still Miss Someone	3:35		Nanci Griffith	Johnny Cash; Roy Cash	Country		AMG
Try the Love	3:45		Nanci Griffith	Pat McLaughlin	Country		AMG
The Streets of Baltimore	2:37		Nanci Griffith	Harlan Howard; Tompall Glaser	Country		AMG
Farrow, Darcy	2:33		Nanci Griffith	Steve Gillette; Tom Campbell	Country		AMG
If I Had a Hammer	2:46		Nanci Griffith	Lee Hays; Pete Seeger	Country		AMG

19 item(s) selected to rip to C:\Documents and Settings\Administrator\My Documents\My Music

Stopped

Click

5 Insert the CD you want to rip into your PC's CD-ROM drive.

6 In WMP, click the **Rip** tab to show the contents of the CD.

7 Put a check mark by the tracks you want to copy.

8 When you've selected which tracks to rip, click the **Rip Music** button.

End

-TIP-
Connect to the Internet
Before you rip a CD, you should make sure your PC is connected to the Internet. This lets WMP download track names and CD cover art for the songs you're ripping.

-NOTE-
Music Files
WMP stores your ripped music files in your My Music folder. It creates a subfolder for the artist, and within that another subfolder for each of the artist's CDs.

CREATING A PLAYLIST

Files in your Windows Media Player library can be combined into *playlists*. You can create playlists from the files you have stored on your hard disk, in any order you want—just like listening to a radio station's playlist.

Start

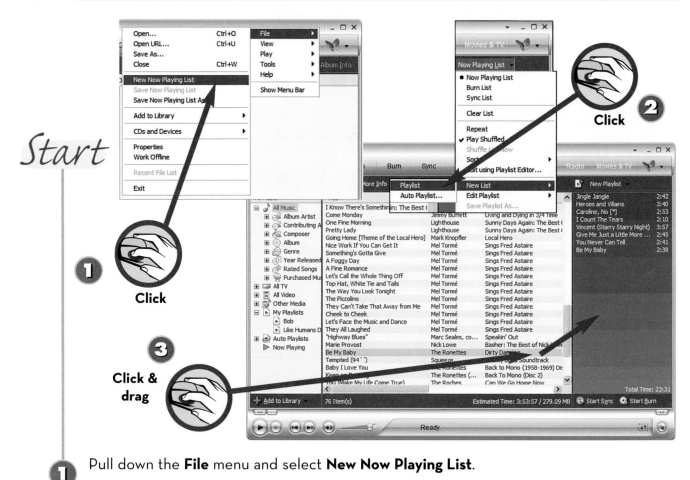

1 Pull down the **File** menu and select **New Now Playing List**.

2 Click the **Now Playing List** button and select **New List**, **Playlist**.

3 Click and drag songs from the Contents pane onto the List pane to create your playlist.

Continued

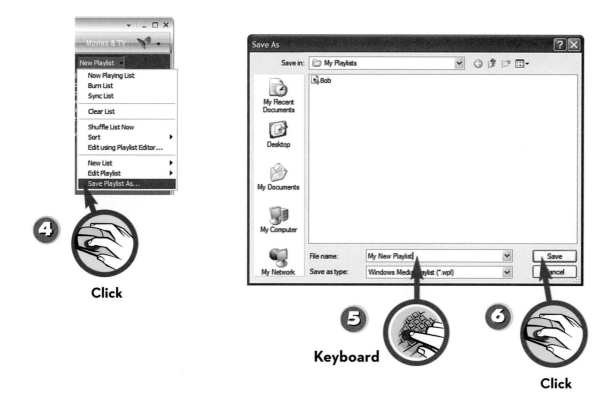

Click

Keyboard

Click

4 Click **New Playlist** and select **Save Playlist As**.

5 Enter a playlist name.

6 Click **Save**.

End

PLAYING A PLAYLIST

After you've created a playlist, you can play back any or all songs in that playlist—in any order.

Click

Start

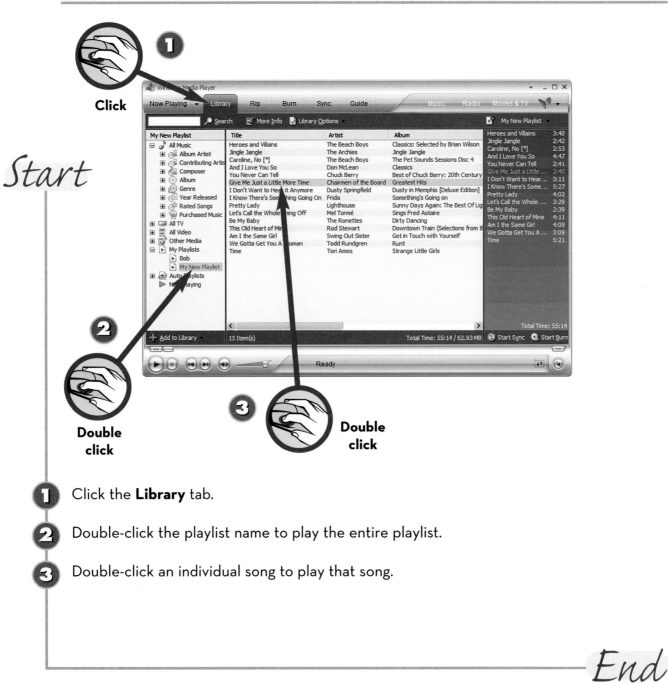

Double click

Double click

① Click the **Library** tab.

② Double-click the playlist name to play the entire playlist.

③ Double-click an individual song to play that song.

End

TIP

Random Play

To play the songs in a playlist in random order, pull down the **Play** menu and check the **Shuffle** option.

BURNING A MUSIC CD

If you have a recordable CD drive (called a *CD burner*) in your PC, you can make your own audio mix CDs. You can take any combination of songs on your hard disk; "burn" them onto a blank CD; and then play that CD in your home, car, or portable CD player.

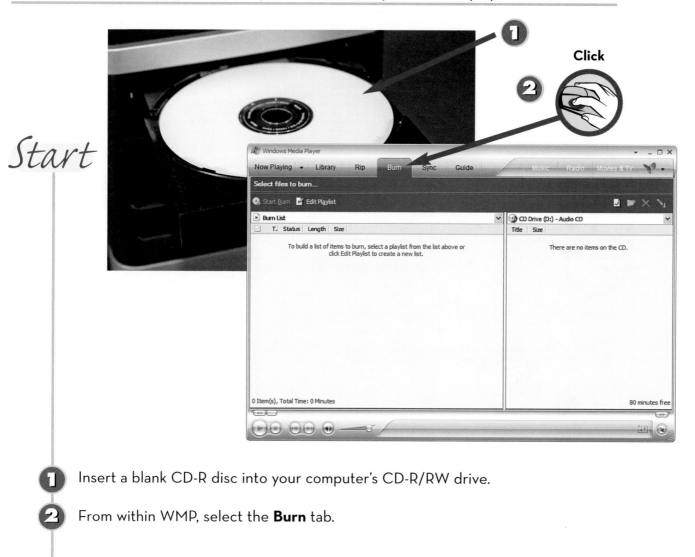

Start

Click

1. Insert a blank CD-R disc into your computer's CD-R/RW drive.

2. From within WMP, select the **Burn** tab.

Continued

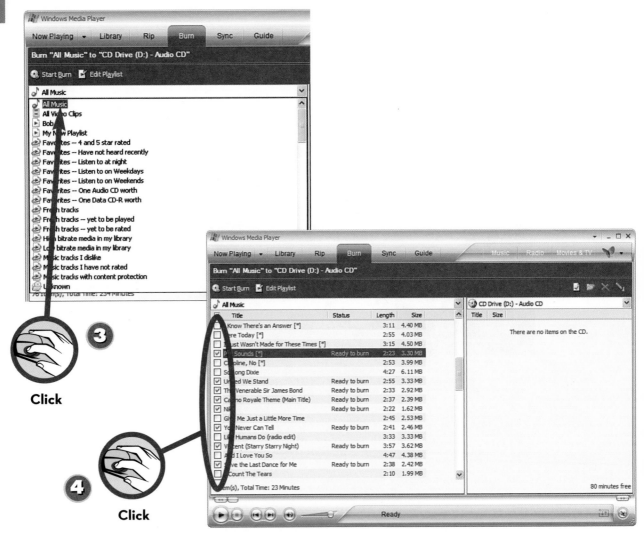

Click

Click

3 Pull down the **Items to Burn** list (on the left) and select **All Music**.

4 Check those songs you want to burn to CD.

Continued

Click

6

Click

5

Windows Media Player — □ ×

Now Playing ▾ | Library | Rip | Burn | Sync | Guide   Music   Radio   Movies & TV ▾

Burn "All Music" to "CD Drive (D:) - Audio CD"

⊙ Start Burn ✎ Edit Playlist   ☑ ▸ ✕ ↘

♪ All Music   ▾   CD Drive (D:) - Audio CD   ▾

☑	Title	Status	Length	Size
☐	Like Humans Do (radio edit)		3:33	3.33 MB
☑	Vincent (Starry Starry Night)	Ready to burn	3:57	3.62 MB
☑	And I Love You So	Ready to burn	4:47	4.38 MB
☑	Save the Last Dance for Me	Ready to burn	2:38	2.42 MB
☑	I Count The Tears	Ready to burn	2:10	1.99 MB
☑	Brand New Me	Ready to burn	2:26	2.80 MB
☑	Just a Little Lovin'	Ready to burn	2:18	3.20 MB
☑	So Much Love	Ready to burn	3:31	4.85 MB
☐	I Don't Want to Hear it Anymore		3:11	4.39 MB
☐	Don't Forget About Me		2:52	3.97 MB
☐	Breakfast in Bed		2:57	4.09 MB
☐	Just One Smile		2:42	3.74 MB
☑	Twenty-Four Hours from Tulsa	Ready to burn	3:02	2.78 MB
☐	little by little		2:20	2.67 MB
☐	I Know There's Something Going On		5:27	7.49 MB

Right panel:
🔘 CD Drive (D:) - Audio CD
  🔘 Audio CD
  🔘 Data CD
  🔘 HighMAT Audio

8 Item(s), Total Time: 25 Minutes   80 minutes free

▶ ⏸ ⏮ ⏭ ⏯ ——○——   Ready   ⟷ ✕

5 Select your CD-R/RW drive from the **Device** list (on the right), then select **Audio CD**.

6 Click the **Start Burn** button.

End

TIP

Use CD-R Discs

To play your new CD in a regular (non-PC) CD player, record in the CD-R format and use a blank CD-R disc specifically labeled for audio use. (CD-RW discs will not play in most home CD players.)

TIP

Burn a Playlist

A quicker way to select songs is to create a playlist first and then select that single playlist on the Burn tab.

CONNECTING AN IPOD TO YOUR PC

To use the iPod with your PC, you first have to install Apple's iTunes software, which comes on the accompanying CD. When you connect your iPod to your PC, your computer automatically launches the iTunes software and transfers any new songs and playlists you've added since the last time you connected.

Start

Connect

Connect

Plug   Play

① Connect one end of the USB cable to your iPod.

② Connect the other end of the USB cable to a USB port on your PC.

Continued

Click

3 The iTunes software will now launch on your PC and automatically sync its songs and playlists to your iPod.

4 Close the iTunes software and disconnect your iPod when the sync is complete.

End

TRANSFERRING SONGS TO YOUR IPOD VIA ITUNES

The key to managing the music on your iPod is mastering Apple's iTunes software. To transfer songs to your iPod, all you have to do is check them. The next time you connect your iPod, all the checked songs in your Library will be downloaded.

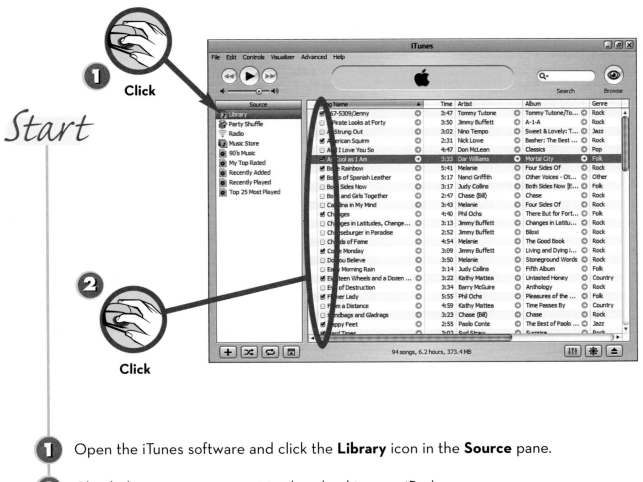

Start

1 Click

2 Click

1 Open the iTunes software and click the **Library** icon in the **Source** pane.

2 Check those songs you want to download to your iPod.

End

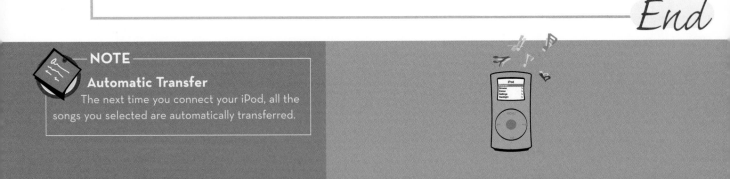

NOTE

Automatic Transfer
The next time you connect your iPod, all the songs you selected are automatically transferred.

CREATING SMART PLAYLISTS FOR YOUR IPOD

You can store thousands of songs on your iPod, which makes it a little difficult to find the music you want. One way to organize your music is to create playlists of your favorite songs. *Smart* playlists let you select songs by artist, album, genre, and so on.

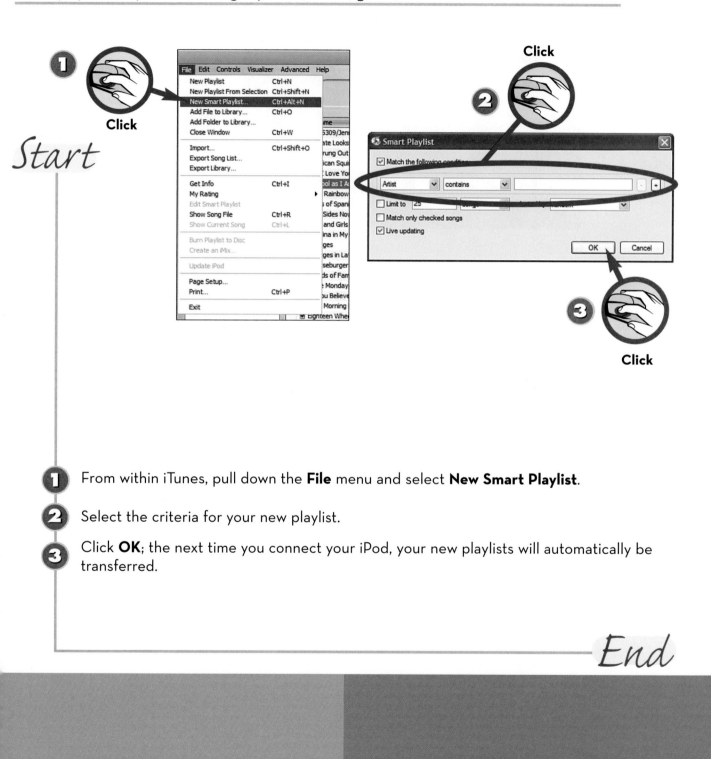

1 From within iTunes, pull down the **File** menu and select **New Smart Playlist**.

2 Select the criteria for your new playlist.

3 Click **OK**; the next time you connect your iPod, your new playlists will automatically be transferred.

End

CONNECTING OTHER PORTABLE MUSIC PLAYERS

You can connect any brand of portable music player to your PC. For most non-iPod players, you can use Windows Media Player to transfer music from your PC to your portable device.

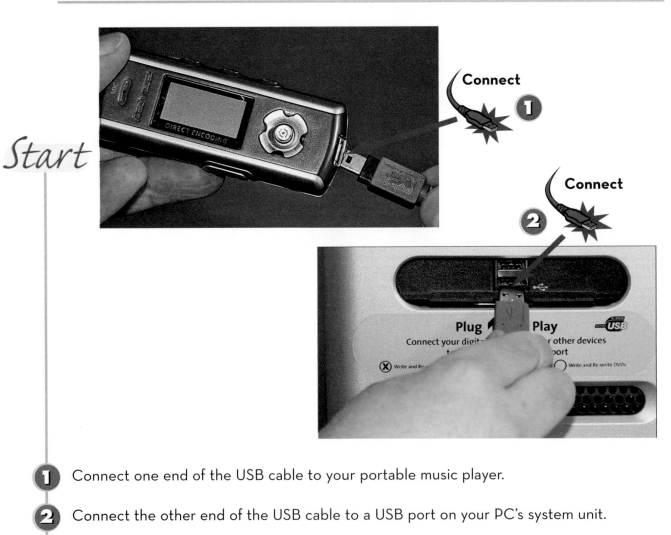

Start

Connect 1

Connect 2

1 Connect one end of the USB cable to your portable music player.

2 Connect the other end of the USB cable to a USB port on your PC's system unit.

Continued

NOTE

MP3 Players

Portable music players—especially those that store songs in flash memory—are often generically called *MP3 players*, after the popular MP3 file format.

Click (6)

Click (3)

(4) **Click**

(5) **Click**

(6) **Click**

(3) In Windows Media Player, click the **Sync** tab.

(4) Pull down the **Sync** list (on the left side) and select either **All Music** or a specific playlist; then check those songs you want to transfer to your music player.

(5) Pull down the **Device** list (on the right side) and select your portable audio player.

(6) Click the **Start Sync** button to transfer the selected files to your portable audio player.

End

TIP

Device Setup

The first time you connect a portable audio player to your PC, Windows Media Player starts the Device Setup Wizard. This helps you configure either automatic or manual synchronization between your music player and WMP.

TIP

Proprietary Software

Many portable audio players come with their own software programs for transferring files from your PC. You can use either your player's program or Windows Media Player to perform this task.

PLAYING A DVD

If your PC has a DVD drive, you can use your PC to watch prerecorded DVD movies. When you insert a DVD in your DVD drive, your PC should sense the presence of the DVD, launch Windows Media Player, and start playing the movie. (You can also initiate playback from within WMP by pulling down the Play menu and selecting DVD.)

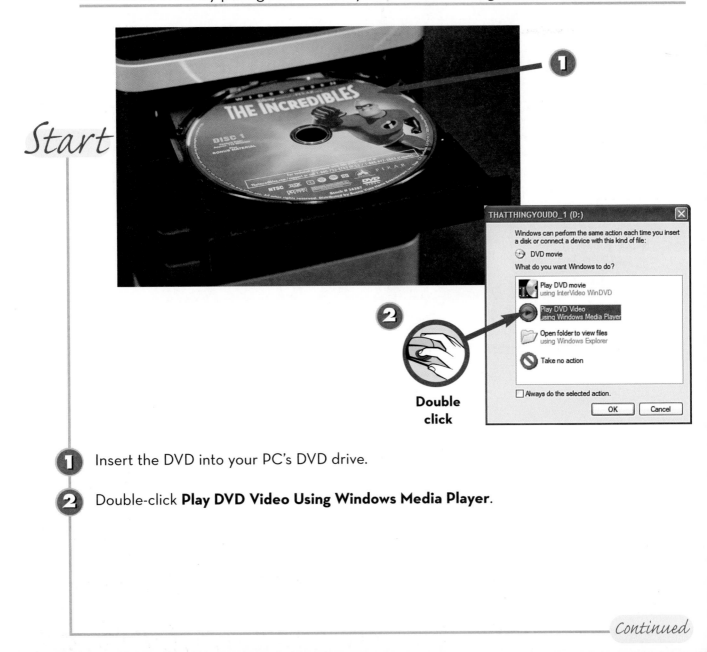

Start

Double click

① Insert the DVD into your PC's DVD drive.

② Double-click **Play DVD Video Using Windows Media Player**.

Continued

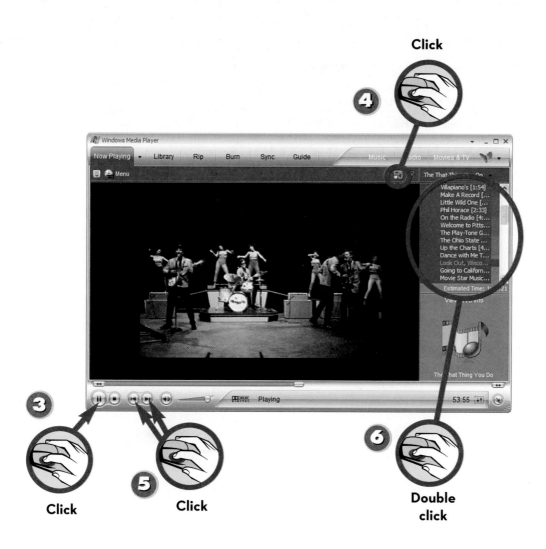

Click

Click

Click

Double click

3 The movie should start playing automatically. To pause the movie, click the **Pause** button; then click **Play** to resume playback.

4 To view the movie full-screen, click the **Full Screen** button; press **Esc** to return to normal viewing mode.

5 Click the **Next** button to go to the next chapter on the DVD, or click the **Previous** button to go to the previous chapter.

6 Go to any specific chapter by double-clicking the chapter name.

End

TIP
Main Menu
To view the DVD's main menu, pull down WMP's **View** menu and select **DVD Features**, **Title Menu**.

TIP
Change Soundtracks
To change languages or soundtracks on a DVD, pull down the **View** menu and select **DVD Features**, **Audio and Language Tracks**. This displays a list of available audio options; select the track you want to listen to.

part

WORKING WITH PICTURES

More and more people are trading in their old film cameras for new digital cameras—and connecting those cameras to their PCs. You can use your digital camera and PC together to transfer all the photos you take to your hard disk and then edit your pictures to make them look even better.

By default, Windows XP stores all your picture files in the My Pictures folder. This folder includes a number of features specific to the management of picture files, found in the Picture Tasks panel.

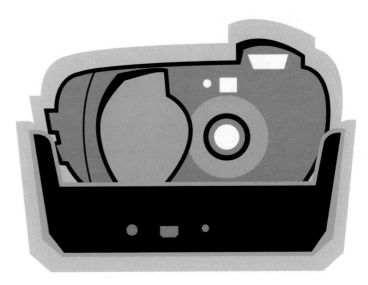

MY PICTURES FOLDER

Order prints
online

View as a
slideshow

Change how My Pictures displays your photos

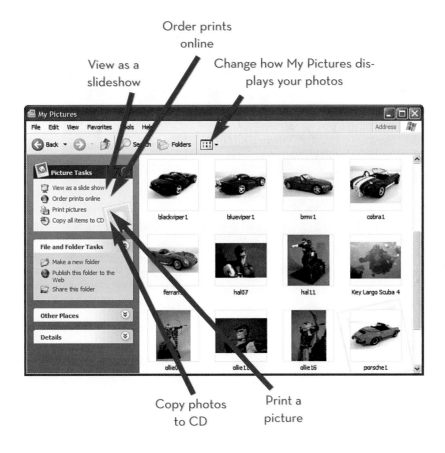

Copy photos
to CD

Print a
picture

TRANSFERRING PICTURES FROM A DIGITAL CAMERA

Connecting a digital camera or scanner to your PC is extremely easy, especially if you have a newer model with a USB or FireWire connection. With this type of setup, Windows will recognize your camera or scanner as soon as you plug it in and will install the appropriate drivers automatically.

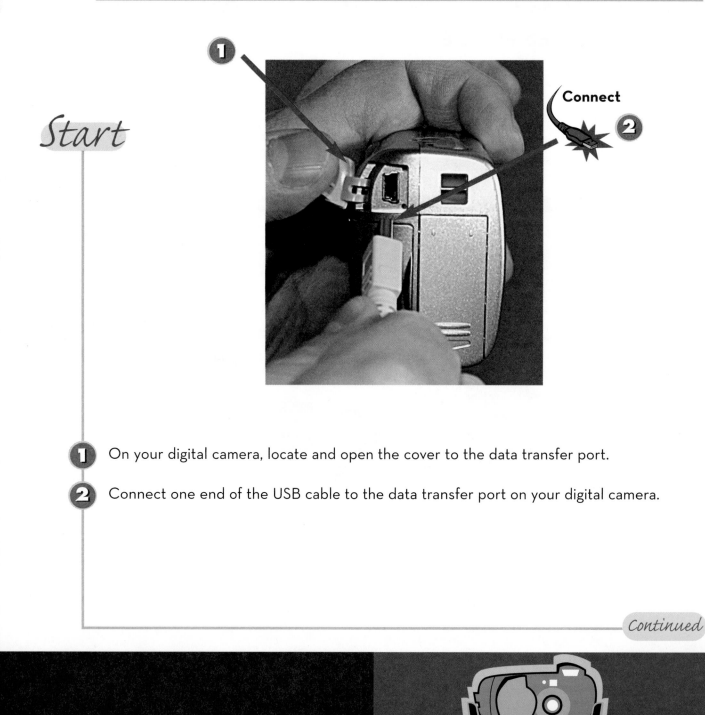

Start

Connect

1 On your digital camera, locate and open the cover to the data transfer port.

2 Connect one end of the USB cable to the data transfer port on your digital camera.

Continued

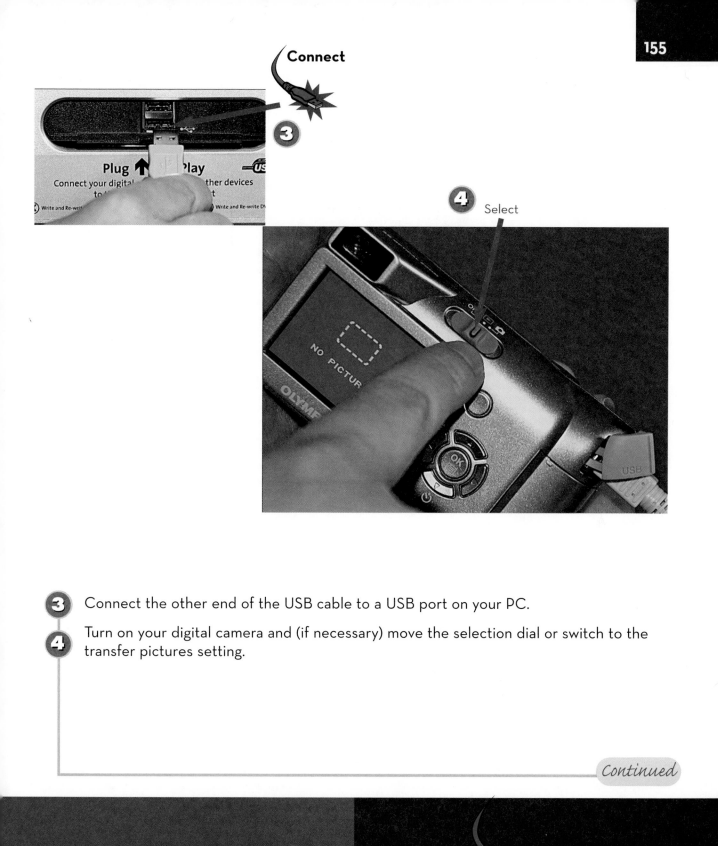

Connect

Select

3 Connect the other end of the USB cable to a USB port on your PC.

4 Turn on your digital camera and (if necessary) move the selection dial or switch to the transfer pictures setting.

Continued

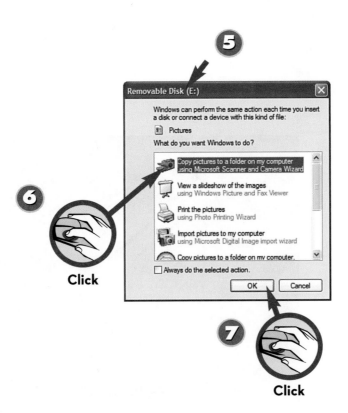

Click

Click

5 This should automatically open the Removable Disk dialog box.

6 Click **Copy Pictures to a Folder on My Computer Using Microsoft Scanner and Camera Wizard**.

7 Click **OK**.

Continued

TIP

Copying Manually

If the Device Connect Autoplay dialog box doesn't open automatically when you connect your camera, open it manually by clicking the **Start** menu, selecting **My Pictures**, and then clicking **Get Pictures from Camera or Scanner**.

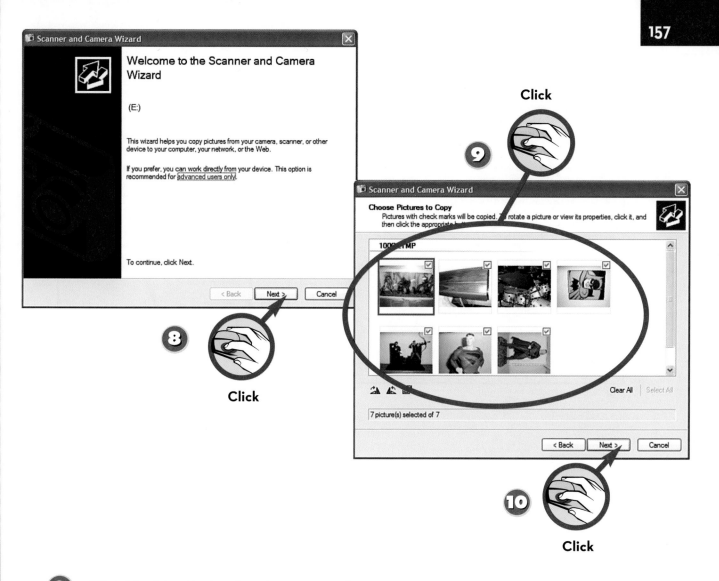

8 Click **Next** to display the photos stored on your camera.

9 Check those photos you want to copy.

10 Click **Next**.

Continued

TIP
Rotating Pictures
If a picture was taken sideways, you can rotate the photo to the portrait orientation by clicking one of the Rotate buttons at the bottom of the Choose Pictures to Copy screen.

Keyboard

Click

Click

Click

11 Enter a name for this group of pictures.

12 Click the **Browse** button and select the destination folder for your pictures.

13 Click **OK**.

14 Click **Next** to copy the selected pictures.

Continued

-TIP-
Naming Picture Groups
Windows automatically names all picture files in the same group starting with the name you supply and then adding **001**, **002**, **003**, and so on.

-TIP-
Delete Pictures from Your Camera
After you've transferred all the pictures from your camera to your PC, you can delete the pictures stored on your camera to free up space for more photos. Just check the **Delete Pictures from My Device After Copying Them** option.

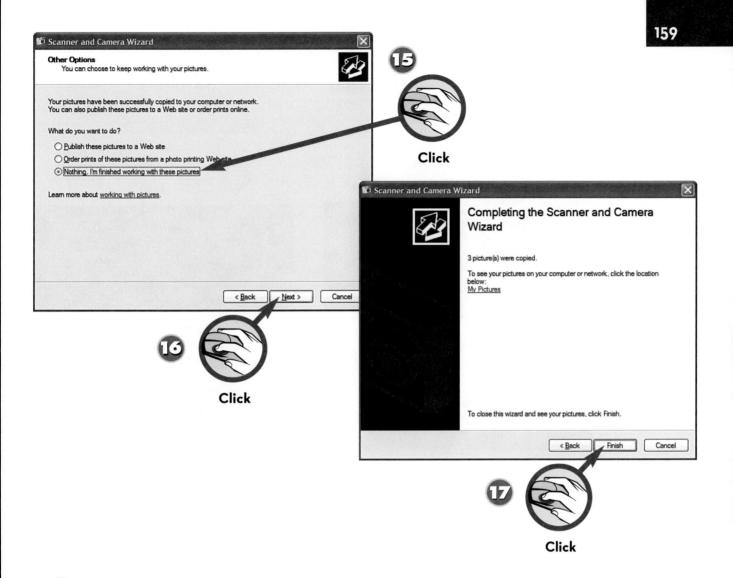

15 After the photos are copied, select **Nothing, I'm Finished Working with These Pictures**.

16 Click **Next**.

17 Click **Finish** to complete the wizard and view your photos.

End

TRANSFERRING PICTURES FROM A MEMORY CARD

If your PC includes a memory card reader, a faster and easier way to copy your digital photos is via your camera's memory card. When you insert a memory card, your PC recognizes the card as if it were another disk on your system. You can then copy files from the memory card to your computer's hard disk.

Start

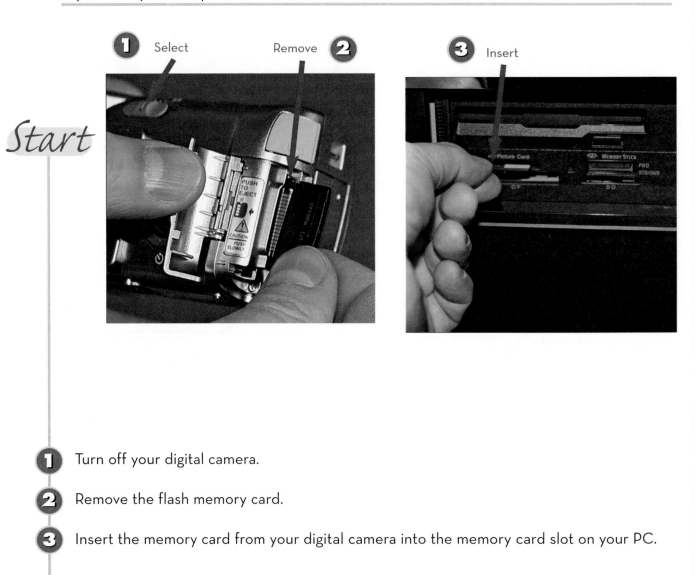

1 Select

2 Remove

3 Insert

1 Turn off your digital camera.

2 Remove the flash memory card.

3 Insert the memory card from your digital camera into the memory card slot on your PC.

Continued

Click

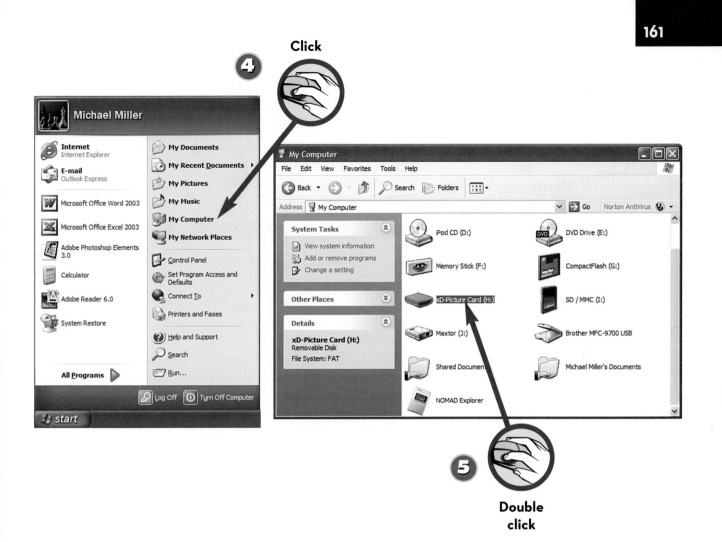

Double click

4 Click **Start** and select **My Computer**.

5 Double-click the icon for the memory card reader drive.

Continued

─ **NOTE** ─────────
Using the Wizard
In some instances, Windows automatically launches the Scanner and Camera Wizard when you insert a memory card with photos stored on it. If this is the case, use the wizard to transfer the photos your PC.

─ **TIP** ─────────
Printing from a Memory Card
Many color photo printers include memory card slots that let you print directly from your camera's memory card, bypassing your computer entirely.

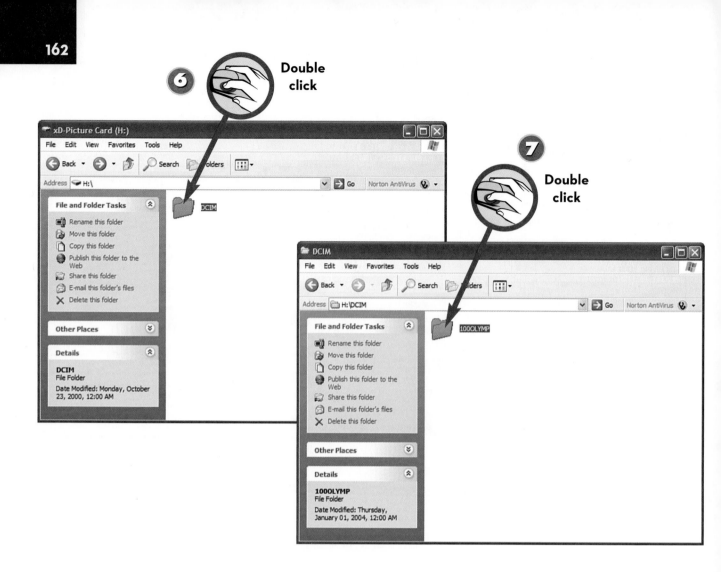

6 Double-click the **DCIM** folder.

7 Double-click the subfolder within the DCIM folder to see your photos.

Continued

TIP

Different Folder Names
Some cameras might use a name other than DCIM for the main folder.

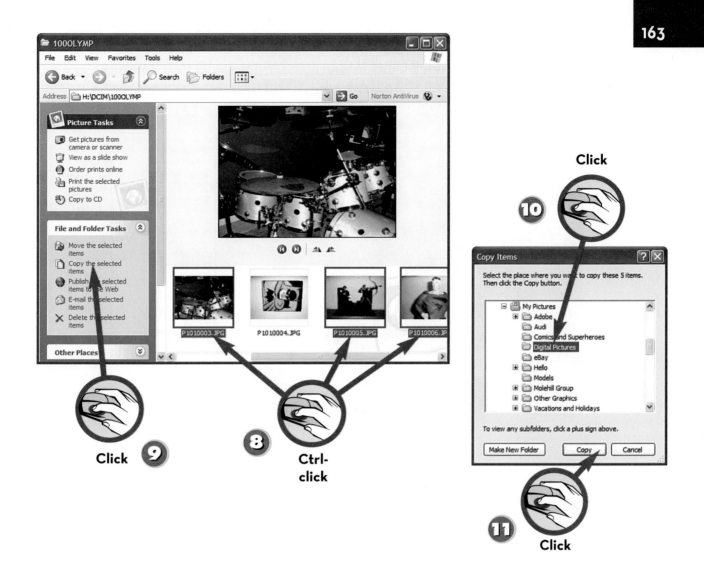

Click

8 Hold down the **Ctrl** key and click each photo you want to transfer.

9 Click **Copy the Selected Items**.

10 Select the destination folder for the photos.

11 Click the **Copy** button.

End

TIP
Buy a Bigger Card
To store more pictures (and higher-resolution pictures) on your camera, invest in a higher-capacity flash memory card. The bigger the card, the more photos you can store before transferring to your computer.

SCANNING A PICTURE

If your photos are of the old-fashioned print variety, you can still turn them into digital files using a flatbed scanner. When you initiate a scan, Windows automatically launches the Scanner and Camera Wizard, which lets you control how your picture is scanned.

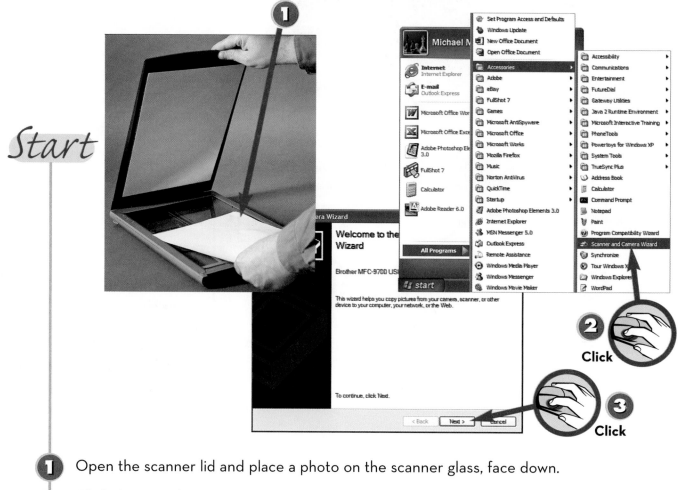

Start

1 Open the scanner lid and place a photo on the scanner glass, face down.

2 Click the **Start** button and select **All Programs**, **Accessories**, **Scanner and Camera Wizard**.

3 Click **Next**.

Continued

TIP

Scan Automatically

Some scanners activate the Scanner and Camera Wizard automatically when you press the Scan button on the scanner.

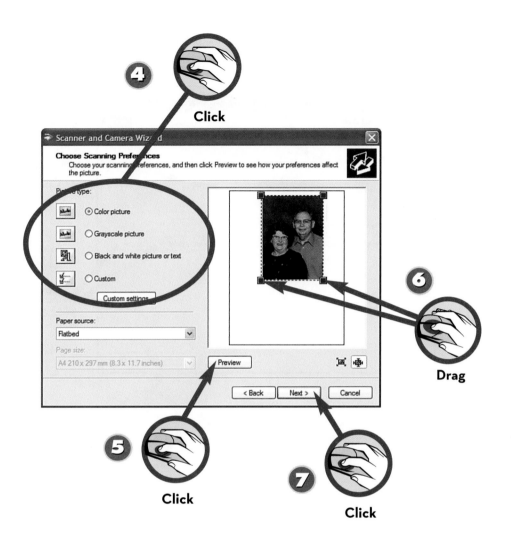

Click

Drag

Click

Click

4 Select a picture type.

5 Click the **Preview** button. Your scanner will now make a preview scan.

6 If necessary, drag the borders of the preview picture to crop the area selected.

7 Click **Next** to continue.

Continued

-TIP-
Reposition the Item
If you don't like the preview scan, reposition the item on your scanner and click the Preview button again to start a new scan.

-TIP-
Higher Resolution
By default, Windows scans your item at 150dpi (dots per inch). If you plan to print the photo, click the **Custom Settings** button and select a higher resolution, such as 300dpi.

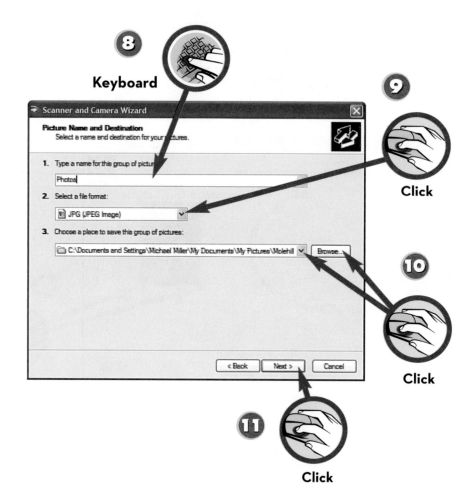

8 Keyboard

9 Click

10 Click

11 Click

8 Enter the name for this group of pictures.

9 Select a file format from the list.

10 Click the **Browse** button to select the destination folder for the photos, or select a location from the pull-down list.

11 Click **Next**.

Continued

TIP

File Formats

For the best quality for photo prints, save your scan in TIF format. For use on the Web or to send photos via email, save your scan in JPEG format.

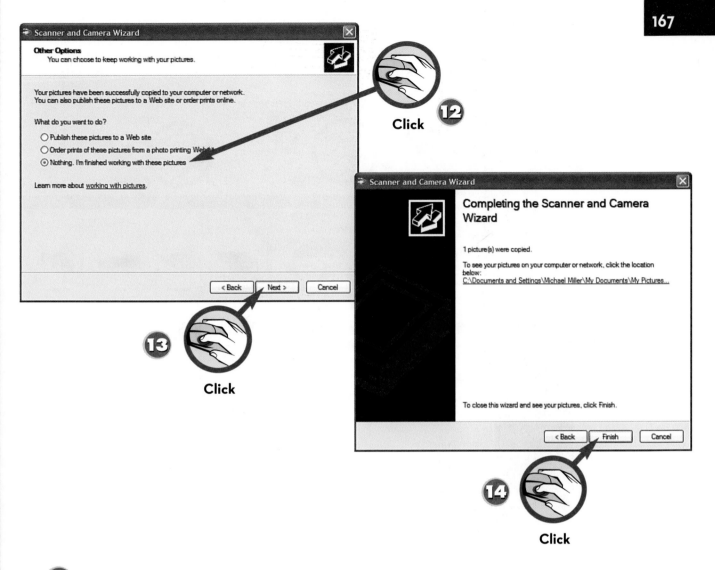

Click **12**

Click **13**

Click **14**

12 When the scan is complete, select **Nothing, I'm Finished Working with These Pictures**.

13 Click **Next**.

14 Click **Finish** to exit the wizard.

End

TIP

Other Options

The other options at the conclusion of the wizard let you transfer your scanned photo to a website or order photo prints of the item.

PRINTING A PHOTO

Any photo editing program will let you print your pictures from within the program. You can also print directly from Windows XP via the Photo Printing Wizard. You launch this wizard from the My Pictures folder.

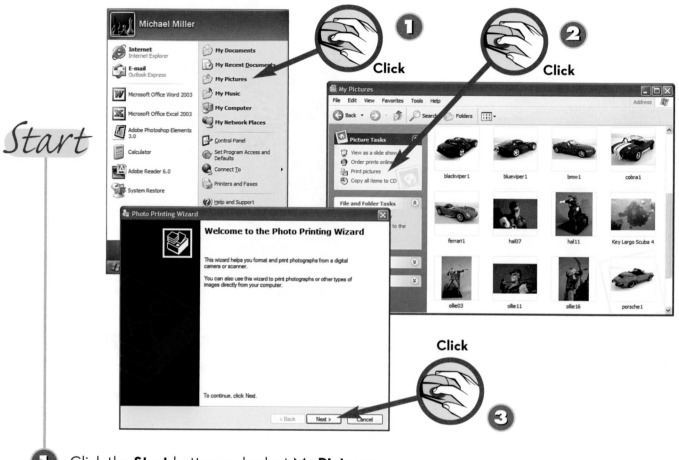

Start

Click ❶

Click ❷

Click ❸

❶ Click the **Start** button and select **My Pictures**.

❷ From the My Pictures folder, click **Print Pictures**.

❸ When the Photo Printing Wizard appears, click **Next**.

Continued

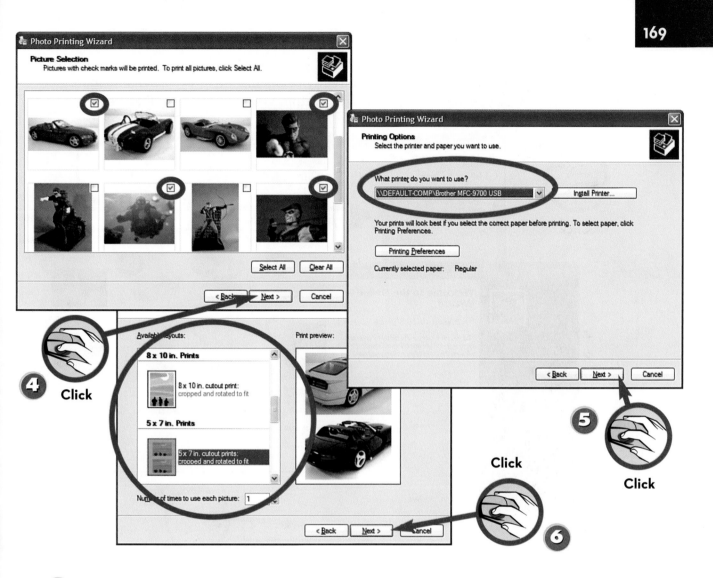

4 Check those photos you want to print and then click **Next**.

5 Select the printer you want to use and then click **Next**.

6 Select a layout for your photos and then click **Next** to start printing.

End

TIP

Different Sizes

You can choose to print your photos full-page, at a specific print size, or as multiple prints on a single contact sheet.

ORDERING PRINTS ONLINE

If you don't have your own photo-quality printer, you can use a professional photo-processing service to print your photos. You can go directly to one of the Internet's many photo-processing sites, or you can order prints from within Windows XP's My Pictures folder.

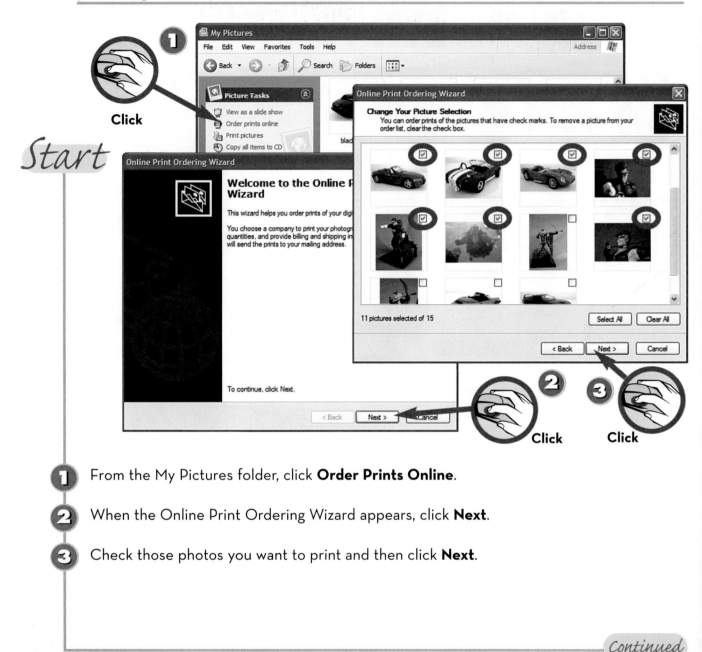

Start

Click

Click

Click

1. From the My Pictures folder, click **Order Prints Online**.

2. When the Online Print Ordering Wizard appears, click **Next**.

3. Check those photos you want to print and then click **Next**.

Continued

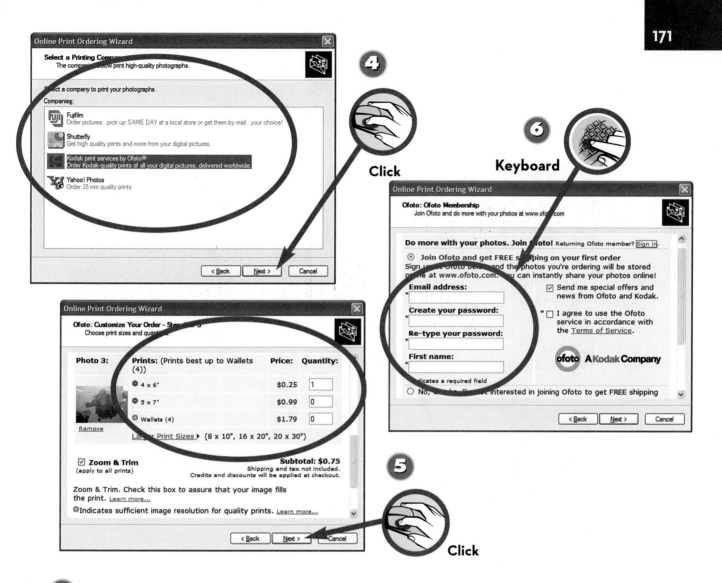

Click

Keyboard

Click

4 Select the printing company you want to order from and then click **Next**.

5 Select the size and quantity for your prints and then click **Next**.

6 Complete the rest of the online ordering process from the site you selected.

End

TIP
Other Online Photo Sites
You can also order prints directly from many online photo sites, including Kodak EasyShare Gallery (www.kodakgallery.com), Shutterfly (www.shutterfly.com), and Snapfish (www.snapfish.com).

QUICK FIXING A PHOTO WITH ADOBE PHOTOSHOP ELEMENTS

The pictures you take with your digital camera don't always turn out perfect. To edit your digital photos, use a photo editing program, such as Adobe Photoshop Elements.

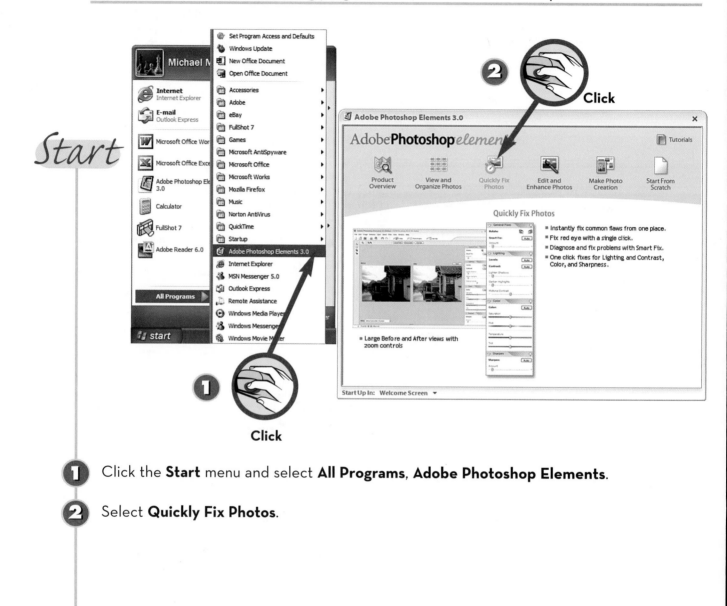

Start

Click

Click

1. Click the **Start** menu and select **All Programs, Adobe Photoshop Elements**.

2. Select **Quickly Fix Photos**.

Continued

Click

Click

Click

3️⃣ Click the **Open** button on the toolbar.

4️⃣ Select the photo you want to edit.

5️⃣ Click **Open**.

Continued

TIP

Other Photo Editing Programs

Other popular photo editing programs include IrfanView (www.irfanview.com), Paint Shop Pro (www.jasc.com), Microsoft Picture It! Photo (www.microsoft.com/products/imaging/), and Roxio PhotoSuite (www.roxio.com).

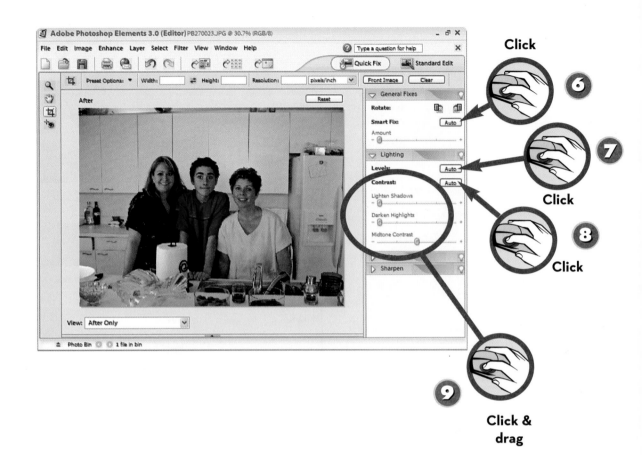

Click

6

7

Click

8

Click

9

**Click &
drag**

6 To perform a one-step "smart fix" of the entire picture, click the Smart Fix **Auto** button.

7 To automatically adjust the brightness, contrast, and color levels, click the Levels **Auto** button.

8 To automatically adjust only the brightness and contrast, click the Contrast **Auto** button.

9 To manually adjust the brightness and contrast, adjust the **Lighten Shadows**, **Darken Highlights**, and **Midtone Contrast** sliders.

Continued

TIP

Different Editing Modes

Photoshop Elements 3.0 has two editing modes. The Quick Fix mode lets you make quick and easy fixes; the Standard Edit mode lets you make more difficult changes to your photos. Switch modes by clicking the buttons in the upper-right corner of the screen.

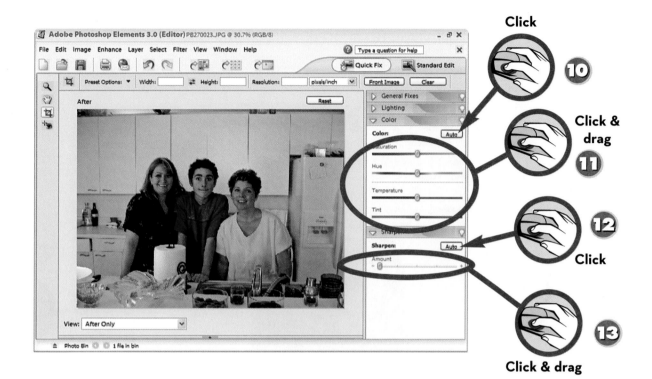

Click — 10

Click & drag — 11

12 — **Click**

Click & drag — 13

10 To automatically adjust the picture's color and tint levels, click the Color **Auto** button.

11 To manually adjust the color and tint levels, adjust the **Saturation**, **Hue**, **Temperature**, and **Tint** sliders.

12 To slightly sharpen the overall picture, click the Sharpen **Auto** button.

13 To manually sharpen the picture, drag the **Amount** slider in the Sharpen section.

End

TIP
Resize Your Picture Onscreen
To enlarge your picture to fit on your computer screen, click the **Zoom** button (with the magnifying glass icon) and then click **Fit on Screen**. To view the picture at its actual size, click **Actual Pixels**.

TIP
Photoshop Elements
The latest version of Photoshop Elements is version 3.0. Learn more at www.adobe.com, or read my companion book *Bad Pics Fixed Quick* (Que Publishing, 2004).

REMOVING RED-EYE

One of the most common problems with pictures of people is red-eye, which is often created when you use your camera's built-in flash. Fortunately, Adobe Photoshop Elements has a tool that lets you quickly and easily fix all red-eye problems.

Click

Start

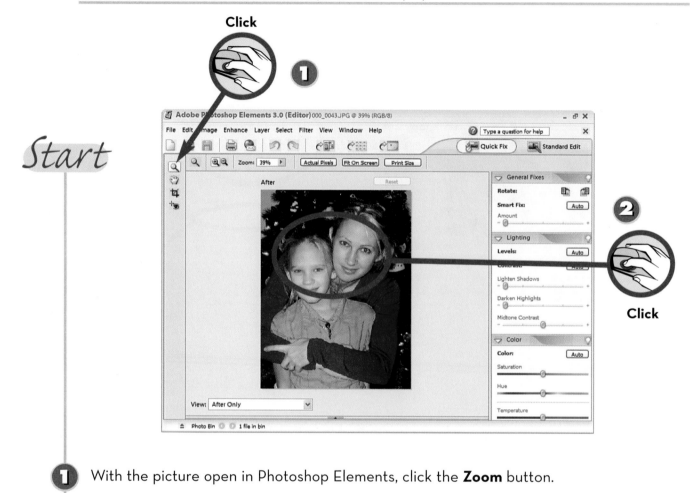

Click

1 With the picture open in Photoshop Elements, click the **Zoom** button.

2 Click one or more times on the subject's face to enlarge this area of the photo.

Continued

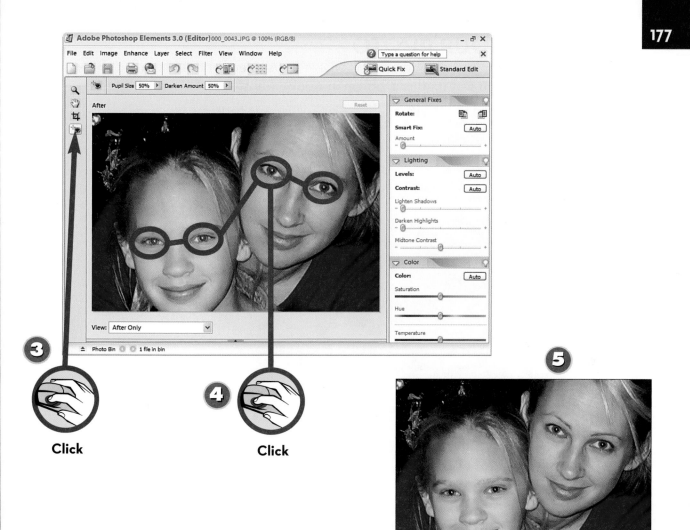

3 Click

4 Click

5

3 Click the **Red Eye Removal Tool** button.

4 Click the red area of the eye.

5 The red-eye is now removed.

End

TIP

Alternative Methods

If clicking the eye area doesn't remove the red-eye, click and drag the cursor to surround the eye area. When you release the mouse button, the red-eye should be gone.

CROPPING YOUR PHOTO

Another common problem is poor framing, where the subject of the picture is either too far away or off center. You can fix this problem in Adobe Photoshop Elements by cropping unwanted areas out of the final picture.

Start

Click

1 With the picture open in Photoshop Elements, click the **Crop Tool** button.

Continued

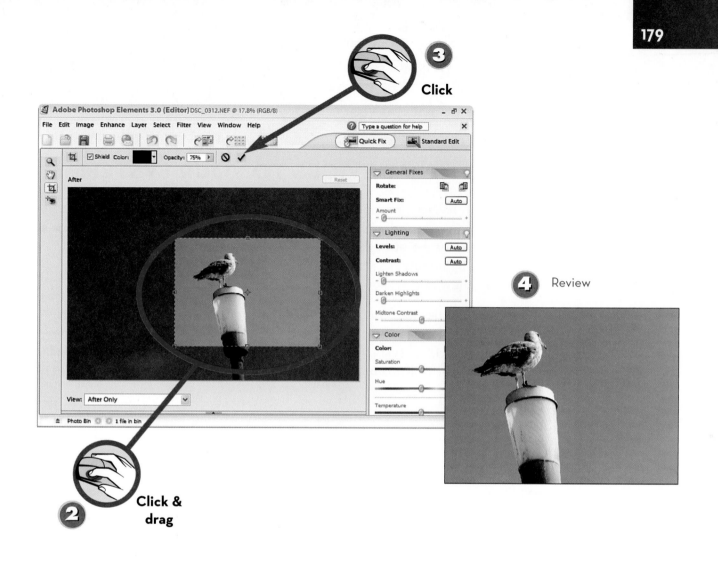

Click ③

Review ④

Click & drag ②

② Click and drag the cursor over the part of the area you want to keep.

③ Click the **OK** button in the options bar to crop the image.

④ The picture is now cropped to your specifications.

End

TIP

Crop to Size

To crop your picture to specific dimensions, click the **Preset Options** button and select a print size. You can also enter custom width and height dimensions in the Crop toolbar.

part 10

ADDING NEW DEVICES TO YOUR SYSTEM

If you just purchased a brand-new, right-out-of-the-box personal computer, it probably came equipped with all the components you could ever desire—or so you think. At some point in the future, however, you might want to expand your system—by adding a second printer, a scanner, a PC camera, or something equally new and exciting.

Everything that's hooked up to your PC is connected via some type of *port*. A port is simply an interface between your PC and another device, either internally (inside your PC's system unit) or externally (via a connector on the back of the system unit). Different types of hardware connect via different types of ports.

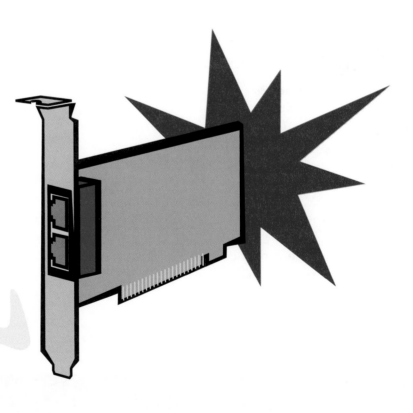

COMPUTER CONNECTIONS

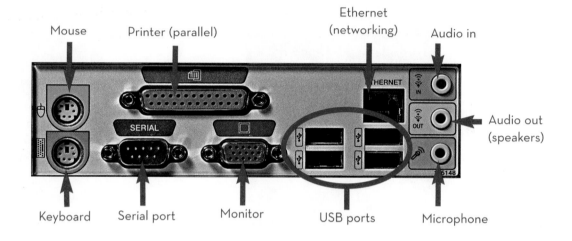

Mouse

Printer (parallel)

Ethernet
(networking)

Audio in

SERIAL

Audio out
(speakers)

Keyboard

Serial port

Monitor

USB ports

Microphone

ADDING A DEVICE VIA USB OR FIREWIRE

The most common external connector today is the USB port; almost every type of peripheral comes in a USB version. USB is popular because it's so easy to use. When you're connecting a USB device, not only do you not have to open your PC's case, but you also don't even have to turn off your system when you add the new device.

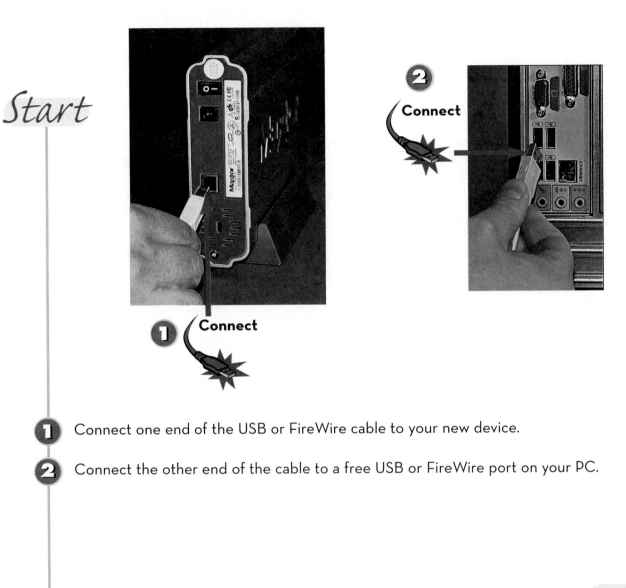

Start

Connect

2 Connect

1 Connect one end of the USB or FireWire cable to your new device.

2 Connect the other end of the cable to a free USB or FireWire port on your PC.

Continued

TIP

Follow Directions

As easy as most USB devices are to connect, you should still read the device's instructions and follow the manufacturer's directions for installation.

Click **Click**

Click

Click

3. Windows should automatically recognize the new peripheral and launch the Found New Hardware Wizard.

4. Check **Install the Software Automatically**.

5. Click **Next** and follow the onscreen instructions to complete the installation.

6. When the installation is complete, click **Finish**.

End

NOTE

FireWire Connections

FireWire is slightly faster than USB, which makes it ideal for connecting devices that move a lot of data, such as hard drives and camcorders. Connecting a device via FireWire is similar to connecting it via USB.

TIP

USB Hubs

If you connect too many USB devices, you can run out of USB connectors on your PC. If that happens, buy an add-on USB hub, which lets you plug multiple USB peripherals in to a single USB port.

ADDING NEW INTERNAL HARDWARE

Adding an internal device—usually through a plug-in card—is slightly more difficult than adding an external device, primarily because you have to use a screwdriver and get under the hood of your system unit. Other than the extra screwing and plugging, however, the process is pretty much the same as with external devices.

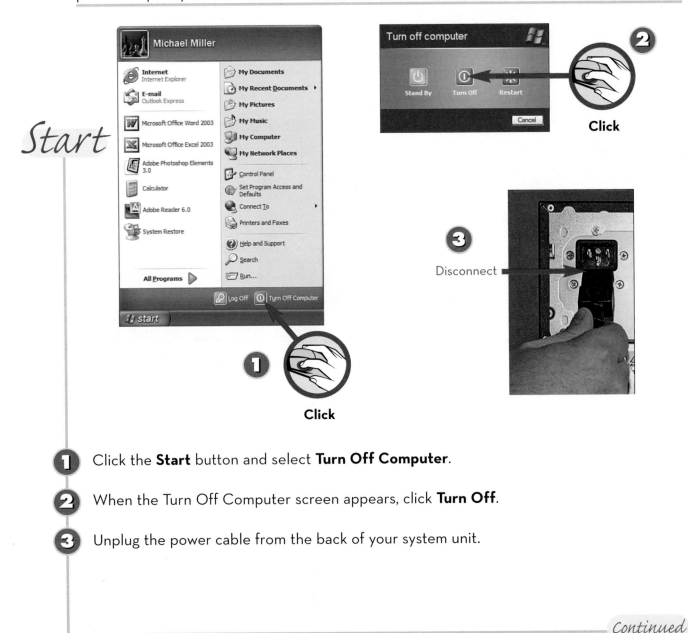

Start

Click

Click

Disconnect

1. Click the **Start** button and select **Turn Off Computer**.

2. When the Turn Off Computer screen appears, click **Turn Off**.

3. Unplug the power cable from the back of your system unit.

Continued

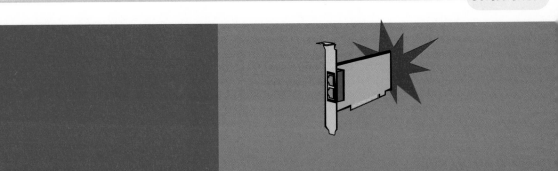

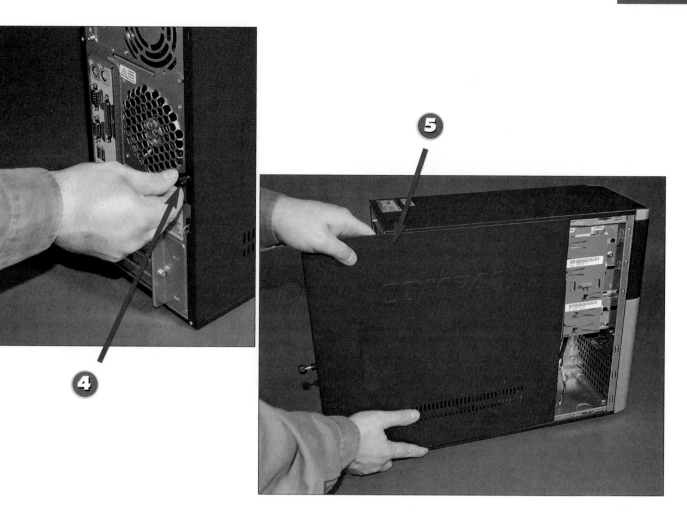

4 Unscrew the screws attaching the case of your system unit.

5 Remove the system unit's case.

Continued

⚠ CAUTION

Turn Off the Power!

Never touch anything inside your computer while the power is still on and connected. Always turn off your PC and unplug the power cord, just to be safe.

NOTE

Device Drivers

A *device driver* is a small software program that lets your PC control a given device. If Windows doesn't include a particular driver, you typically can find the driver on the installation CD or on the manufacturer's website.

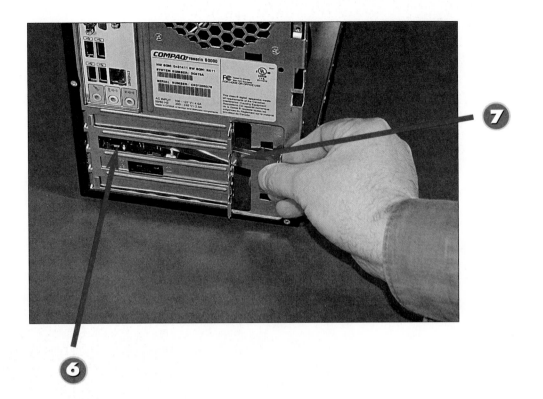

 Find an open card slot inside the system unit that fits the type of card you'll be installing.

7 Unscrew and remove the cover plate for the open slot. (Save the screw.)

Continued

NOTE

Common Upgrades

The most common types of internal computer upgrades are sound cards and video cards. You can also add cards to provide additional ports for your system—USB, FireWire, serial, or parallel.

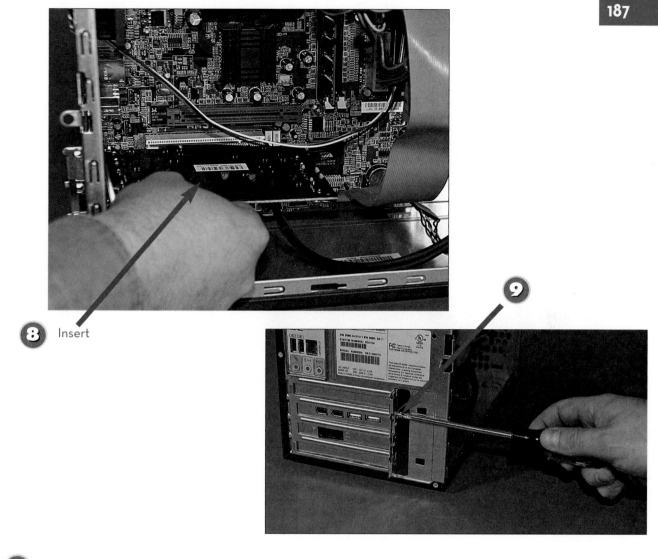

8 Insert

8 Insert the new card into the open slot, making sure it's firmly seated.

9 Screw the card into place.

Continued

 10 Put the case back on the system unit.

11 Screw the case back together.

Continued

TIP

Test It Before You Finish It

You probably want to see whether the new component configures and works properly before you close your system unit. For that reason, you might want to leave the case off until you're convinced everything is working okay and you don't need to do any more fiddling around inside your PC.

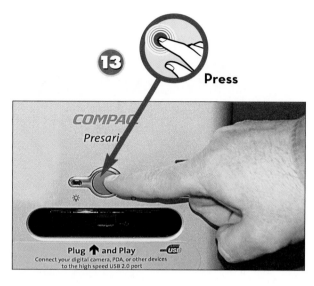

Connect

Press

COMPAQ
Presari

Plug ↑ and Play
Connect your digital camera, PDA, or other devices
to the high speed USB 2.0 port

12 Reattach the power cable to the system unit.

13 Turn your computer back on. As Windows starts, it should recognize the new device and either install the proper drivers automatically or ask you to supply the device drivers (via CD-ROM).

End

TIP
Installation Programs
Some peripherals come with their own installation programs either on CD or floppy disk. Always follow the manufacturer's instructions when installing a new device.

189

USING THE ADD HARDWARE WIZARD

In most cases, both your PC and Windows will recognize any new hardware you install without any manual prompting. If, however, Windows doesn't recognize your new device, you can install it manually via the Add Hardware Wizard.

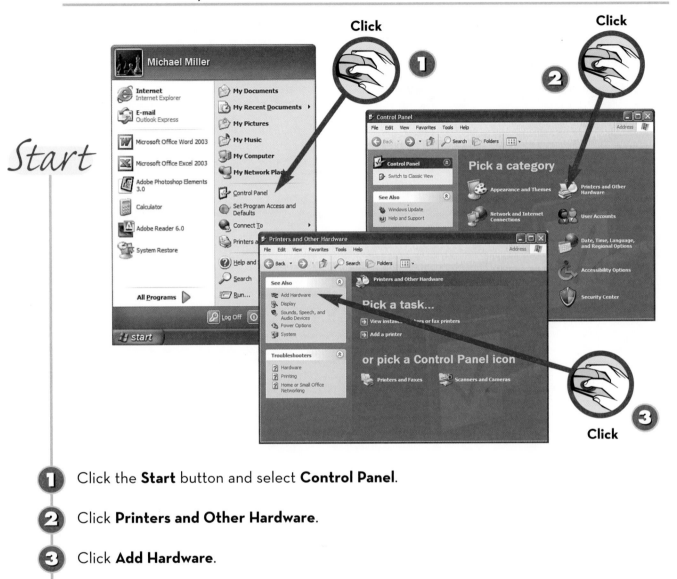

1 Click the **Start** button and select **Control Panel**.

2 Click **Printers and Other Hardware**.

3 Click **Add Hardware**.

Continued

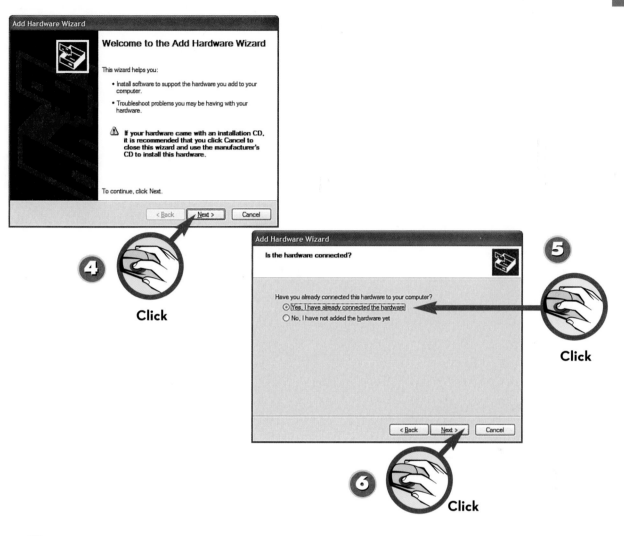

Click

Click

Click

When the Add Hardware Wizard launches, click the **Next** button.

If you're asked whether you've already installed any new hardware, select **Yes, I Have Already Connected the Hardware**.

Click **Next**.

Continued

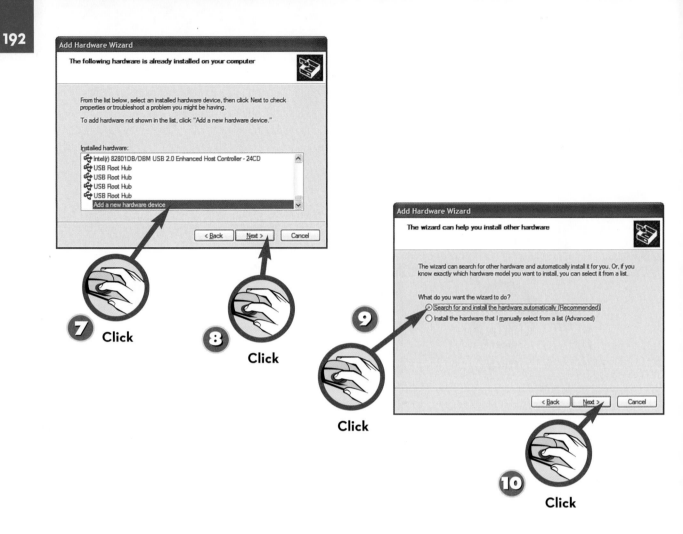

7 Windows now displays a list of installed devices. Scroll to the bottom of this list and select **Add a New Hardware Device**.

8 Click **Next**.

9 When the next screen appears, select **Search for and Install the Hardware Automatically**.

10 Click **Next**.

Continued

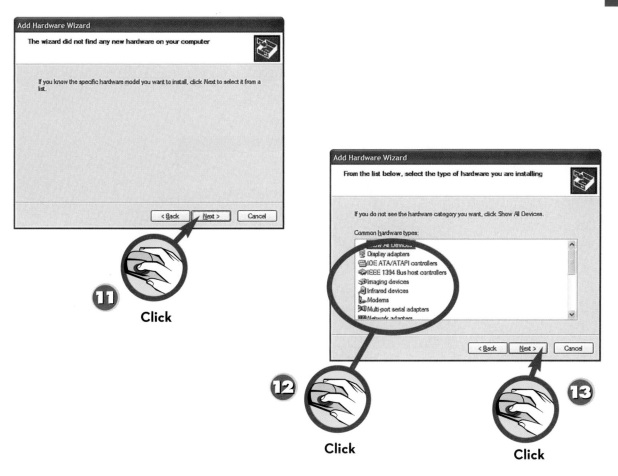

Click

Click

Click

11 If Windows can identify the new hardware, the wizard continues with the installation. If Windows can't find a new device, click **Next** to begin a manual installation.

12 Select the type of device you want to install.

13 Click **Next**.

Continued

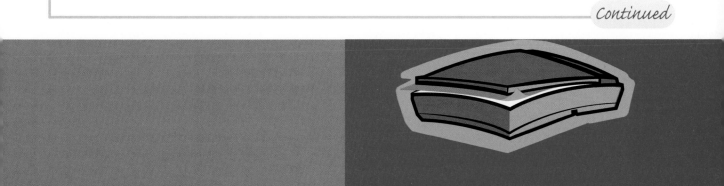

Click

14

Add Hardware Wizard

Select the device driver you want to install for this hardware.

Select the manufacturer and model of your hardware device and then click Next. If you
have a disk that contains the driver you want to install, click Have Disk.

Manufacturer
(Standard system devices)
Aztech Systems
CH Products Game Ports
Creative Technology Ltd.

Model
Game Port for Creative
Sound Blaster 16 or AWE32 or compatible (WDM)

15

This driver is digitally signed.
Tell me why driver signing is important

Have Disk...

Click

< Back   Next >   Cancel

16

Click

14 On the next screen, select the manufacturer and specific device.

15 If you want to install disk-based drivers that came with the device, click the **Have Disk** button.

16 To use a built-in Windows driver, click the **Next** button.

Continued

TIP

Use the Supplied Drivers

In most cases, you should use the drivers supplied by the device's manufacturer.

Click

17 Follow then onscreen instructions to complete the installation; then click **Finish** when done.

End

⚠️ CAUTION

Downloading New Drivers

If your new device doesn't appear to work, you might have to download updated device drivers from the manufacturer's website.

SETTING UP A WIRELESS HOME NETWORK

When you need to connect two or more computers together, you need to create a computer *network*. A network is all about sharing; you can use your network to share files, share peripherals (such as printers), and share a broadband Internet connection.

There are two ways to connect your network—wired or wireless. A wireless network is more convenient (no wires to run), which makes it the network of choice for most home users. Wireless networks use radio frequency (RF) signals to connect one computer to another. The most popular type of wireless network uses the Wi-Fi standard and can transfer data at either 11Mbps (802.11b) or 54Mbps (802.11g).

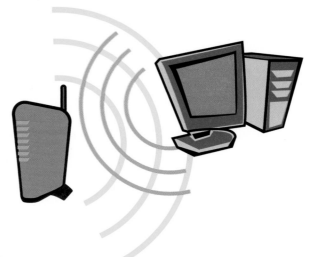

HOW A WIRELESS NETWORK WORKS

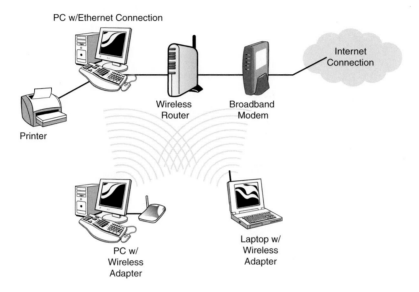

PC w/Ethernet Connection

Printer

Wireless Router

Broadband Modem

Internet Connection

PC w/ Wireless Adapter

Laptop w/ Wireless Adapter

SETTING UP YOUR NETWORK'S MAIN PC

The focal point of your wireless network is the *wireless router*, sometimes called a *base station* or an *access point*. The wireless PCs on your network must be connected to or contain *wireless adapters*, which function as mini-transmitters/receivers to communicate with the base station.

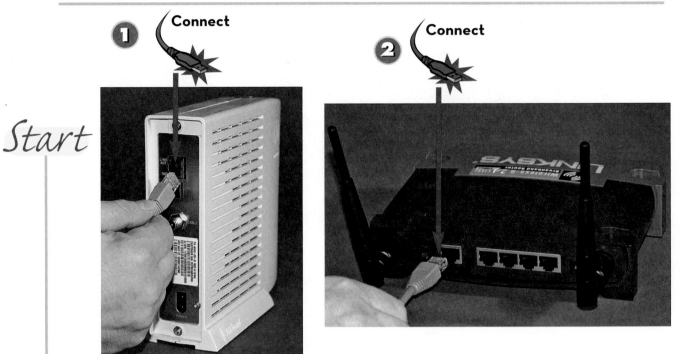

Start

1 Connect one end of an Ethernet cable to the Ethernet port on your broadband modem.

2 Connect the other end of the Ethernet cable to one of the Ethernet ports on your wireless router.

Continued

Connect

3

Connect

4

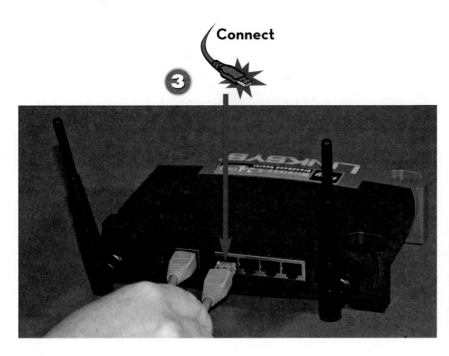

3 Connect one end of an Ethernet cable to another Ethernet port on your wireless router.

4 Connect the other end of the Ethernet cable to the Ethernet port on your main PC.

Continued

NOTE

Ethernet Connections

Your main PC connects to the wireless router via an Ethernet cable. If your main PC doesn't have a built-in Ethernet port, you'll need to install an internal network interface card or an external Ethernet adapter via USB.

Connect

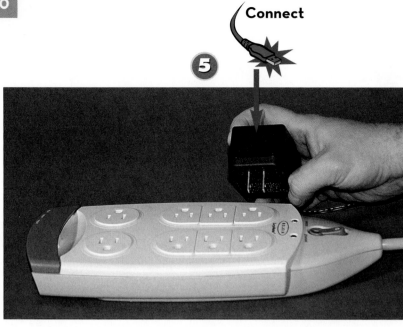

5

6

Click

5 Connect your wireless router to a power source and, if it has a power switch, turn it on.

6 On your main PC, click the **Start** button and click **Control Panel**.

Continued

TIP
Wired and Wireless Connections
Most wireless routers include four or more wired Ethernet connectors in addition to wireless capabilities.

TIP
Broadband Routers
Some broadband modems include built-in wireless routers. If you have one of these, you don't need to buy a separate router.

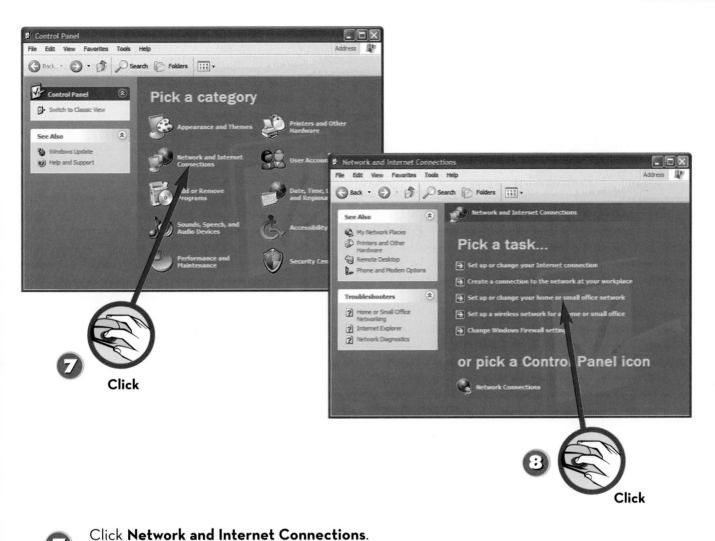

 7 Click **Network and Internet Connections**.

8 Click **Set Up or Change Your Home or Small Office Network**.

Continued

TIP
Installation Software
Many wireless routers come with their own installation software. You should run this software before—or, in some cases, instead of—running Windows's Network Setup Wizard.

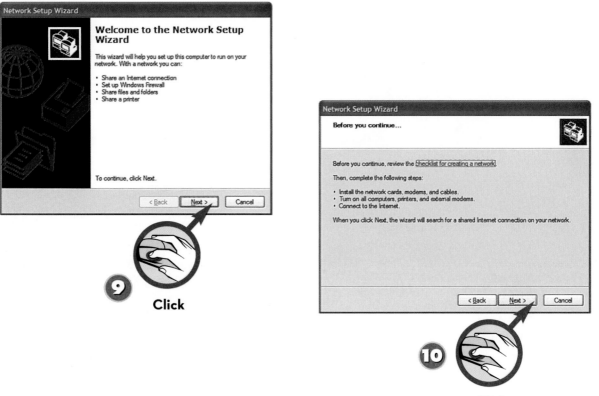

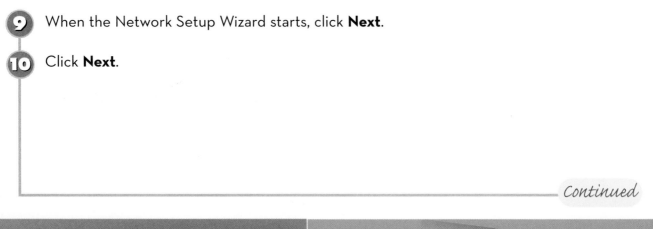

9 When the Network Setup Wizard starts, click **Next**.

10 Click **Next**.

Continued

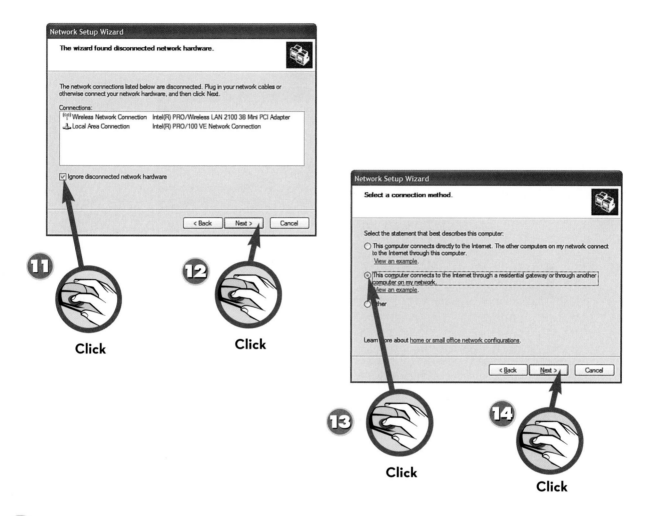

11 Check **Ignore Disconnected Network Hardware**.

12 Click **Next**.

13 Check **This Computer Connects to the Internet Through a Residential Gateway or Through Another Computer on My Network**.

14 Click **Next**.

Continued

NOTE

LANs and WANs

The type of home network that connects computers geographically close together is called a *local area network (LAN)*. A larger network in which computers are in multiple locations is called a *wide area network (WAN)*.

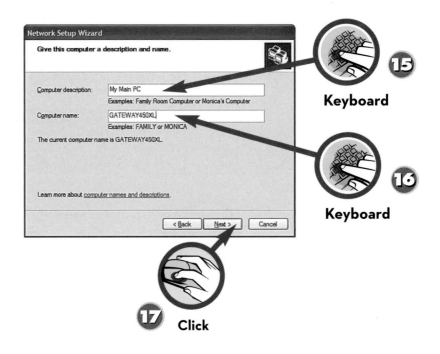

Keyboard 15

Keyboard 16

Click 17

15 Enter a description for your main PC.

16 Enter a name for your main PC.

17 Click **Next**.

Continued

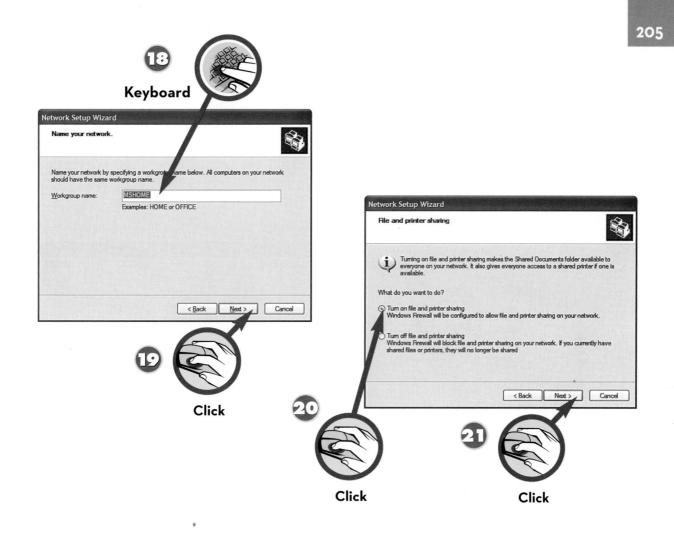

Keyboard

Click

Click

Click

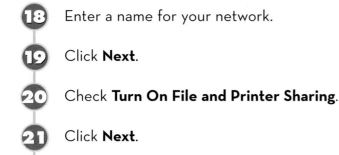

18 Enter a name for your network.

19 Click **Next**.

20 Check **Turn On File and Printer Sharing**.

21 Click **Next**.

Continued

NOTE

Measuring Network Speed

How quickly data is transferred across a network is measured in megabits per second (Mbps). The bigger the Mbps number, the faster the network—and faster is always better than slower.

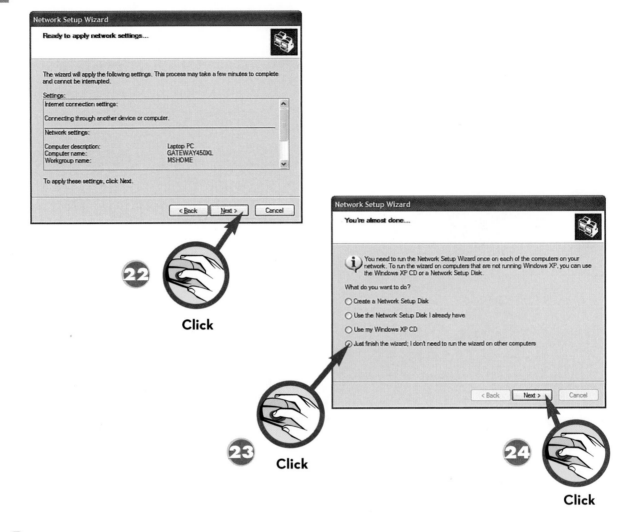

Click

Click

Click

 Click **Next**.

Check **Just Finish the Wizard**.

Click **Next**.

Continued

NOTE

Wi-Fi Networks

Wi-Fi is short for *wireless fidelity*. Learn more about the Wi-Fi standard at the Wi-Fi Alliance website (www.wi-fi.org). This website also lets you search for public Wi-Fi hotspots near you.

Network Setup Wizard

Completing the Network Setup Wizard

You have successfully set up this computer for home or small office networking.

For help with home or small office networking, see the following topics in Help and Support Center:

- Using the Shared Documents folder
- Sharing files and folders

To see other computers on your network, click Start, and then click My Network Places.

To close this wizard, click Finish.

[< Back] [**Finish**] [Cancel]

 Click

 Click **Finish** when done.

End

TIP

Wireless Security

To keep outsiders from tapping into your wireless network, you can add wireless security. Open the **Control Panel**, select **Network and Internet Connections**, and click **Set Up a Wireless Network for a Home or Small Office**. (Available in Windows XP with Service Pack 2 installed.) This runs a wizard that adds an encrypted network key to your wireless connections.

CONNECTING ADDITIONAL PCS TO YOUR WIRELESS NETWORK

Each additional PC on your network requires its own wireless adapter. You'll also need to run the Network Setup Wizard on each network PC.

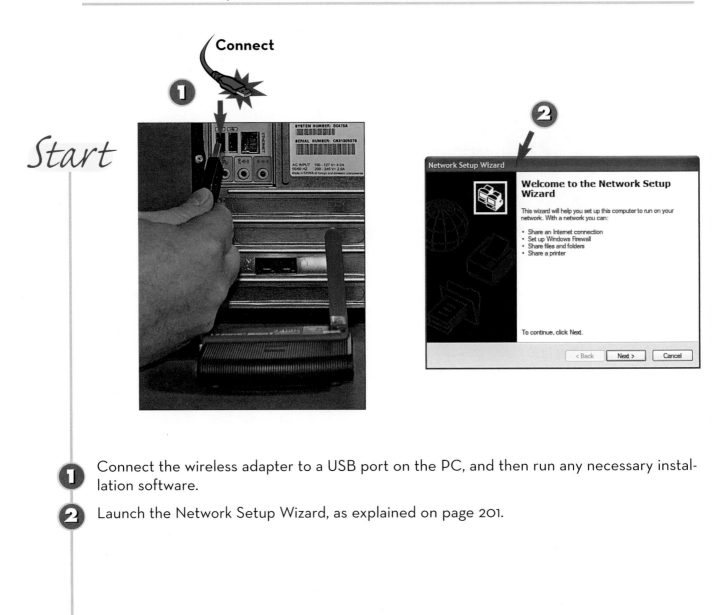

Start

Connect

Welcome to the Network Setup Wizard

This wizard will help you set up this computer to run on your network. With a network you can:

- Share an Internet connection
- Set up Windows Firewall
- Share files and folders
- Share a printer

To continue, click Next.

① Connect the wireless adapter to a USB port on the PC, and then run any necessary installation software.

② Launch the Network Setup Wizard, as explained on page 201.

Continued

TIP

Wireless Adapters

A wireless adapter can be a small external device that connects to the PC via USB, an expansion card that installs inside your system unit, or a PC card that inserts into a laptop PC's card slot.

3

Network Setup Wizard

Completing the Network Setup Wizard

You have successfully set up this computer for home or small office networking.

For help with home or small office networking, see the following topics in Help and Support Center:

- Using the Shared Documents folder
- Sharing files and folders

To see other computers on your network, click Start, and then click My Network Places.

To close this wizard, click Finish.

< Back | Finish | Cancel

4

Click

3 Follow the same steps as before to complete the wizard.

4 Click **Finish**.

End

TIP

Configuring Older PCs

If a computer is running Windows 98, Windows Me, or Windows 2000, you need to run the Network Setup Wizard from the Windows XP installation CD.

SHARING FILES AND FOLDERS ACROSS YOUR NETWORK

After you have your network up and running, it's time to take advantage of it—by copying or moving files from one computer to another. To share files between the PCs on your network, you have to enable Windows XP's file sharing on the PC that contains those files.

Start

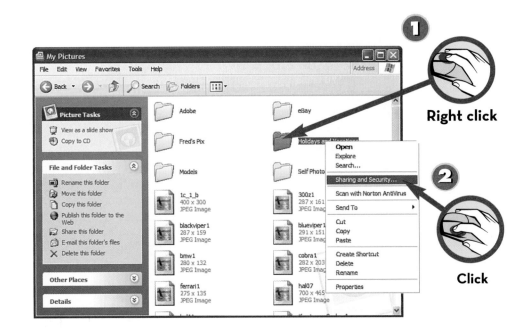

Right click

Click

1. Use My Computer or My Documents to navigate to the folder that contains the file you want to share; then right-click the folder icon.

2. Select **Sharing and Security** from the pop-up menu.

Continued

Click

3

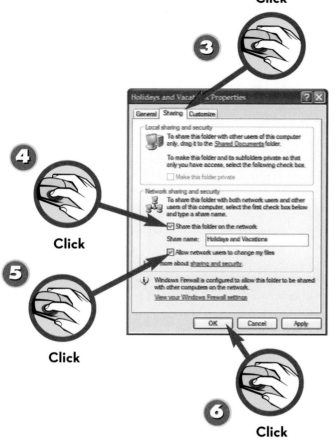

4

Click

5

Click

6

Click

Click

3 Click the **Sharing** tab.

4 Check **Share This Folder on the Network**.

5 Check **Allow Network Users to Change My Files**.

6 Click **OK**.

End

TIP
Share Carefully
Be cautious about turning on file sharing. When you let a folder be shared, anyone accessing your network can access the contents of the folder.

TIP
Repeat the Procedure
You'll need to repeat this procedure for every folder on every computer on your network that contains files you want to share.

part 12

PROTECTING YOUR COMPUTER

When you connect your PC to the Internet, you open up a whole new world of adventure and information for you and your family. Unfortunately, you also open up a new world of potential dangers—viruses, spam, computer attacks, and more.

Fortunately, it's easy to protect your computer and your family from these dangers. All you need are a few software utilities—and a lot of common sense!

To track your PC's security, open the Windows **Control Panel** and select **Security Center**. The Security Center (found in Windows XP with Service Pack 2 installed) will tell you what steps you need to take to better protect your system.

WINDOWS SECURITY CENTER

Firewall
settings

Windows automatic
update settings

Virus protection
settings

Click for more
recommendations

DEFENDING AGAINST COMPUTER ATTACKS WITH A FIREWALL

Connecting to the Internet is a two-way street. Not only can your PC access other computers online, but other computers can also access *your* PC—to access your private data or damage your system hardware and software. You protect against attacks with a firewall program, such as the one included in Windows XP.

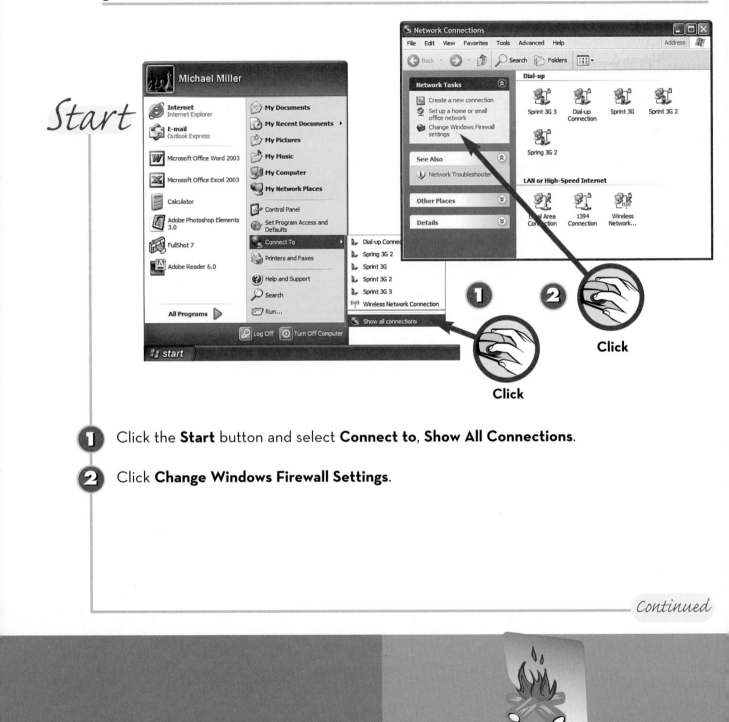

1. Click the **Start** button and select **Connect to**, **Show All Connections**.

2. Click **Change Windows Firewall Settings**.

Continued

Click

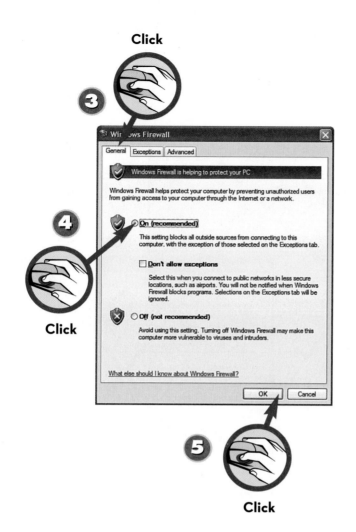

Click

Click

3 Click the **General** tab.

4 Check the **On** option.

5 Click **OK**.

End

 TIP

Other Firewall Programs

Many third-party firewalls offer more protection than the Windows Firewall. These programs include BlackICE PC Protection (blackice.iss.net), Sygate Personal Firewall (www.sygate.com), and ZoneAlarm (www.zonelabs.com).

PROTECTING AGAINST COMPUTER VIRUSES

A *computer virus* is a malicious software program designed to do damage to your computer system by deleting files or even taking over your PC to launch attacks on other systems. A virus attacks your computer when you launch an infected software program. Here are some tips for protecting your system from computer viruses.

Start

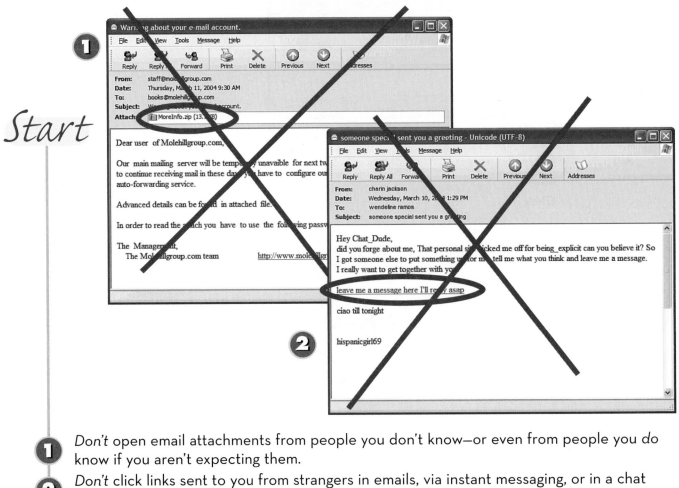

1 *Don't* open email attachments from people you don't know—or even from people you *do* know if you aren't expecting them.

2 *Don't* click links sent to you from strangers in emails, via instant messaging, or in a chat room—even if the messages appear to be legitimate.

Continued

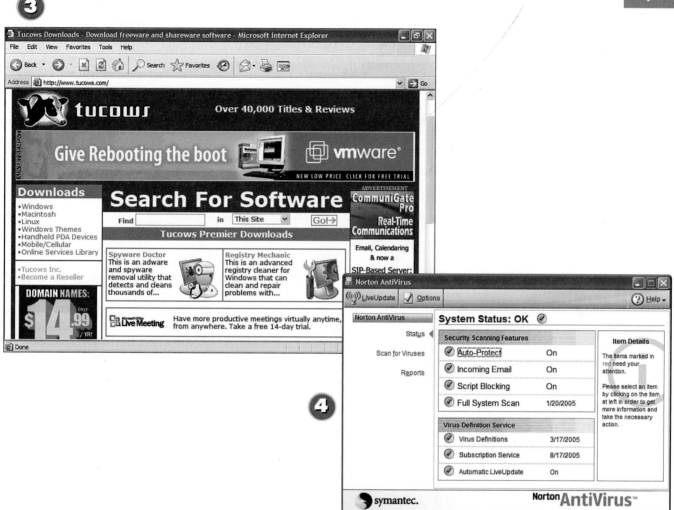

3 *Do* download files from reliable websites only, such as Tucow (www.tucows.com) and Download.com (www.download.com).

4 *Do* install and use antivirus software, such as Norton AntiVirus (www.symantec.com) or McAfee VirusScan (www.mcafee.com).

End

-TIP-
Email Attachments Are Bad!
The single largest source of computer viruses is infected email attachments. If you remember nothing else from this chapter, remember this: *Never open an unexpected file attachment*, even if it's from someone you know. Period!

-TIP-
Update Your Antivirus Program
Whichever antivirus program you choose, you'll need to go online periodically to update the virus definition database the program uses to look for known virus files. New viruses are created every week!

FIGHTING EMAIL SPAM

If you're like most users, well over half the messages delivered to your email inbox are unsolicited, unauthorized, and unwanted—in other words, *spam*. These spam messages are the online equivalent of the junk mail you receive in your postal mailbox, and they're a huge problem.

Start

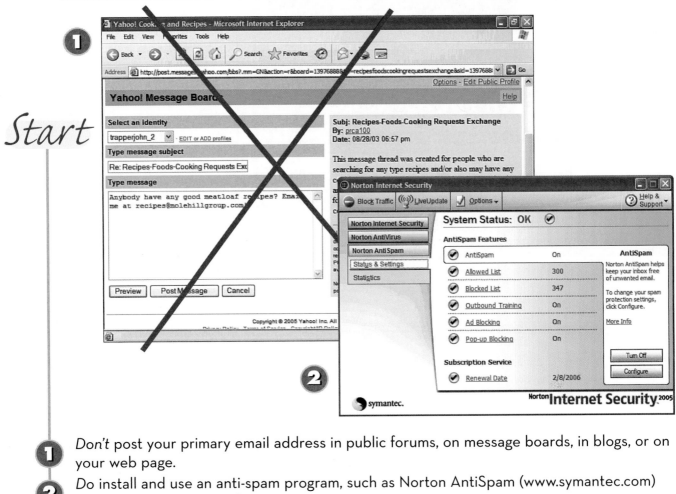

1 *Don't* post your primary email address in public forums, on message boards, in blogs, or on your web page.

2 *Do* install and use an anti-spam program, such as Norton AntiSpam (www.symantec.com) or SpamKiller (www.mcafee.com).

Continued

Click

4

3

Click

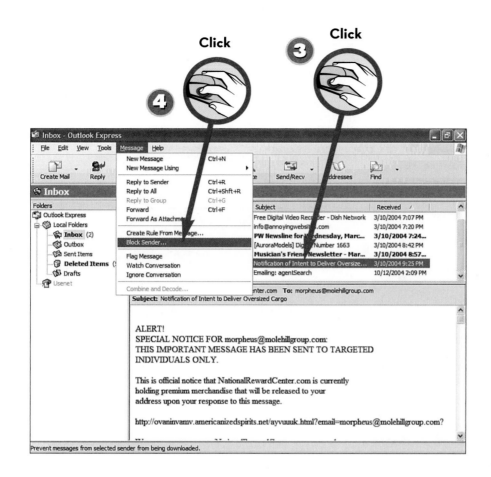

To block future spam messages in Outlook Express, start by selecting the unwanted message.

Pull down the **Message** menu and select **Block Sender**.

End

TIP
Use a Spamblock
To confuse email address-harvesting software, you can insert a *spamblock* into your address. For example, if your email address is johnjones@myisp.com, you might change the address to read johnSPAMBLOCKjones@myisp.com.

TIP
Use Two Addresses
Another trick is to use two email addresses—a public one you use when you post on the Web or register on websites and a private one you give out only to friends and relatives.

CLEANING SPYWARE FROM YOUR SYSTEM

Another growing nuisance is the proliferation of *spyware* programs. These programs install themselves on your computer and then surreptitiously send information about the way you use your PC to some interested third party. Spyware typically is installed in the background when you're installing another program, or when you visit certain websites.

Start

1 *Don't* use peer-to-peer file trading networks; their software is often infested with spyware.

2 *Do* install and use an anti-spyware program, such as Microsoft AntiSpyware (www.microsoft.com/athome/security/spyware/software/) or Ad-Aware (www.lavasoftusa.com).

End

BLOCKING POP-UP ADS

Although they're not dangerous, pop-up ads are extremely annoying. Fortunately, the latest version of Internet Explorer contains a pop-up blocker that effectively keeps those annoying ads from popping up while you're surfing the Web.

Start

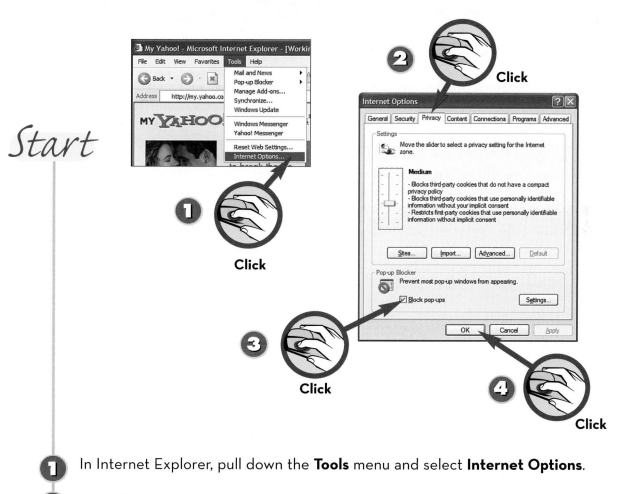

Click

Click

Click

Click

1. In Internet Explorer, pull down the **Tools** menu and select **Internet Options**.

2. Click the **Privacy** tab.

3. Check the **Block Pop-ups** option.

4. Click **OK**.

End

⚠ **CAUTION** ─────────────────────────────────

Don't Go Phishing

Another potential problem is that of online identity theft, which can happen if you respond to "phishing" emails—messages mocked up to look like legitimate notices from your bank or other institution. When you click a link to update your personal information, you're taken to a phony website and your info is stolen. Avoid the problem by never clicking links in email messages!

part 13

TAKING CARE OF YOUR COMPUTER

"An ounce of prevention is worth a pound of cure" is a bit of a cliché, but it's also true—especially when it comes to your computer system. Spending a few minutes a week on preventive maintenance can save you from costly computer problems in the future.

To make this chore a little easier, Windows XP includes several utilities to help you keep your system running smoothly. You should use these tools as part of your regular maintenance routine—or if you experience specific problems with your computer system.

WINDOWS XP'S SYSTEM TOOLS

Disk Cleanup

Disk Cleanup is calculating how much space you will be able to free on My Hard Disk (C:). This may take a few minutes to complete.

Calculating...

Cancel

Scanning: Compress old files

Disk Cleanup

Disk Defragmenter

Disk Defragmenter

File   Action   View   Help

Volume	Session Status	File System	Capacity	Free Space	% Free Space
My Hard Disk (C:)		NTFS	37.26 GB	20.00 GB	53 %

Estimated disk usage before defragmentation:

Estimated disk usage after defragmentation:

| Analyze | Defragment | Pause | Stop | View Report |

■ Fragmented files   ■ Contiguous files   ☐ Unmovable files   ☐ Free space

Check Disk My Hard Disk (C:)

Check disk options

☑ Automatically fix file system errors
☑ Scan for and attempt recovery of bad sectors

Start   Cancel

ScanDisk

DELETING UNNECESSARY FILES

Even with today's humongous hard disks, you can still end up with too many useless files taking up too much hard disk space. Fortunately, Windows XP includes a utility that identifies and deletes unused files. The Disk Cleanup tool is what you should use when you need to free up extra hard disk space for more frequently used files.

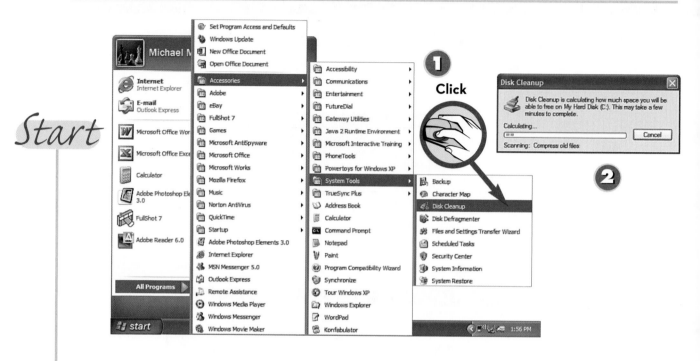

Start

1 Click the **Start** button and select **All Programs**, **Accessories**, **System Tools**, **Disk Cleanup**.

2 Disk Cleanup starts and automatically analyzes the contents of your hard disk drive.

Continued

Click

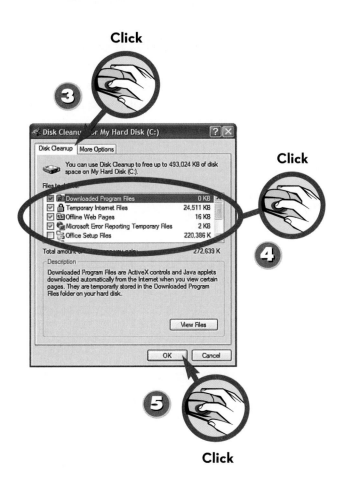

Click

Click

When Disk Cleanup is finished analyzing, it presents its results in the Disk Cleanup dialog box; click the **Disk Cleanup** tab.

Check which types of files you want to delete.

Click **OK** to delete the files.

End

TIP

Which Files to Delete?

You can safely choose to delete all these files except the setup log and Content Indexer files, which are often needed by the Windows operating system.

DEFRAGMENTING YOUR HARD DISK

If you notice that your system takes longer and longer to open and close files or run applications, it's probably because little fragments of files are spread all over your hard disk. You
fix the problem when you put all the pieces of the puzzle back in the right boxes—which
you do by defragmenting your disk.

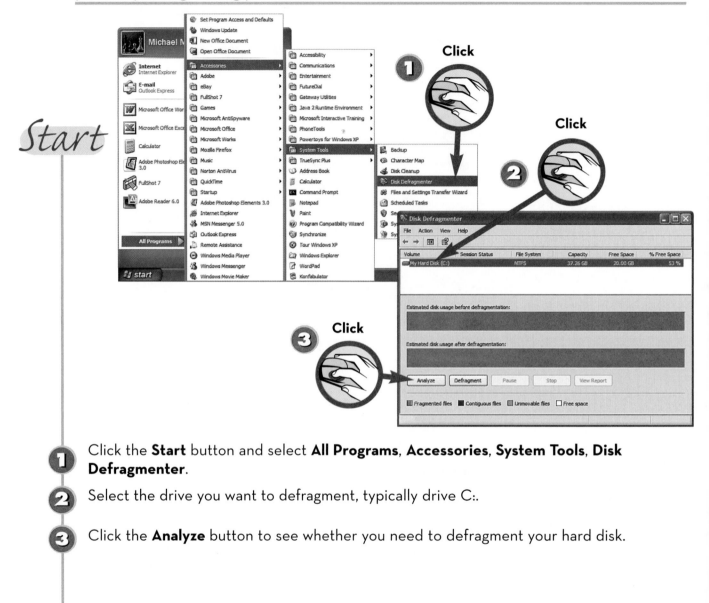

Start

① Click the **Start** button and select **All Programs**, **Accessories**, **System Tools**, **Disk Defragmenter**.

② Select the drive you want to defragment, typically drive C:.

③ Click the **Analyze** button to see whether you need to defragment your hard disk.

Continued

TIP
It Takes Time
Defragmenting your drive can take an
hour or more, especially if you have a large
hard drive or your drive is really fragmented.

Click

4 If your disk needs defragmenting, click the **Defragment** button.

5 After defragmenting, the program shows a new map of your hard disk.

End

NOTE

Pieces of the Puzzle

File fragmentation is like taking the pieces of a jigsaw puzzle and storing them in different boxes along with pieces from other puzzles. The more dispersed the pieces are, the longer it takes to put the puzzle together.

NOTE

Fragmented Files

Files can get fragmented whenever you install, delete, or run an application, or when you edit, move, copy, or delete a file.

CHECKING YOUR HARD DISK FOR ERRORS

Any time you run an application, move or delete a file, or accidentally turn off the power while the system is running, you run the risk of introducing errors to your hard disk. Fortunately, you can find and fix most of these errors directly from within Windows XP, using the ScanDisk utility.

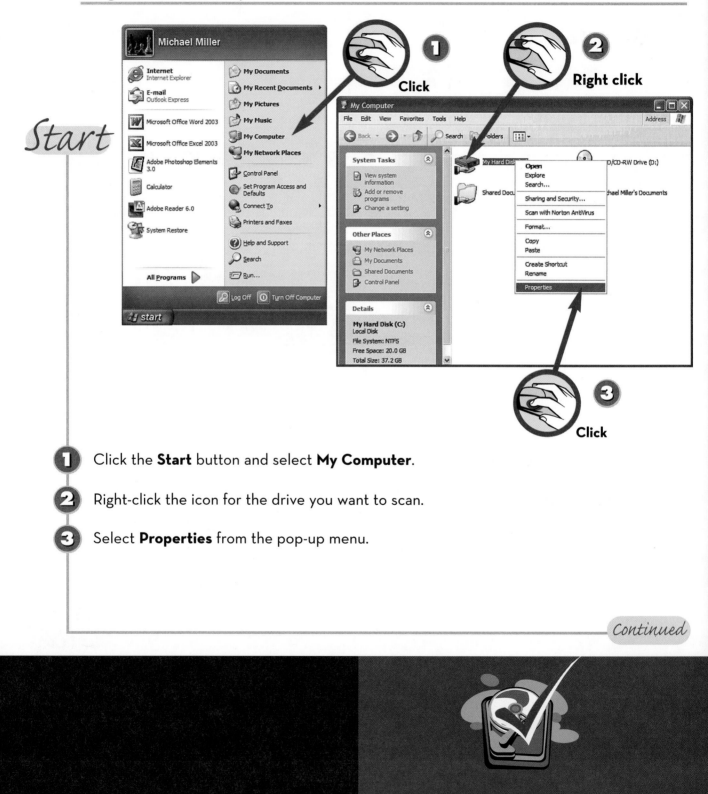

1 Click the **Start** button and select **My Computer**.

2 Right-click the icon for the drive you want to scan.

3 Select **Properties** from the pop-up menu.

Continued

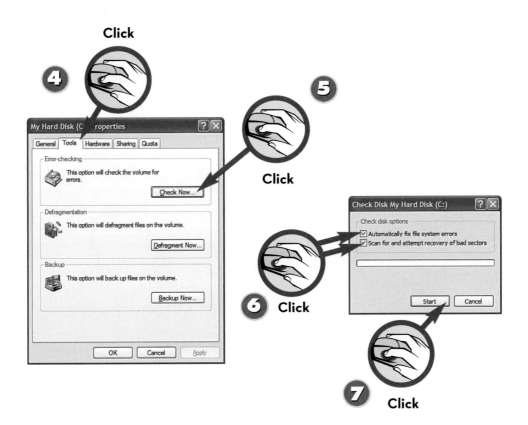

Click

Click

Click

Click

4 When the Properties utility opens, click the **Tools** tab.

5 Click the **Check Now** button in the Error-Checking section.

6 Check **Automatically Fix File System Errors** and **Scan for and Attempt Recovery of Bad Sectors**.

7 Click **Start**.

End

TIP
Scanning and Fixing
ScanDisk not only scans your hard disk for errors, but also automatically fixes any errors it finds.

TIP
How Often to Run?
It's a good idea to run all these system utilities at least once a month, just to ensure that your system stays in tip-top condition.

RESTORING YOUR COMPUTER AFTER A CRASH

If your computer system ever crashes or freezes, your best course of action is to run the System Restore utility. This utility can automatically restore your system to the state it was in before the crash occurred—and save you the trouble of reinstalling any damaged software programs. It's a great safety net for when things go wrong!

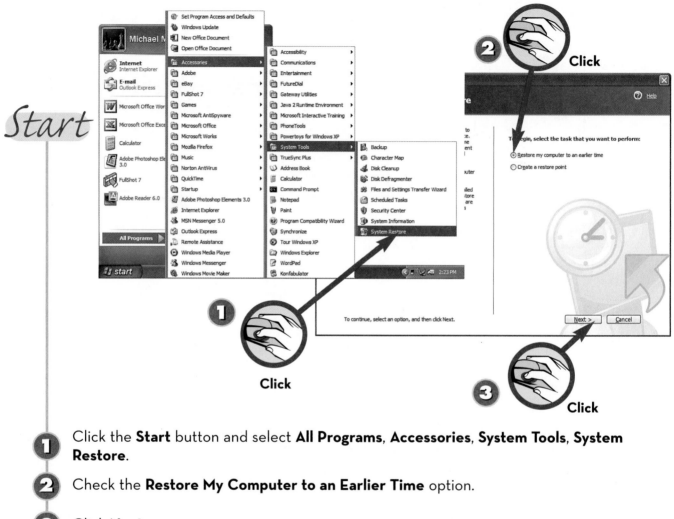

1 Click the **Start** button and select **All Programs**, **Accessories**, **System Tools**, **System Restore**.

2 Check the **Restore My Computer to an Earlier Time** option.

3 Click **Next**.

Continued

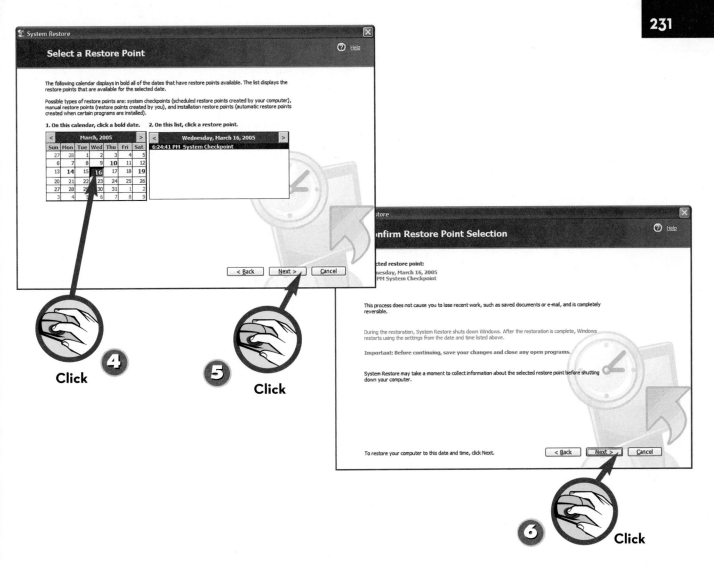

Click 4

Click 5

Click 6

4 Click a bold date on the calendar from before your system started acting up; this will be your restore point.

5 Click **Next**.

6 When the confirmation screen appears, click **Next** to begin the restore process.

End

A

add-in board   A device that plugs in to your computer's system unit and provides auxiliary functions. (Also called a *card*.)

address   The location of an Internet host. An email address might take the form johndoe@xyz.com; a web address might look like www.xyztech.com. See also **URL**.

application   A computer program designed for a specific task or use, such as word processing, accounting, or missile guidance.

attachment   A file, such as a Word document or graphic image, attached to an email message.

B

boot   The process of turning on your computer system.

broadband   A high-speed Internet connection; it's faster than a typical dial-up connection.

browser   A program, such as Internet Explorer, that translates the Hypertext Markup Language of the Web into viewable web pages.

bug   An error in a software program or the hardware.

burner   A device that writes CD-ROMs or DVD-ROMs.

C

cable modem   A high-speed, broadband Internet connection via digital cable TV lines.

card   Also called an *add-in board*, this is a device that plugs in to your computer's system unit and provides auxiliary functions.

CD-R (compact disc recordable)   A type of CD drive that lets you record only once onto a disc, which can then be read by any CD-ROM drive or audio CD player.

CD-ROM (compact disc read-only memory)   A CD that can be used to store computer data. A CD-ROM, similar to an audio CD, stores data in a form readable by a laser, resulting in a storage device of great capacity and quick accessibility.

CD-RW (compact disc rewritable)   A type of CD that can be recorded, erased, and rewritten to by the user, multiple times.

central processing unit (CPU)   The group of circuits that directs the entire computer system by (1) interpreting and executing program instruction and (2) coordinating the interaction of input, output, and storage devices.

computer   A programmable device that can store, retrieve, and process data.

CRT   Cathode ray tube is a type of video display device that uses a vacuum tube display.

cursor The highlighted area or pointer that tracks with the movement of your mouse or arrow keys onscreen.

D

data Information that is convenient to move or process.

database A program for arranging facts in the computer and retrieving them—the computer equivalent of a filing system.

desktop The entire screen area on which you display all your computer work. A typical computer desktop can contain icons, a taskbar, menus, and individual application windows.

device A computer file that represents some object—physical or nonphysical—installed on your system.

digital subscriber line (DSL) A high-speed Internet connection that uses the ultra-high frequency portion of ordinary telephone lines, allowing users to send and receive voice and data on the same line at the same time.

disk A device that stores data in magnetic or optical format.

disk drive A mechanism for retrieving information stored on a magnetic disk. The drive rotates the disk at high speed and reads the data with a magnetic head similar to those used in tape recorders.

diskette A portable or removable disk.

domain The identifying portion of an Internet address. In email addresses, the domain name follows the @ sign; in website addresses, the domain name follows the www.

download A way to transfer files, graphics, or other information from the Internet to your computer.

dpi (dots per inch) A measurement of printer resolution; the more dots per inch, the higher the resolution.

driver A support file that tells a program how to interact with a specific hardware device, such as a hard disk controller or video display card.

DVD An optical disc, similar to a CD, that can hold a minimum of 4.7GB, enough for a full-length movie.

E

email Electronic mail; a means of corresponding with other computer users over the Internet through digital messages.

encryption A method of encoding files so only the recipient can read the information.

Ethernet The most common computer networking protocol; Ethernet is used to network, or hook together, computers so they can share information.

executable file A program you run on your computer system.

F

favorite   A bookmarked site in Internet Explorer.

file   Any group of data treated as a single entity by the computer, such as a word processor document, a program, or a database.

firewall   Computer hardware or software with special security features to safeguard a computer connected to a network or to the Internet.

FireWire   A high-speed bus used to connect digital devices, such as digital cameras and video cameras, to a computer system. Also known as *iLink* and *IEEE-1394*.

folder   A way to group files on a disk; each folder can contain multiple files or other folders (called *subfolders*).

freeware   Free software available over the Internet. This is in contrast with *shareware*, which is available freely but usually asks the user to send payment for using the software.

G

gigabyte (GB)   One billion bytes.

graphics   Pictures, photographs, and clip art.

H

hard disk   A sealed cartridge containing a magnetic storage disk(s) that holds much more memory than removable disks—up to 400GB or more.

hardware   The physical equipment, as opposed to the programs and procedures, used in computing.

home page   The first or main page of a website.

hover   The act of selecting an item by placing your cursor over an icon without clicking.

hub   Hardware used to network computers together, usually over an Ethernet connection.

hyperlink   A connection between two tagged elements in a web page, or separate sites, that makes it possible to click from one to the other.

I–J

icon   A graphic symbol on the display screen that represents a file, peripheral, or some other object or function.

instant messaging   Text-based, real-time one-on-one communication over the Internet.

Internet   The global network of networks that connects millions of computers and other devices around the world.

Internet service provider (ISP)   A company that provides end-user access to the Internet via its central computers and local access lines.

K–L

keyboard   The typewriter-like device used to type instructions to a personal computer.

kilobyte (KB)   A unit of measure for data storage or transmission equivalent to 1,024 bytes; often rounded to 1,000.

LAN (local area network)   A system that enables users to connect PCs to one another or to minicomputers or mainframes.

laptop   A portable computer small enough to operate on one's lap. Also known as a *notebook* computer.

LCD (liquid crystal display)   A flat-screen display where images are created by light transmitted through a layer of liquid crystals.

M-N

megabyte (MB)   One million bytes.

megahertz (MHz)   A measure of microprocessing speed; 1MHz equals 1 million electrical cycles per second.

memory   Temporary electronic storage for data and instructions, via electronic impulses on a chip.

microcomputer   A computer based on a microprocessor chip. Also known as a *personal computer*.

microprocessor   A complete central processing unit assembled on a single silicon chip.

modem (modulator demodulator)   A device capable of converting a digital signal into an analog signal, which can be transmitted via a telephone line, reconverted, and then "read" by another computer.

monitor   The display device on a computer, similar to a television screen.

motherboard   The largest printed circuit board in a computer, housing the CPU chip and controlling circuitry.

mouse   A small handheld input device connected to a computer and featuring one or more button-style switches. When moved around on a flat surface, the mouse causes a symbol on the computer screen to make corresponding movements.

network   An interconnected group of computers.

O-P

operating system   A sequence of programming codes that instructs a computer about its various parts and peripherals and how to operate them. Operating systems, such as Windows, deal only with the workings of the hardware and are separate from software programs.

parallel   A type of external port used to connect printers and other similar devices.

path   The collection of folders and subfolders (listed in order of hierarchy) that hold a particular file.

peripheral   A device connected to the computer that provides communication or auxiliary functions.

pixel   The individual picture elements that combine to create a video image.

Glossary

Plug and Play (PnP)   Hardware that includes its manufacturer and model information in its ROM, enabling Windows to recognize it immediately upon startup and install the necessary drivers if not already set up.

pop-up   A small browser window, typically without menus or other navigational elements, that opens seemingly of its own accord when you visit or leave another website.

port   An interface on a computer to which you can connect a device, either internally or externally.

printer   The piece of computer hardware that creates hard copy printouts of documents.

Q-R

RAM (random access memory)   A temporary storage space in which data can be held on a chip rather than being stored on disk or tape. The contents of RAM can be accessed or altered at any time during a session but will be lost when the computer is turned off.

resolution   The degree of clarity an image displays, typically expressed by the number of horizontal and vertical pixels or the number of dots per inch (dpi).

ROM (read-only memory)   A type of chip memory, the contents of which have been permanently recorded in a computer by the manufacturer and cannot be altered by the user.

root   The main directory or folder on a disk.

router   A piece of hardware or software that handles the connection between two or more networks.

S

scanner   A device that converts paper documents or photos into a format that can be viewed on a computer and manipulated by the user.

serial   A type of external port used to connect communication devices, such as modems, PalmPilots, and so on.

server   The central computer in a network, providing a service or data access to client computers on the network.

shareware   A software program distributed on the honor system; providers make their programs freely accessible over the Internet, with the understanding that those who use them will send payment to the provider after using them. See also **freeware**.

software   The programs and procedures, as opposed to the physical equipment, used in computing.

spam   Junk email. As a verb, it means to send thousands of copies of a junk email message.

spreadsheet   A program that performs mathematical operations on numbers arranged in large arrays; used mainly for accounting and other record keeping.

spyware   Software used to surreptitiously monitor computer use (that is, spy on other users).

system unit   The part of your computer system that looks like a big beige or black box. The system unit typically contains the microprocessor, system memory, hard disk drive, floppy disk drives, and various cards.

T-U-V

terabyte (TB)   One trillion bytes.

upgrade   To add a new or improved peripheral or part to your system hardware. Also to install a newer version of an existing piece of software.

upload   The act of copying a file from a personal computer to a website or Internet server. The opposite of *download*.

URL (uniform resource locator)   The address that identifies a web page to a browser. Also known as a *web address*.

USB (universal serial bus)   An external bus standard that supports data transfer rates of 12Mbps and that can connect up to 127 peripheral devices, such as keyboards, modems, and mice.

virus   A computer program segment or string of code that can attach itself to another program or file, reproduce itself, and spread from one computer to another. Viruses can destroy or change data and in other ways sabotage computer systems.

W-X-Y-Z

web page   An HTML file, containing text, graphics, and/or mini-applications, viewed with a web browser.

website   An organized, linked collection of web pages stored on an Internet server and read using a web browser. The opening page of a site is called a *home page*.

Wi-Fi   The radio frequency (RF)-based technology used for home and small business wireless networks, and for most public wireless Internet connections. It operates at either 11Mbps (802.11b) or 54Mbps (802.11g). Short for "wireless fidelity."

window   A portion of the screen display used to view simultaneously a different part of the file in use or a part of a different file than the one in use.

Windows   The generic name for all versions of Microsoft's graphical operating system.

World Wide Web (WWW)   A vast network of information, particularly business, commercial, and government resources, that uses a hypertext system for quickly transmitting graphics, sound, and video over the Internet.

Zip file   A file that has been compressed for easier transmission.

Numbers

5.1 surround sound, 11

A

Absolute Beginner's Guide to eBay, Third Edition, 116

access points, 198

accounts (user), creating, 52-53

Accounts command (Tools menu), 120

AccuWeather.com, 112

Ad-Aware, 220

adapters, wireless, 198, 208

Add a Contact Wizard, 128-129

Add Hardware Wizard, 190-195

Add to Favorites command (Favorites menu), 106

additional PCs, connecting to home networks, 208-209

Adobe Photoshop Elements
    cropping pictures, 178-179
    fixing photos with, 172-175
    removing red-eye, 176-177

anti-spam programs, 218-219

AntiSpyware (Microsoft), 220

antivirus programs, 216-217

Arrange Icons by command (View menu), 61

attachments (email), 217

auctions (eBay), 116-119

audio CDs. *See* CDs

audio systems, connecting, 18

B

backgrounds (desktop), 50

Bad Pics Fixed Quick, 175

bargain shopping at shopping.com, 114-115

base stations, 198

bidding for items on eBay, 116-119

black-and-white printers, 13

BlackICE PC Protection, 215

blocking pop-up ads, 221

boards (cards), 6

booting computers, 24-25

broadband connections, 99

broadband modems, 22

broadband routers, 200

burning music CDs, 141-143

C

cables, connecting, 23

cameras (digital)
    deleting pictures from, 158
    transferring pictures from, 154-159

cards, 6
    sound cards, 11
    video cards, 12

cases, opening, 6

cathode ray tube (CRT) monitors, 12

CD burners, 141

CD drives, 8

CD-R discs, 143

CDs
    burning, 141-143
    CD-R discs, 143
    playing, 134-135
    ripping to hard disk, 136-137

checking spelling, 92

clicking the mouse
    double-clicking, 31
    dragging and dropping, 33
    hovering, 34
    pointing and clicking, 30
    right-clicking, 32

closing windows, 38

color printers, 13

color schemes, 51

composing email, 126

compressed folders, extracting files from, 72-73

compressing files, 71

computer system components. See *also* connecting computer systems
    cards, 6
    cases, 6
    CD and DVD drives, 8
    connections, 181
    device drivers, 185
    FireWire, 182-183
    hard disk drives, 7
    internal hardware, 184-189
    keyboards, 9
    laptops/notebooks, 4
    monitors, 12
    motherboards, 6
    mouse, 10
    ports, 5
    printers, 13
    sound cards, 11
    speakers, 11
    system units, 4-5
    USB, 182-183
    video cards, 12

computer viruses, 216-217

connecting computer systems, 14, 180
    Add Hardware Wizard, 190-195
    audio systems, 18-19
    computer connections, 181
    device drivers, 185
    FireWire, 182-183
    internal hardware, 184-189
    iPods, 144-145
    logging on to Windows XP, 26
    modems, 22
    monitors, 17
    mouse and keyboard, 16
    parallel printers, 20
    powering on, 24-25
    system power cables, 23
    typical connections, 15
    USB, 21, 182-183

connecting to Internet, 94-101. See *also* web surfing

contacts, adding to Windows Messenger, 128-129

Control Panel, 46-47

Copy command (Word Edit menu), 87

Copy Items dialog box, 66

copying files/folders, 66

crashes, restoring computers after, 230-231

cropping pictures, 178-179

CRT (cathode ray tube) monitors, 12

cursors, 10

Cut command (Word Edit menu), 87

D

defragmenting hard disk drives, 226-227

deleted files, restoring, 69

deleting
    files, 68, 224-225
    folders, 68
    pictures, 158

desktop, 29
    backgrounds, 50
    changing size of, 48
    color schemes, 51
    screensavers, 54-55
    shortcuts, 41
    themes, 49

Device Connect Autoplay dialog box, 156

device drivers, 185, 195

devices, adding to computer systems, 180
    Add Hardware Wizard, 190-195
    computer connections, 181
    device drivers, 185
    FireWire, 182-183
    internal hardware, 184-189
    iPods, 144-145
    USB, 182-183

digital cameras
    deleting pictures from, 158
    transferring pictures from, 154-159

digital photos. See pictures

Disk Cleanup, 224-225

Disk Defragmenter, 226-227

displaying files, 60

documents (Word)
    creating, 82-83
    definition of, 83
    keyboard shortcuts, 87
    opening, 78, 85

Index

documents

paragraph formatting, 90

printing, 93

saving, 84

spell checking, 92

styles, 91

templates, 82

text editing, 87

text entry, 86

text formatting, 88-89

double-clicking the mouse, 31

downloading

device drivers, 195

Windows Media Player, 135

dragging and dropping, 33

drivers, 185, 195

drives

CD and DVD drives, 8

hard disk drives, 7

DVD drives, 8

DVDs, 150-151

E

eBay, 116-119

Edit menu (Word), 87

editing Word documents, 87

electrostatic shock, 187

email

attaching files to, 127

attachments, 217

composing, 126

email accounts, 120-123

phishing emails, 221

reading, 124

replying to, 125

sending, 126

spam, 218-219

emptying Recycle Bin, 70

Ethernet connections, 199

extensions, 65

extracting files from compressed folders, 72-73

Extraction Wizard, 72-73

F

favorite web pages

returning to, 107

saving, 106

Favorites menu commands, Add to Favorites, 106

feedback ratings (eBay), 117

file attachments (email), 217

file extensions, 65

File menu commands

New, 82

New Now Playing List, 138

New Smart Playlist, 147

Open, 85

Save, 84

Save As, 84

files, 58

compressing, 71

copying, 66

deleting, 68

displaying, 60

extensions, 65

extracting from compressed folders, 72-73

fragmentation, 227

moving, 67

My Documents folder, 59

renaming, 65

restoring deleted files, 69

sending via email, 127

sharing across wireless home networks, 210-211

sorting, 61

unnecessary files, deleting, 224-225

.zip files, 71

financial information, finding online, 113

firewalls, 214-215

FireWire, 182-183

fixing photos with Adobe Photoshop Elements, 172-175

flash memory cards, 160-163

folders, 58

compressed folders, extracting files from, 72-73

copying, 66

creating, 64

deleting, 68

Folders pane, 63
moving, 67
My Documents, 59-60
My Music, 137
My Pictures, 153
navigating, 62-63
Recycle Bin, 69-70
renaming, 65
sharing across wireless home networks, 210-211
sorting, 61
subfolders, 58
Font command (Word Format menu), 89
Font dialog box (Word), 89
Format menu commands (Word)
Font, 89
Paragraph, 90
formatting
hard disk drives, 7
Word documents, 89-91
fragmented files, 227

G-H

glossary, 232-237
Google, 109

hard disk drives
defragmenting, 226-227
formatting, 7
ripping CDs to, 136-137
scanning for errors, 228-229
hardware. *See* computer system components; connecting computer systems
health information, finding online, 113
help, 34, 56-57
History list (Internet Explorer), 108
home networks (wireless), 196-197
additional PCs, connecting, 208-209
broadband routers, 200
compared to wired networks, 204
Ethernet connections, 199
file/folder sharing, 210-211
main PC, setting up, 198-207

Network Setup Wizard, 202-206
network speed, 205
security, 207
Wi-Fi networks, 206
wireless adapters, 198, 208
wireless routers, 198
hovering, 34

I

icons, 44
identity theft, 221
IE. *See* Internet Explorer
illegal characters, 64
images. *See* pictures
inkjet printers, 13
insertion points (Word), 86
instant messaging, 130-131
internal hardware, adding, 184-189
Internet Accounts dialog box, 120
Internet Explorer, 95
bargain shopping at shopping.com, 114-115
bidding for items on eBay, 116-119
favorite pages, 106-107
History list, 108
home page, changing, 103
news, finding online, 110-113
web searches, 109
web surfing, 102-105
Internet pop-up ads, blocking, 221
Internet service providers (ISPs), 98
Internet, connecting to, 94-101. *See also* web surfing
iPods
connecting to PCs, 144-145
playlists, 147
transferring songs to, 146
ISPs (Internet service providers), 98
iTunes
Music Store, 134
playlists, creating, 147
songs, transferring to iPods, 146

Index

J-K-L

junk email, 218-219

keyboard shortcuts, 87
keyboards, 9, 16
Kodak EasyShare Gallery, 171

LANs (local area networks), 203
laptops, 4
laser printers, 13
LCD monitors, 12
local area networks (LANs), 203
local sports websites, 111

M

maintenance, 222
    computer systems, restoring after crashes,
        230-231
    hard disk drives, defragmenting, 226-227
    hard disk drives, scanning for errors, 228-229
    System Tools, 223
    unnecessary files, deleting, 224-225
MarketWatch, 113
maximizing windows, 38
medical information, finding online, 113
memory cards, 160-163
menu bars, 43
menus, 43
messages (email)
    attaching files to, 127
    attachments, 217
    composing, 126
    email accounts, 120-123
    phishing emails, 221
    reading, 124
    replying to, 125
    sending, 126
    spam, 218-219
messaging (instant messaging), 130-131

Messenger
    adding contacts to, 128-129
    instant messaging, 130-131
Microsoft AntiSpyware, 220
Microsoft Windows XP. *See* Windows XP
Microsoft Word. *See* Word
Microsoft Works. *See* Works
minimizing windows, 38
modems, 22
monitors, 12, 17
motherboards, 6
Motley Fool, 113
mouse, 10
    connecting, 16
    double-clicking, 31
    dragging and dropping, 33
    hovering, 34
    pointing and clicking, 30
    right-clicking, 32
Move Items dialog box, 67
movies, playing, 150-151
moving
    files/folders, 67
    windows, 35
MP3 players, connecting to, 148-149
MSN Money, 113
MSN Music, 134
music
    CDs, 134-137, 141-143
    iPods, 144-147
    online music stores, 134
    playlists, 138-140
    portable music players, connecting to, 148-149
My Computer, 45
My Documents command (Start menu), 60
My Documents folder, 59
My Music folder, 137
My Pictures folder, 153

N

naming files/folders, 65
Napster, 134

navigating folders, 62-63

Network Setup Wizard, 202-208

networks. *See* home networks

New command (Word File menu), 82

New Connection Wizard, 96-101

New Now Playing List command (File menu), 138

New Smart Playlist command (File menu), 147

news, finding online, 110-113

Norton AntiSpam, 218

notebook computers, 4

O

online identity theft, 221

online music stores, 134

Online Print Ordering Wizard, 170-171

online shopping
   eBay, 116-119
   shopping.com, 114-115

Open command (Word File menu), 85

Open dialog box (Word), 85

opening
   cases, 6
   documents in Works, 78
   Microsoft Works programs, 76
   programs, 40
   Windows Media Player, 135
   Word documents, 85

operating systems, 28. *See also* Windows XP

ordering prints online, 170-171

Outlook Express
   composing email, 126
   email accounts, 120-123
   email attachments, 127
   reading email, 124
   replying to email, 125
   sending email, 126

P

Paragraph command (Word Format menu), 90

Paragraph dialog box (Word), 90

paragraphs, formatting in Word documents, 90

parallel printers, 20

Paste command (Word Edit menu), 87

PayPal, 119

phishing emails, 221

Photo Printing Wizard, 168-169

photos. *See* pictures

Photoshop Elements
   cropping pictures, 178-179
   fixing photos with, 172-175
   removing red-eye, 176-177

pictures, 152
   cropping, 178-179
   deleting from cameras, 158
   desktop backgrounds, 50
   fixing with Adobe Photoshop Elements, 172-175
   icons, 44
   My Pictures folder, 153
   ordering prints online, 170-171
   printing, 168-169
   removing red-eye, 176-177
   resizing, 175
   rotating, 157
   scanning, 164-167
   screensavers, 54-55
   transferring from digital cameras, 154-159
   transferring from memory cards, 160-163

playing
   CDs, 134-135
   DVDs, 150-151
   playlists, 140

playlists
   burning, 143
   creating, 138-139
   iPod playlists, 147
   playing, 140

pointing and clicking mouse, 30

pop-up ads, blocking, 221

portable music players (non-iPod), 148-149. *See also* iPods

ports, 5, 180

power cables, connecting, 23

powering on, 24-25

preventive maintenance. *See* maintenance

Print Layout command (Word View menu), 89

printers, 13
    parallel printers, 20
    USB printers, 21

printing
    pictures, 168-169
    Word documents, 93

prints, ordering online, 170-171

protecting computers. *See* security

Q-R

quick fixing photos with Adobe Photoshop Elements, 172-175

random play (Windows Media Player), 140

reading email, 124

rebooting, 24

Recycle Bin
    emptying, 70
    restoring files from, 69

red-eye, removing, 176-177

Removable Disk dialog box, 156

renaming files/folders, 65

replying to email, 125

resizing
    desktop, 48
    pictures, 175
    windows, 37

resolution, 48

restoring
    computers after crashes, 230-231
    files, 69

right-clicking mouse, 32

ripping CDs, 136-137

rotating pictures, 157

routers
    broadband, 200
    wireless, 198

S

Save As command (Word File menu), 84

Save command (Word File menu), 84

saving
    favorite web pages, 106
    Word documents, 84

ScanDisk, 228-229

Scanner and Camera Wizard, 161, 164-167

scanning hard disk drives for errors, 228-229

scanning pictures, 164-167

screensavers, 54-55

scrolling windows, 36

searching the web, 109

security, 212
    electrostatic shock, 187
    email spam, 218-219
    firewalls, 214-215
    identity theft, 221
    phishing emails, 221
    pop-up ads, blocking, 221
    Security Center, 213
    spyware, 220
    viruses, 216-217
    wireless home networks, 207

Security Center, 213

sending
    email, 126
    files via email, 127

setting up computers. *See* connecting computer systems

sharing files/folders across home networks, 210-211

shipping costs (online merchants), 115

shopping online
    eBay, 116-119
    shopping.com, 114-115

shortcuts (desktop), 41

Shutterfly, 171

shutting down, 27

sizing
  desktop, 48
  pictures, 175
  windows, 37
Smart Playlists (iTunes), 147
Snapfish, 171
sniping, 119
sorting files/folders, 61
sound cards, 11
sound systems, 18-19
spam, 218-219
spamblock, 219
SpamKiller, 218
speakers, 11, 18-19
special characters in filenames, 64
spell checking, 92
sports websites, 111
spyware, 220
Start menu commands, 39, 60
styles, applying in Word documents, 91
subfolders, 58
surfing the web
  bargain shopping at shopping.com, 114-115
  bidding for items on eBay, 116-119
  favorite pages, 106-107
  Google, 109
  History list, 108
  Internet Explorer, 102-105
  news, finding online, 110-113
  pop-up ads, blocking, 221
surround sound, 11
switching between programs, 42
Sygate Personal Firewall, 215
system power cables, 23
System Restore, 230-231
System Tools, 223
  Disk Cleanup, 224-225
  Disk Defragmenter, 226-227
  ScanDisk, 228-229
  System Restore, 230-231
system units, 4-5

T

Task Launcher (Works), 75
tasks (Works), 77
templates
  Word, 82
  Works, 77
Templates dialog box (Word), 83
text (Word documents)
  editing, 87
  entering, 86
  formatting, 88-89
themes, 49
To Do lists (Works), 79
toolbars, 44
tools. See System Tools
ToolTips, 34
transferring
  pictures from digital cameras, 154-159
  pictures from memory cards, 160-163
  songs to iPods, 146
turning on computer systems, 24-25

U-V

unnecessary files, deleting, 224-225
upgrades. See devices, adding to computer systems
USB, 21, 182-183
user accounts, creating, 52-53

video cards, 12
View menu commands
  Arrange Icons by, 61
  Print Layout, 89
viruses, 216-217

W-X-Y-Z

WANs (wide area networks), 203
weather, finding online, 112

How can we make this index more useful? Email us at indexes@quepublishing.com

web surfing
    bargain shopping at shopping.com, 114-115
    bidding for items on eBay, 116-119
    favorite pages, 106-107
    Google, 109
    History list, 108
    Internet Explorer, 102-105
    news, finding online, 110-113
    pop-up ads, blocking, 221

webMD Health, 113

Wi-Fi Alliance website, 206

Wi-Fi networks, 206

wide area networks (WANs), 203

windows
    closing, 38
    maximizing, 38
    minimizing, 38
    moving, 35
    resizing, 37
    scrolling, 36

Windows Media Player (WMP), 133
    CDs, burning, 141-143
    CDs, playing, 134-135
    CDs, ripping, 136-137
    downloading, 135
    DVDs, playing, 150-151
    iPods, 144-147
    launching, 135
    playlists, 138-140
    portable music players (non-iPod), 148-149

Windows Messenger
    adding contacts to, 128-129
    instant messaging, 130-131

Windows XP, 28. *See also* windows
    color schemes, 51
    Control Panel, 46-47
    desktop, 29, 48-50
    desktop shortcuts, 41
    Disk Cleanup, 224-225
    Disk Defragmenter, 226-227
    double-clicking, 31
    dragging and dropping, 33
    Folders pane, 63
    help, 56-57
    hovering, 34
    logging on to, 26
    menus, 43
    My Computer, 45
    My Documents, 59-60
    pointing and clicking, 30
    programs, opening, 40
    programs, switching between, 42
    Recycle Bin, 69-70
    right-clicking, 32
    ScanDisk, 228-229
    screensavers, 54-55
    Security Center, 213
    Start menu, 39
    System Restore, 230-231
    toolbars, 44
    user accounts, 52-53

wired networks, 204

wireless adapters, 198, 208

wireless fidelity (Wi-Fi), 206

wireless home networks. *See* home networks

wireless routers, 198

WMP. *See* Windows Media Player

Word, 80
    documents, 82-85
    keyboard shortcuts, 87
    paragraph formatting, 90
    printing, 93
    spell checking, 92
    styles, 91
    templates, 82
    text editing, 87
    text entry, 86
    text formatting, 88-89
    workspace, 81

word processing. *See* Word

words, adding to Word dictionary, 92

Works, 74. *See also* Word
    documents, 78
    programs, opening, 76
    project management, 79
    Task Launcher, 75
    tasks, 77

writing email messages, 126

.zip files, 71

ZoneAlarm, 215

Index